What people  about

China, the USA and C...de

A book that anyone concerned about the human future would do well to read. Written lucidly and rich in its insights, it offers a distinctive interpretation of the US-China relationship, in many ways the defining relationship of our time. Though the two societies may have vastly different cultures and histories, William Briggs is at pains to show that both are set on a capitalist trajectory, and that neither the American neo-liberal or Chinese authoritarian model has much to commend it. These two capitalist titans, he tells us, are now locked in an increasingly turbulent relationship which, if mismanaged, could inflict immense devastation on an already deeply fractured world. His thought provoking yet dispassionate analysis is a welcome antidote to the now fashionable but highly dangerous sport of China bashing.

Professor Joseph Camilleri, Emeritus Professor of Politics at La Trobe University in Melbourne and one of Australia's leading international relations scholars and authors

We live in a precarious time. As insecurity, poverty, and inequality are growing, the world is engulfed by the antagonisms between capital and labor as well as between nation-states. Capitalism has brought the planet to the brink through climate change and pandemics. Briggs correctly argues that the rise of China has been based on a capitalist economic system. Rather than helping to resolve the world's urgent problems, China's challenge to the US hegemony brings the world closer to the dangerous interplay between two superpowers. Will the current historical era prove to be capitalism's last crusade and what has to change to bring hope to the future? To understand these important questions, one has to read this book.

Professor Minqi Li, Department of Economics, University of Utah, author of *The Rise of China* and the *Demise of the Capitalist World Economy 2015 Monthly Review*

What I like about this book is that it looks at China, the United States and their relations through the lens of big-picture history. I like the way it considers not only countries, but more importantly economic and political systems. The role of capitalism in the rise of the American state is well known, and Briggs's interpretation is well worth looking at. Even more interesting is his portrayal of contemporary China, which claims to be 'socialism with Chinese characteristics', as essentially a capitalist state in a globalised capitalist world. He contends, rightly in my view, that the "threats" are more against China than from it, the threatener being a state that sees its hegemony challenged by any rising power. We don't know if it will lead to war, but we'd best watch out.

The author is an extraordinarily prolific and capable author, who has written very widely on many topics relating to political theory and economy.

This is an excellent account by somebody who really knows what he is talking about and provides an enlightening alternative to the heavily biased mainstream press.

Emeritus Professor Colin Mackerras, Foundation Professor, Griffith University, School of Modern Asian Studies, Department of International Business and Asian Studies

China, the USA and Capitalism's Last Crusade

When Survival Is All That Matters

China, the USA and Capitalism's Last Crusade

When Survival Is All That Matters

William Briggs

Winchester, UK
Washington, USA

JOHN HUNT PUBLISHING

First published by Zero Books, 2021
Zero Books is an imprint of John Hunt Publishing Ltd., No. 3 East St., Alresford,
Hampshire SO24 9EE, UK
office@jhpbooks.com
www.johnhuntpublishing.com
www.zero-books.net

For distributor details and how to order please visit the 'Ordering' section on our website.

Text copyright: William Briggs 2020

ISBN: 978 1 78904 767 7
978 1 78904 768 4 (ebook)
Library of Congress Control Number: 2020945893

A CIP catalogue record for this book is available from the British Library.

Design: Stuart Davies

UK: Printed and bound by CPI Group (UK) Ltd, Croydon, CR0 4YY
Printed in North America by CPI GPS partners

We operate a distinctive and ethical publishing philosophy in
all areas of our business, from our global network of authors to
production and worldwide distribution.

Contents

Also by William Briggs

Classical Marxism in an Age of Capitalist Crisis: the Past is Prologue 978-1-138-34428-0 (Routledge 2018)
Removing the Stalin Stain 978-1-78904-521-5 (Zero Books 2020)
A Cauldron of Anxiety 978-1-78904-609-0 (Zero Books 2021)

For Rose

Introduction

The sun sets and the sun rises. It sets on the old and rises on the young. The old often cling to a fading power, or the memory of power, and the young feel their strength and test their strength. And so it is with the United States and China. The global hegemon no longer enjoys absolute dominion and yet remains fearsomely powerful. Its military might is unparalleled. Its economic clout is enormous. It still has political sway over much of the world, and holds hundreds of millions in thrall, but even so, the sun is setting on it and is rising on China. It is a truth and, for the United States, an unpalatable truth. There is another truth. The USA will not give up its hold on power lightly and this truth must concern us all.

The passing of American global domination is not something to be lamented. Nor is the rise of China as a global superpower anything to be applauded. While this book focuses heavily on the waxing and waning of power it most certainly does not take sides. It cannot. These arguments are connected to a broader observation, that economic formations are impermanent structures. As such, the book sees the rise and fall of capitalist empires within the broader framework of economic and political history. Empires rise and fall, and so too do entire economic formations have a beginning, a middle and an end.

There has been a veritable avalanche of books and commentaries on the rise of China and its implications for the world. This book is different. While it is about the rise and fall of empires, it is about much more than that. It is about capitalism, about power, about the clash between capital and the nation-state, about ideology, about war and about peace. It has a wide scope. It asks and answers questions that resonate and certainly have relevance for today and into the future. Its relevance is immediately obvious. The world today exists in an atmosphere of threat and insecurity. Global powers face off and it is not difficult to see parallels from the not so distant past.

Great power rivalries are once more bubbling to the surface. The wheel turns and history, it would seem, repeats. The names might have changed but there is a disturbing sense of *déjà vu* accompanying the headlines, the opinion pieces and statements from government agencies and from world leaders. The growth of capitalism, its globalising effect and the antagonisms it engenders is not something new. The turn of the twentieth century was just such a time. Globalisation and the integration of capitalist relations was met with a ferocious return to economic and political nationalism as imperialist rivalries and the requirements of nation states to reposition themselves clashed. Globalisation was paused, but not reversed. Capitalism does not and nor can it work that way. Millions died in the cause of determining which capitalist power would prevail. The alliances that confronted each other in WWI no longer exist, but the problems and contradictions that plunged the world into war remain virtually unchanged.

While it is obvious that today's 'great powers' are different players, the rules of that macabre game have not changed. Since the end of WWII, the United States has enjoyed the unchallenged status of dominant capitalist economy. For the better part of half a century it waged an ideological campaign against 'communism' in the form of the Stalinist regime in the Soviet Union and simultaneously came to dominate the global economy. It was that heady time of '*pax Americana*'. The problem with all of this is that empires come, and empires go. It is clear for all to see that the American era is on the wane. As capitalism still rules, then what will follow *pax Americana*? What happens if the usurped refuses to be replaced? These are questions that are central to the arguments that motivate this work. The ruling class in the United States will not simply say, 'Oh well, we had a good run. It looks like it's over to you, China.' There will be no simple and smooth passing of batons. The shift in power, influence and the geo-political centre of gravity will be painful and it will be the working people who will, as always, be made to suffer the most, economically, materially and not inconceivably at the hands of competing military machines.

This book explores several interconnected themes. It looks at the nature of capitalism, of the nation-state and its relationship to capital and power, of the rise of China, and how this might be observed through the lens of Marxist theory. It is about threats, real and perceived, about the rise in insecurity and inequality, about the very real threat that hangs over the planet and its people as capitalism desperately seeks to survive. It is about history, although it is not a history book. It is about economics, although it is not an economics text. It is about the political economy of late capitalism and about the dangers that go with nuclear threats. It is about politics, the economy, the future, and above all it is about how we, the people, might forge a future.

War and Peace – questions and answers

The Cold War ended in 1991. The Soviet Union collapsed and the real or imagined threat from what had been termed 'communism' disappeared. For some, like Francis Fukuyama (1992), this meant the 'end of history' and the ultimate and eternal victory of democracy and capitalism. The threat of war receded. Ideological opponents of capitalism had been vanquished. We were told that all would be well in what was, after all, the best of all possible worlds. Before history 'ended' there had been a real sense of danger. The *Bulletin of the Atomic Scientists* (Spinazze 2020) has, each year, set the hands of the 'doomsday clock'. In 1984, at the height of the Cold War, the clock was set at 3 minutes to midnight. They were days of fear and anxiety. With the collapse of the Soviet Union the hands of the clock were moved out to 17 minutes to midnight. The world seemed to breathe a little easier. Then, even as the years

3

of peace and stability that marked that 'post-history' era went by, something began to happen. As this decade dawned, the world discovered that the clock's hands had been moved on to 2 minutes to midnight. This is closer to annihilation point than at the height of US-Soviet rivalries and the chilling threats of mutually assured destruction. Then in 2020, the hands moved once more, to 100 seconds to midnight! This can but send shivers up and down the collective spines of us all and it begs the question; why?

This book seeks to answer that question and in doing so will ask and answer other connected questions. Why do half of the world's millennials fear a nuclear attack in the coming decades (ICRC 2020)? Why do they believe that they will live to see WWIII? Why is there so clearly a Cold-War mentality in a world when there are no appreciable ideological causes? Why have those born in the last 20 years only known the USA and its allies to have been at war? Why is it that the Pentagon and US policymakers have changed their military doctrine and now claim that global 'great power' rivalries must re-occupy centre stage in military thinking and preparedness, and that the 'war on terror' is no longer central to their thinking? Why is the USA spending over a trillion dollars on re-equipping its nuclear arsenal? Why are low yield 'useable' nuclear weapons being virtually mass-produced? Why is there such a threat perception being pursued by governments and the media around the world that sees China as a threat to global peace and security? Why does the influential International Institute for Strategic Studies (IISS) make the statement that 'for its part, the USA is not likely voluntarily, reluctantly or after some sort of battle, to pass any strategic baton to China' (IISS 2019)? All these questions are, understandably, keeping people awake at night. They all have a common thread, a common cause, a common answer. That common cause is capitalism. Capitalism has always existed with crisis and contradiction but has reached a point of near breakdown. While this is unfolding, the major capitalist economy and the most powerful nation-state the world has ever seen is threatened by a rising economy and political power. China looms as a real threat to the continued power of the USA. There can be no 'sharing' of power and influence. It is not how capitalism works.

Key issues

Among a range of questions that the book will address are key issues around which the discussion must inevitably flow. The first of these is just how capitalism works. Nation-state economies may develop at different paces and assume developmental strategies that appear to be more dependent upon local conditions and internal factors, but ultimately they conform to inherent laws of capitalist development.

The second issue is that capitalism, while doubtless an enduring and dominant economic formation, is not some immutable force. Such a proposition was first promoted and validated in Marxism's theory of historical materialism (Engels 1966, Plekhanov 1976). Entire socio-political-economic formations have risen and fallen, to be replaced by new and more efficient, more effective formations. A central element of this historical materialist view includes the development of society and economy, from primitive communism, to slavery, to feudalism, to bourgeois or capitalist society and into the future to socialism and finally communism. It is a progression that has been criticised by some as being either too euro-centric or too simplistic, but Karl Marx was careful to point out that what he was presenting was simply a guideline to historical research. As a guideline it remains rather effective. That 'big picture' view of the world can be used as a model to examine what happens within economic formations as well. This is especially so when we observe the sun setting on the American century and see the sun rising on China's.

Capitalism had a beginning, a middle and inevitably will have an end. Just as feudalism replaced slave society, and capitalism replaced feudalism, then so capitalism will be replaced. And, just as each economic formation resisted change, then so too will capitalism resist. This simple observation assumes some significance for the discussion that follows. The rise of China within the overarching capitalist world system is in many ways a microcosm of that larger, historical change that haunts capitalism.

The USA has enjoyed total domination, economically, politically and militarily, for well over half a century. China is threatening this power on all fronts. The USA will resist and is resisting any paradigm shift. The growth in influence of China, economically, and within international politics and international relations, most assuredly threatens the USA. It could be no other way. An old order is coming to an end. Whether Chinese capitalism and Chinese power is better, or preferable, or whether it poses a threat to all that is 'good and pure' is not the issue. What is important is that its rise is being resisted. The waves of vitriol that have been unleashed are often less than edifying. The anti-China syndrome has assumed a life of its own. Governments, media, opinion-moulders, all join the queue to produce ever more chilling stories. All of this is understandable. The world capitalist order is changing, but there is a degree of inevitability to it all, just as there is an inevitability to the passing of capitalism. The difference between these two examples is the passing of capitalism will herald a better future, or at least will offer a future for us all. Changing the capitalist guard will not make life more secure or offer us greater social or economic equality.

So why is this book relevant?

If the noise around the US-China dispute is simply about changing the guard, then why the fuss? This brings us to the centre of the discussion and with it some rather unsubtle messages being broadcast by capital and its supporters. It can be accepted that the United States, as global hegemon, would not be prepared to give up its place of primacy. It can be accepted that it would seek to 'call in favours' from traditional allies to ensure that China's rise is resisted. Some of the anti-China rhetoric is ridiculous and some of it justified. A blurring of lines is unavoidable. China's domestic policies and the treatment of its working class is simply unjustifiable, but then many of America's domestic policies and the treatment of its working class are hardly a blueprint for how to manage an equitable and just society. China is accused of seeking to manipulate political and economic decisions in other countries. They may, just possibly, have learned this from studying US foreign policy. What is certain is that an anti-Chinese sentiment has been engendered and that this has some echoes to historical moments that have preceded mass slaughter. The lead ups to both world wars are cases in point.

China has been accused of many things but to argue or claim that it represents socialism, or communism, is perhaps the most ludicrous. China is a capitalist economy. The USA is a capitalist economy, as are just about all the nation states on earth. Washington knows this. Wall Street knows this. All world leaders know this and yet on an almost daily basis the lie is trotted out that China is a 'communist' country and, by definition, an enemy of the free market, the free world and all that is worth defending. The USA and its allies, in building and presenting the case against China, are treading a dangerous path, but a path that has been deliberately chosen. It is a path that could so easily lead to war and devastation for both parties and for the world. While China is hardly a paragon of virtue and is hard to defend, the threatening posture of the USA is quite another matter.

The vehemence of the US attacks on China are all the more

alarming when considered against the backdrop of the crisis that confronts capitalism. If it were simply a matter of one superpower being removed and another put into place, then it would be irritating for the losing side, but life would go on. However, we are at a confluence of extraordinary events. At once the greatest hegemon the world has seen is losing power, while at the same time an entire economic formation is experiencing a crisis that it cannot overcome. It is a dangerous time to be alive. Change is in the air.

Another element of the book and one that makes it especially relevant is the fact that it closely describes and discusses how capitalism developed, and how its various contradictions effect that development. An understanding of how Marxists regard capitalism is important to this work. As Karl Marx and Friedrich Engels explained, capitalism cannot but end up 'creating a world in its own image' (Marx 1977: 71). The paths taken to reach that point may differ depending on any number of factors, but the end point is simply...capitalism. These different paths have been described by some as proving that there are 'different' forms of capitalism. Much has been written about China's rise, from just such a standpoint. Some argue that what we see in China is 'state' capitalism (Naughton and Tsai 2015). Others assert that there is a 'Confucian' capitalism, while a body of thought insists that globalisation is leading to a 'hybrid' capitalism in China (Yeung 2004). The Chinese government still maintains the charade that they are 'building socialism with Chinese characteristics' but in the economic sense that China exists in the world today, it is a capitalist system, pure and simple. This argument will be developed, in some detail, as will the claim that capitalism has all but run its race. It will be shown that capitalism, once a relatively progressive system, has exhausted its capacity for development and is in a process of 'breakdown'. This systemic disintegration coupled with the rise of China and the relative decline of the USA sets the scene for an intensely dangerous period ahead.

War is a very real possibility, as is attested to by documents from Washington and the Pentagon (National Defense Strategy 2018). What ought to be unthinkable is being thought and openly discussed. The potential to unleash devastation in order to maintain power and hegemony must be linked to the real and imminent dangers to the planet that stem from climate change. The same centres of power that can countenance using 'low yield' nuclear weapons to secure military victories and thus maintain an economic supremacy are the same people that hold all the cards when it comes to changing policies that might just save the planet from environmental disaster. It is hardly an optimistic scenario. At the same time, despite war and disaster being imminent, they are conditions that are not inevitable.

This book presents an overview of the world and of its discontents in the twenty-first century. It will show that the USA will continue its economic and therefore its political decline. It will show that China's rise is one that the world must simply acknowledge. Significantly, it will not take sides, although the potential for crisis and catastrophe is manifestly an issue of the United States' making. It will show that capitalism and the nation-state, regardless of how powerful that nation-state might be, are locked in an unresolvable set of contradictions that will hasten the demise of both state and economic system. All of these issues are important and make the book more than relevant.

Structure

The main premise remains that the rise of China and the subsequent eclipse of America is inevitable and that this is a reflection of the historical materialist view of the rise and fall of economic formations. The discussion that will support that primary argument is arranged through a series of discrete but interrelated chapters. The work begins with some theoretical observations. Consequently Chapter 1 takes as its focus the issue of capitalism and presents an analysis of what capitalism is, and how it developed. The chapter also discusses the relationship between capitalism and the state and of how the state exists to facilitate capitalist development. While capitalism and the capitalist state have not developed evenly across all nations, the fact remains that states ultimately conform to capitalist norms.

Chapter 2 continues this theoretical exposition by presenting and describing how this materialist conception of history operates. I argue that this becomes a valuable tool in understanding how history and especially the history of economic formations has progressed. Its strength lies in helping to appreciate how things work – or in other words in understanding the world. The chapter explains how issues such as globalisation are inevitabilities in the historical development of capitalism and that globalisation and the clash of nationalism reveal what is, effectively, a final and inescapable crisis for capitalism.

From here, the discussion will move from the domain of the theoretical world to observe how these theories are played out in real life and in real time. Chapter 3 uses the theoretical arguments relating to the often-conflicted relationship between state and capitalism. Nation states, in the twenty-first century, are increasingly engaged in rivalries and have resorted to regressive policies of nationalism and economic nationalism. This has echoes to past eras of capitalist development and particularly to the period of economic nationalist upsurge that came immediately before WWI. The history of capitalism has unfolded alongside the rise and fall of economic empires. The sun finally set on the British Empire, as it had to. Inevitably there was a new paradigm.

The two protagonists, the USA and China, become the focus of attention in the next chapters. Chapter 4 looks briefly at the astonishing history of the United States and tracks its journey from an optimistic birth of an idea, of how that idea came to represent how it viewed itself and the world, to the point where it became a global power. It looks at the concept of American 'exceptionalism' and of how it shaped the development of the USA and of how it still embodies the 'idea' that remains, in the minds of many: America. The chapter looks at the rise of American capitalism, its slave past and pauses, momentarily, to discuss the arguments that have come to dominate debate in that country.

Chapter 5 further tracks the path of the United States' economic rise. It has at times been both expansionist and isolationist although it has always had a very exceptional way of viewing isolationism. The chapter describes how the USA managed to acquire such power – economic, political and military – the like of which has never been rivalled. Just as British capitalism and imperialism waned, so too are we witnessing the beginning of the decline of the American megalith. The power that the USA still wields is enormous and has implications for the entire world and especially for the power that waits in the wings: China.

China is clearly the major player in contemporary international relations and the global economy. Chapter 6 begins a discussion of China and its rise as a global superpower. The chapter looks at the political and economic history of China, from the turn of the last century until the opening up to capitalist relations in the late 1970s. It traces the turbulent twentieth century of Chinese history, set against an earlier backdrop of imperialist domination and reactions against imperialism. It was a period of rebellion, of rising nationalism and oppression as China began its ever so long march. The chapter describes the growth of both Chinese capitalism and the creation of a Chinese working class and of political responses to the events of the twentieth century. Focus is given to the creation and activities of the Chinese Communist Party (CCP), its relationship with

Stalinism, its shift in theory from the working class to the peasantry and of its eventual seizure of power. The chapter also traces developments in Chinese politics and economics from the time of the 1949 revolution until 1978 and the shift in economic policies that ensued.

This economic shift in China is the focus of Chapter 7. The chapter also looks at the often confused and confusing characterisation of capitalism in China. Is it 'state' capitalism or is China now a capitalist economy in the fullest meaning of that term? How that question is answered is of more than mere 'academic' interest. If, as it will be shown, the Chinese economy is fully capitalist, then it puts the lie to the absurd claim that it has anything to do with socialism or communism. It also places it full square at odds with the USA. Which economy, which entity, will enjoy supremacy?

Chapter 8, then, looks at the dangerous interplay between these two giants and their struggle. This by no means infers that the protagonists have the same immediate aims and motivations. The USA, for its part, has a long and bloodied history of intervention, war and interference in the affairs of just about everyone. China's track record has been vastly different. It does not share the belligerent history of its rival. Many of the propagandist claims levelled at China do not hold up to scrutiny. However, while this may be the case, there is little to suggest a peaceful accord, or any sense of harmonious relationships developing. Daggers, both figuratively and literally, have been drawn. The world waits with bated breath and as is inevitably the case, sides are being taken and alliances are being forged.

This scenario is bleak. The potential for cataclysm is real. There is more than a chance of war. However, war, while imminent, is not inevitable. Chapter 9 examines this dangerous perspective. If looked at purely through the prism of realist international relations theory, then there is really no hope and yet dystopia cannot be an option. This in no way seeks to diminish or dismiss the very real chance of disaster. A real and present danger hangs over us all. What the chapter does is explain how things have reached this point, how capitalism as an economic formation has reached its 'use-by-date'. It shows that the prize that both the USA and China so desire is a poisoned chalice. Insecurity, poverty, inequality and a growing sense of antagonism between capital and labour are growing. Capitalism is bringing the planet to the brink through climate change and pandemics which are linked to climate disruption. Something has to change and in this the chapter indicates that there is hope for the future.

Chapter 1

Capitalism and the state

Our media, political leaders and governments assail us on an almost daily basis with 'analysis', either to keep us 'informed' or possibly more likely, to assuage our collective fears. There are issues that escape too much scrutiny. Issues of the state, of capitalism, of the relationship between the two are seldom offered up for any serious analysis. The state and capitalism are presented as simple facts of life, givens, and as such require no more than a passing reference. This omission by our leaders and opinion makers is by no means accidental but is a deliberate and strategic element of the ideology of the state and of capital. It may make life simple but cannot help but leave confusion, especially when changes are in the wind and those changes are monumental.

The task that this chapter undertakes is to look critically at the state and capitalism and at the relationship between the two. It has a direct implication for what is transpiring in the world today as capitalist nations vie with one another for economic and political hegemony. It also has implications for changes and challenges to capitalism itself. Capitalism has long dwelt in a world of crisis. It has been crisis that has driven it forward and it is crisis that is ultimately the rock upon which it is set to founder. The key to capitalism's ability to maintain its dominance is not that it is in any way an admirable system. It has no special gifts of resilience. It is not a mystical phenomenon. That key is in its relationship with the state. The state, for its part, exists to facilitate the smooth operation and development of capitalism. Each needs the other and they have developed alongside each other.

There has been more than a little debate concerning state

development, of what has been described as the 'relative autonomy' of the state, and of the potential for people to use the state and its institutions to ameliorate some of the more negative aspects of capitalism. A brief examination of some elements of state theory is required. It is required to help understand just what the state is and what its role is in maintaining a sense of equilibrium and an ideological framework that has ensured relative stability between antagonistic classes in society. Understanding the state is central to understanding what is taking place within the global political economy and within interstate relations. Finally, it is important to appreciate how the state responds to an increasingly globalising capitalism.

Capitalism, its development and, ultimately, whether it can survive, is central to the arguments that follow. Therefore, the chapter offers a view of how capitalism developed, its initial progressive position and the contradictions that have at once impelled its growth and signal its breakdown. This development has seen the requirements of capitalism, as an incessantly globalising force, come more into conflict with the nation-state. What we are seeing in the twenty-first century is a resurgence of regressive nationalism and economic nationalism. Great power rivalries have inevitably resurfaced as nations and nation states do battle for power and economic influence in a crisis-riven global setting.

Capitalism rules – but how?

The rise of the modern state mirrors the development of capitalism, or is it the other way around? This is not a riddle, although it has a certain chicken and egg feel to it. Capitalism could not have become the dominant political force without the state. Capitalism is the dominant idea, the overriding ideological force. The state ultimately is the state of and for the ruling idea. Each needs the other. What then is this thing called 'the state' and how does the relationship between state and capital work?

That question, like so many things in our world, seems at first glance to be almost inconsequential. But as with so many things, complexity is never far away. The state, it would seem, is simply the state. It is the source of governance and the administrator of society. It is an entity unto itself. At least that is how things have been presented. However, despite the claims made to the effect that the state enjoys a degree of autonomy, the relationship is far less simple. A brief overview of what the state is and how people see it is required. Whenever the state is discussed, it seems that the discussion almost always starts with Max Weber (2004) and his famous description of what constitutes the legitimate state. Much has been made of his definition that the state is that organised institution that enjoys the right to claim a monopoly on the use of coercion and violence in a given territory. Traditionally this 'violence' was and remains the province of police or military. In today's reality this can also include the privatisation of security but this 'right' to the use of force has remained closely guarded by the state and its institutions. Weber had much more to say than this, but violence and the state remain closely linked as does the coercive nature of the state, which is more or less evident depending on any number of internal or external factors.

While there are many interpretations of the state, this work is based on a Marxist world view. That ought to simplify the issue, but unfortunately does not. Marxism maintains that the state is ultimately about power and class interests. Colin Hay (1999: 153-5) has identified four ever-so-slightly different and competing interpretations of the state that all fit within a Marxist world view. This might have something to say about the divergent schools of Marxist thought but Hay's four 'states' are worth considering. Hay's interpretations of states are: the state as the repressive arm of the bourgeoisie; the state as an instrument of the ruling class; the state as the ideal collective capitalist and the state as a factor of social cohesion.

Much time and energy has been spent in argument and disputation about these four interpretations of the role and purpose of the state. In all likelihood, the time spent has served very little purpose. We need to keep in mind that, as Marx and Engels (1964: 36) made clear, the state evolves and responds to issues depending upon social, political and economic necessities as they arise. It might be argued that much of the 'theoretical' work concerning the state by various interpreters of Marx are simply different shades of the same colour, or possibly theorists seeking to put a personal stamp on things. At the end of the day it is abundantly clear that the state advantages class interests and, depending upon historical and economic conditions, can present in any of the above formulations.

Marxists, however, are not the only ones to have considered the state, its role and purpose. Two influential schools of thought need to be, if only cursorily, outlined. The first of these is often described as the *pluralist* concept. Under such a vision, liberty is seen as the most important value that a society can hold, and state sovereignty should represent an 'ideal' means of regulating society. Under such an arrangement, no single political group or interest group is able to exercise complete control, but negotiation and dialogue can resolve conflicts within society (Dahl 1967). In contrast, *elite theory* (Michels 1962) argues that the state inevitably becomes controlled by a small and powerful group of actors. C Wright Mills (1963: 167-9) depicts the scenario whereby the executive branch of government, major capitalist interests and representatives of the military establishment jointly exercise power.

It takes little imagination to see aspects of both theories playing out in states in this twenty-first century. Just as Marx and Engels explained, the state evolves to meet the requirements that present themselves. When economic conditions allow it, the state appears, to an extent, to fit some of the requirements of the pluralist world view. Economic conditions, over the past few decades, however, have been such that there is less and less 'obvious' liberality in the structure of the state. This is reflected in people's responses to their own states. There have been monumental upheavals across many countries and continents. These would have been virtually unthinkable just a decade ago, but economic conditions and crisis have meant that the state has been compelled to become more authoritarian. Under such conditions and as conditions worsen rather than improve, the elitist theory of the state assumes a sharper detail.

The question, then, is why does the state feel such a compulsion to change tack so markedly? If the state was simply a representation of the people, their needs and aspirations, then why do news reports feature such unrest and why do we see images of military-style police actions against civilian populations? Why do we see tear gas becoming the crowd control weapon of choice? The answer is tied up with the symbiotic relationship between the state and capitalism. The state exists to facilitate capitalist development and, in this case, to defend capitalism.

Capitalism's irresistible rise

Capitalism has so infused the very psyche of the world that it appears to need neither definition nor explanation. It is just capitalism. If pushed someone might say that it is about free enterprise, or the market, or about an individual's right to make profit from endeavour. They might equate it with democracy and freedom. They might say that they are in favour of it or that they are against it, but are less inclined to offer much by way of explanation of what it is, how it came to dominate our lives, or why it has become all but impossible to imagine a world without capitalism. Opinion polls regularly show that a majority of Americans aged 18-24 no longer regard capitalism in a favourable light. These figures can be replicated throughout other leading capitalist states. For anti-capitalists, these are doubtless encouraging figures, but what is this thing called capitalism, from whence did it spring, how has it come to dominate our world, our lives, consciousness, our every waking moment?

A definition is as good a place to start as any. There are many to choose from but this should certainly suffice. 'Pure capitalism is defined as a system wherein all of the means of production (physical capital) are privately owned and run by the capitalist class for a profit, while most other people are workers who work for a salary or wage (and who do not own the capital or the product)' (Zimbalist and Sherman 1984: 6-7). It must be acknowledged that as an economic system, this format has been most successful. It has created vast wealth and in its early days revolutionised the way people lived and worked. It has a long and often turbulent history. It developed from its early agrarian roots, through the great mercantilist period to grow into its industrialist form, replete with the 'dark satanic' mills that went with the industrial revolution and into the all-encompassing forms that we see around us. Along the way, it appeared to shift, from the brutal slave-trading entity to a seemingly benign bastion of freedom and democracy. Its constant evolution and development, however, does not change the most basic element of capitalism; its need to grow, to produce a profit and to devour anything that might impede this development. Just the same, this forward motion is constantly threatened by internal contradictions that simply cannot be resolved.

Capitalism has, from the very beginning, been enmeshed in this web of irresolvable contradictions. These have at once promoted capitalism's forward motion while, over time, deepened the contradictions and problems that remain an inherent part of the system. Among these contradictions are: the private ownership of the means of production and the social nature of the production process; the drive to maximise profit by expanding the productive processes and surplus value, which necessitates limiting real wages growth; the imperative to increase labour productivity which acts to contribute to the tendency for profit rates to fall; and what becomes especially important not merely for this work, but for the future of capitalism itself, the drive to a globalised economy while relying on the nation-state system to administer capitalist relations. At the same time, and as a response to the expansionary nature of capitalism, its progressive role, as described by Marx in the nineteenth century, has dissipated but its underlying motivation of survival has remained unchanged.

Capitalism's constant striving to overcome these contradictions has meant that it has remained expansionary and outward looking. Marx wrote of the political economy in a setting of a growing capitalism that was still essentially national in character. Significantly, he saw that capital, if it was not only to survive but to grow, was compelled to break from the confines of this national boundary and expand to become, as he described it, a world economy, or as we now categorise it, a global economy (Marx and Engels 1977: 39). What we see in such a telling of the capitalist story is a continual cycle of crisis, recovery, forward motion and then a return to crisis. Marxism is clear in its analysis that the cycle is, however, not endless, and that crisis will ultimately overpower the juggernaut.

The fact is that capitalism has grown to become that very juggernaut and along the way has achieved phenomenal results. These are increasingly being overshadowed by the damage it is inflicting in an era of existential crisis. It is a system that divides opinion. While 'anti-capitalist' arguments abound, it is not without vocal and influential supporters.

Robert Gilpin (2000: 3) described capitalism as the most successful wealth-creating economic system the world has ever seen. It is a statement that is clear, precise and completely true. His work focused on the challenges that capitalism faces in the twenty-first century, especially as it assumes an ever more encompassing global character. Significantly he called for the United States to resume its leadership role within global capitalism (Gilpin 2000: 357). Central to this analysis is a monumental contradiction facing capitalism. It is the contradiction between the relentless tendency towards globalisation and of the necessity of maintaining a sense of hegemony within the nation-state system. The last 2 decades have made this dilemma one of extreme importance, for the capitalist economy, for nation states and for the people of the planet. Gilpin enthusiastically spoke of a new age of global capitalism. 'Americans, other citizens of the industrialized world, and many people in other parts of the international economy have entered what the financial expert and economic commentator Hale has called "The Second Great Age of Global Capitalism"' (2000: 15). An almost messianic zeal sometimes creeps in. 'Thanks to capitalism, Americans as a nation are living dramatically better and longer than they did at the beginning of the twentieth century' (Forbes and Ames: 2009). Such claims are widely debated and disputed. We shall leave them to other forums. It simply shows that capitalism divides thought and is in a perpetual and, for many, an emotional turmoil. Along the way it has revolutionised the world. It is, as Marx and Engels stated in the *Manifesto of the Communist Party*, because of capitalism's 'need of a constantly expanding market for its products [that it] chases the bourgeoisie over the whole surface of the globe. It must nestle everywhere, settle everywhere, establish connexions everywhere' (Marx and Engels 1977: 39).

It soon became clear that for capitalism to not only 'establish these connexions' and expand across the globe, but to maintain a sense of order and 'harmony', force alone was never going to be enough. The relationship between worker and capitalist was and remains one based on exploitation. It is a simple fact of economic life. This is where that special relationship between capital and state becomes so important. Max Weber's view of the state was one of a 'legitimate' use of force and coercion. This does not always mean brute force. It cannot. Force ultimately will be met by force. Many decades of careful work resulted in the great majority of the people coming to willingly accept the rule of capital and the administration of this rule, through the state. The most appealing version of this comes through a sense of common ownership of decision making, regardless of the fact that power devolves upward and has little to do with any idea of participatory democracy. However, the people have learned to accept this as being a system that not only allegedly works to serve their best interests but is one 'controlled' by the people. It is a remarkable sleight of hand. Keeping the show on the road might have been difficult but through a highly skilled ideological apparatus, successive generations have come to believe that there is some common bond that unites us, regardless of where we might be placed in the economic pecking order.

Keeping the peace

The simple fact that capitalism, as an economic system predicated on class division and exploitation, has survived for so long is a testament to the 'beauty' and 'symmetry' in its relationship with the state. Capitalism assumed a position of economic and political dominance in an historically short period of time. It was at times a brutal path. The destructive nature of the industrial revolution has been well-documented but was inevitable, as capitalism destroys in order to build. This burn and build logic translated to capitalist development on a global scale. As Marx and Engels described, capitalism:

> on the one hand enforced destruction of a mass of productive forces; on the other, by the conquest of new markets, and by the more thorough exploitation of the old ones. That is to say, by paving the way for more extensive and more destructive crises, and by diminishing the means whereby crises are prevented (1977: 42).

Capitalism as an inevitably expansionary process must destroy older, pre-existing economic systems in order to create new ones (Marx 1975: 200-1). Otherwise no forward movement is possible.

Such a path was, of course, unpalatable to many. Here is where the state stepped in. Its role became one to make the path appear to be smoother, more palatable. The 'magic' was that it overlaid an ideological framework that made dissent more and more difficult to even consider, let alone enact. Put simply, ideology is essentially an expression of the world view of the dominant class in society. Terry Eagleton offers a definition of ideology as 'processes whereby interests of a certain kind become masked, rationalized, naturalized, universalized, legitimized in the name of certain forms of political power' (Eagleton 1991: 202). There is an intrinsic link, in such a construction, between the notion of ideology as the legitimisation of political power and the shrinking of class consciousness. Marx described how the development of capitalism acted to promote such a state of affairs:

> The advance of capitalist production develops a working-class, which by education, tradition, habit, looks upon the conditions of that mode of production as self-evident laws of Nature. The organisation of the capitalist process of production, once fully developed, breaks down all resistance (1986a: 689).

The importance of ideology is outlined by Richard Miller when he describes Marx's conception of the power of ideology within society, pointing out that 'the economically dominant class requires the existence of false beliefs for its dominance and has resources for perpetuating beliefs that are in its interests' (Miller: 1991: 74). It would have become obvious very early on that an economic and political structure so clearly based around antagonistic class interests could expect to survive by force alone. Capital and the state quickly built that 'better mousetrap'. The twentieth century, for capitalism, was both the best and worst of times. There were moments of crisis that were, in effect, existential moments for capitalism. The century ended, however, with capitalism still largely secure. The state may take a bow. That 'better mousetrap' has served it well.

Capitalism remains dominant, despite a growing tendency toward crisis and inherent instability. The contradiction between the private nature of capitalism and the social nature of the production process remains. There is also a constant need for capitalism to acquire greater returns on its investments as a counter to a tendency for the rate of profit to fall. The inescapable and irreconcilable contradictions of capitalism would indicate that the system itself must proceed to a point of breakdown as portrayed in Marxist theory. Capitalism holds power not through any inherent strengths it might possess. On the contrary capitalism and its tendency towards crisis displays weakness. It is in the lack of effective challenge that capitalism has managed to survive. Capitalism is in a perpetual state of crisis, and yet the working class and its allies remain largely acquiescent. Why?

The answer, already alluded to, can be found in the way the state has acted resolutely to reduce and, if not eliminate, then mask any obvious expressions of class antagonisms. The state operates for and in the interests of the capitalist ruling class. It exists, as Engels pointed out when commenting on apparent ruling class accommodation to the needs of the working class, for a reason (Engels 1984: 27). For a class-based society to function in relative harmony, there must be a degree of acceptance that the *status quo* represents the best interests of all.

Marx and Engels (1964: 78-9) argued that once the bourgeoisie assumed the ascendancy, it became imperative for the state to preserve the existing balance and state of affairs, by force if necessary. At the same time the link between the bourgeoisie and state is 'more internal and essential than the contingent use of control...the state, as such, is intrinsically a bourgeois form of social relationship' (Sayer 1985: 241). This relationship has advantaged capitalism while limiting the use of force to maintain that *status quo*.

The use of ideology as a means of legitimising the economic structures upon which society rests assumes on-going importance. This task is made easier if the views of the working class can be aligned with those of the ruling class. An effective integration of the working class and of its organisations occurs. This integration into the structure of the state serves to both reduce more obvious expressions of class antagonism and at the same time promote capitalist development. As capitalism globalises, the role of securing the acquiescence of the working class acquires an even greater significance. Workers are less able, under such conditions, to develop an independent political perspective. As capitalism developed, the tendency towards limitation of class struggle became ever more pronounced (Moore Jr 1978: 472-5). This is a theme that is revisited by Benjamin Selwyn (2013: 50) who regards the integration of labour into the capitalist state as a two-fold process, with labour's role and power being diminished due to the very real threat and prospect of the dispersal of production. In this sense, he is referring to the globalisation of capitalist relations. It is a process that has long been in evidence, although the enormous upheavals of 2019 and 2020, which saw a resurgent working class in many countries, indicate that cracks are emerging.

Michael Lebowitz (2004: 21-3) eloquently argues that capitalism maintains its position of ideological power by masking the exploitative nature of the economic system itself. The idea of labour power and the extraction of surplus value are never explicitly divulged. Capitalism, therefore, is not visibly exploitative which leads to a degree of 'mystification' of capital itself. Society, according to Lebowitz's argument, does not appear to depend on capital but rather gives the impression of autonomy. Workers are not simply dependent on capital, but on particular sections of capital. As these sections are often in competition with each other then so too are individual groups of workers in competition with other workers. This serves to intensify an already dependent relationship on capital.

State power is maintained by a combination of economic power and control of the broad machinery of state: the institutions of control. The effectiveness of state control and of its ability to evoke a feeling, not merely of acceptance, but of willing acceptance on the part of the working class has been extraordinarily successful.

The capitalist state has been forced to inculcate at least a semblance of social harmony. It has been an objective necessity for the stability of an inherently unstable mechanism to function. Harmony, that elusive quality, is further enhanced by the infusion of a deep sense of nationalism and national symbolism. The nation-state as we have come to recognise it is in historical terms a relatively new formation. The nation-state has come to occupy a special place in the hearts of many. What also needs to be borne in mind is that the nation-state is ultimately a political formation and not a geographical location. The antagonistic nature of capitalist relations has been hidden from view for a long time by exhortations to the unifying nature of the 'nation'. It has little to do with reality and a lot to do with the ability of the state apparatus to promote an illusion of unity. It is the illusion that sees workers believing that they have more in common with their ruling class than with workers in another country. It is an illusion that has permitted the slaughter of millions in the name of nationalism and which could so easily be repeated.

When state and capitalism are in conflict

A range of contradictory factors that go to the very core of capitalism have already been briefly outlined. Of these contradictions, the requirement of capitalism to globalise and integrate while maintaining a strong system of nation states remains singularly important.

Any serious appreciation or understanding of the irresolvable contradictions existing within capitalism cannot but include an appreciation of Marx's theory of the tendency of the rate of profit to fall. Marx was by no means the first to consider this tendency. Both Adam Smith and David Ricardo had written extensively on the question. Marx's proposition was quite straightforward. It asserted that capitalists seek to increase competitiveness by increasing productivity. The means of production (machinery etc.) grows more rapidly than the labour force and so profitability rises. However, the degree of investment needed to meet the cost of the added means of production also grows. Profit, Marx argued (1986c: 211-31), must come from the accumulation of surplus value which can only come from labour. If less labour is used as a means of reducing costs, then there is a downward pressure on profit. Capitalists seek to redress the problem of falling profits through a range of measures: intensifying the degree of exploitation of workers through longer hours, reducing wages and increasing the use of technology. At best this can only mean a limited reprieve before the cycle repeats.

While Marx wrote about the tendency for the rate of profit to fall, he was careful not to indicate that it would be a seamless process. Among the influences that Marx identified as acting against this tendency is the area that he described as 'foreign trade'. This assumes even greater significance when capitalist globalisation is considered. Capitalism is compelled, both in its search for markets and in its struggle against the potential for a fall in profits, to globalise. Susan Jellissen and Fred Gottheil

(2009) argue that it is the tendency for the rate of profit to fall that has acted as a trigger mechanism for globalisation. Their argument is that astute capitalists, in seeking to eliminate the possibly negative consequences of a fall in profits, have no real alternative but to expand; to globalise. Embedded in this strategy, of realising greater profits while simultaneously developing an industrial base, lies another important contradiction; on the one hand destroying the economic and social bases of the less developed states while, on the other hand, replicating the economic bases of the more developed. They share, with Marx, the perspective that this is ultimately a positive outcome and, for Marx, an inevitable one. 'The country that is more developed industrially only shows, to the less developed, the image of its own future' (Marx 1986b: 19).

That capitalism must grow and globalise is obvious. Productive forces have developed on a global scale. Capitalism now skims across the globe. It has no other allegiance but to itself and to its driving purpose of accumulating profit. This again is obvious. So too is the fact that the social and political superstructure, legal jurisdictions, property and all the rest, not the least of which are populations, remain firmly entrenched within the bounds of the nation-state. A clear problem emerges. Are we moving into a new form of capitalism that discards the nation-state and its structures? Are we likely to see the emergence of a new organisational structure? Already there is a clearly defined global working class. Is there a corresponding global ruling class and does this imply the end of the nation-state? It is a debate that has exercised the minds of scholars for some time. Foremost among those that see the nation-state as being effectively 'finished' is William I Robinson. Robinson (1998: 567), described as a *hyperglobalist*, consistently and vigorously argues that the development of an interstate capitalist system was an historical inevitability but that those relations are being superseded by the globalisation of capitalism. Robinson, in collaboration with Jerry Harris (2004), asserts that significant changes in capitalism are well established. They regard these changes as heralding the arrival of a new global capitalist class. Georgina Murray characterises this 'new' capitalism in terms of 'the rise of transnationalised capital, the hegemony of a transnational capitalist class, the emergence of a transnational apparatus, and the appearance of new forms of power inequality' (Murray 2012: 199).

These authors may well be correct. Capitalism may, over time, force such changes but will do so at enormous cost. There is a huge dilemma facing capital. The formation of national states and the establishment of national markets gave a tremendous boost to the development of the productive forces. But, as we well know, economic development did not stop at the national border and capitalism increasingly and swiftly outgrew its national framework. What remains, and these are objective realities, are enormously strong national bourgeoisies, whose task was and remains to achieve domination of the global market. This has, time and again, led to collisions with rival national states and rival bourgeoisies. This, after all, was what triggered WWI. Each major capitalist power sought to become a world power. If we move forward a century or so, we can see disquieting slogans across the globe. 'Make America Great' is effectively being re-badged to fit the national requirements of any number of rivals.

A question remains. Can there be an intelligent way of organising the productive forces of the world? If there is, then all is well and good. The hyperglobalists may well be proven correct. Just what form such a transition may take is yet to be seen but it can, rationally, be only as a continuation of capitalism in a fully globalised form, or in a global socialist system. Either way nation-state power will have to be considered. Who is likely to voluntarily relinquish position, power and life itself? The bourgeoisie cannot solve this problem because in seeking to subordinate the world market to its own profit needs, it strives to eliminate its competitors through competition, trade war and ultimately military conflicts.

Globalised and integrated capitalist relations are not about to go away. World leaders and especially those controlling the dominant economies of the world will speak of the pursuit of 'free trade' as an objective, while manipulating public opinion to support nationalist perspectives and promote retrograde tariff and trade war policies. It is in this pursuit of nationally based responses to global questions that dangers lurk.

Empire and nationalism

The fact that capitalism relies on continual expansion and a globalisation of the productive forces can easily be accepted. The evidence is before us on a day-to day-basis. The growth in nationalist sentiment, the advancement of nationalist symbolism, the move to reinvigorate economic nationalism as state policy are no less evident. The dilemma this presents to capital and state is obvious and the ramifications are potentially deadly. In a great many ways, we are witnessing a tragic repeating of history. The difference being that the stakes are so much higher. The hands of the Atomic Scientists' doomsday clock attest to that grim fact. If history is repeating, then it is important to know how and why? This is not because we are simply an inquisitive species. Knowledge, in this sense, becomes a tool and a tool by which change can be effected.

The history of capitalism has been a history of war, conquest and imperialism. Sometimes aims have been achieved by the blatant use of force. Sometimes by threat and intimidation, and economic power has been exerted to gain political and strategic influence. The events that are shaping our world are closely related to events that unfolded at the turn of the twentieth century. A comparison is in order. In 1902, John Hobson published his *Imperialism: a study* (2005). He wrote of the tendency of states to expand beyond their national boundaries. He was speaking of nationalism being 'transformed' into imperialism. Vladimir Lenin in *Imperialism, the highest stage of capitalism* (1977a) described imperialism as a special stage of capitalism: the monopoly stage of capitalist development. Like most things, the notions of imperialism and nationalism quickly become contested. For many, nationalism becomes almost the enemy of imperialism. There is a certain logic to this. Such a perspective sees imperialism causing a nationalist backlash in the country being adversely affected by an imperialist power. Nationalism, therefore, fights against imperialism. This has led to concepts of progressive nationalism and regressive nationalism. It is a debate that is hardly going to be resolved easily. The point that needs to be borne in mind is that without nationalist symbolism, without the ideological manipulation of populations to serve capitalist advances, then imperialism as we recognise it from the nineteenth century could not have developed. The antithesis of nationalism is not imperialism. It is internationalism.

What we might term the negative power of nationalism was at the very centre of the drive to WWI. Nicolai Bukharin published his *Imperialism and World Economy* in 1917, at the height of the war. He described the interplay of states and:

the struggle between national states, which is nothing but the struggle between the respective groups of the bourgeoisie... One cannot picture this gigantic conflict as the conflict of two bodies in a vacuum. On the contrary, the very conflict is conditioned by the special medium in which the 'national economic organisms' live and grow...the struggle between modern 'national economic bodies' must be regarded first of all as the struggle of various competing parts of world economy (Bukharin 2003).

Critics might argue that Bukharin had the benefit of hindsight, writing as he did during the imperialist war. Even so, events did support his general theoretical position. The lead up to war was a period marked out by intense polemic and debate and not a little of this debate centred on the question of imperialism. Karl Kautsky (1914) developed the theory that what the world was witnessing was the growth of 'ultra-imperialism'. By this he claimed that in international relations, the ferocity of rivalry between states would be negated by their 'cartel' relationship. In other words, the integration of capital across states would ensure a mutual necessity to 'behave' well. Some of the debates around the idea of globalisation and capitalism have a very loud echo in the ideas of Kautsky. History very quickly despatched his theory to a nether world. Imperialist powers sought to resolve their differences at the point of a bayonet.

The period immediately following the end of the Cold War and the collapse of the Soviet Union for the briefest moment in time may have seen the ideological fortunes of Kautsky's theory rise. The appalling doctrine of mutually assured destruction disappeared with the Cold War. There was talk of a new 'unipolar' world. History after all, or at least in Fukuyama's view, had ended and with it the threat of conflict. But no, even in this climate, Kautsky's views remain stubbornly out of step with reality. What happened was that the world seemed to be dividing into trading blocs. Trade is essential to the well-being of capitalism, the global economy and to the people whose livelihoods depend on that trade. The problem with blocs is, however, the same as with competition between individual states. There are ultimately winners and losers. While this is crudely put, its truth remains.

As this twenty-first century has progressed the threat of war has grown rather than diminished. Why? The answer is simple if painful. There are, today, 193 member states of the United Nations. Many are relatively minor players. Some observers might describe them as little more than vassal states to the major nations and most powerful economies in the world. Even so, each of these 193 states are seeking, wherever possible, to gain some comparative advantage, politically or economically. There are small powers, middle powers and great powers. What doesn't exist is a regime of harmony and accord. To consider, even for a moment, that the world is fundamentally different from the world that willingly slaughtered millions for the sake of economic, political and strategic advantage is ludicrous. What drove those states to war was the inability of capitalism to resolve its life-threatening contradictions. None of those contradictions have been resolved but, rather, have become more acute with the passing of the decades. None of this is difficult to see and yet it is a fact that is kept from the public gaze.

War, we have often been told, is a relic of the past. Democracies do not go to war with democracies. The 'democratic peace theory' is often cited to prove that there is really little to see here. If only it were so simple. The United States and its allies have effectively been at war for decades. Whether Syria or Iraq deserve the title democratic or not is not entirely relevant. The carnage that unfolded in the former Yugoslavia was undeniably between states that were multi-party 'democracies'. Points can be made, and arguments used to sway opinion in any direction. The simple fact of the matter is that war is so much a part of the 'normal' that it becomes unremarkable. Chris Hedges (2003) shows, for instance, that the world has only been at 'peace' for 268 of the last 3400 years. That is just 8 per cent of that vast historical period. The twentieth century resulted in 108 million war dead. In 2003, when Hedges' book was published, there were 30 wars taking place. There are 2.1 million global soldiers. Since 1975, the USA has spent between 15-30 per cent of its budget on the military.

When there is war, or the threat of war, then all manner of

'reasons' are trotted out. It may have something to do with the psychological make-up of a given leader. It might have a religious undertone. It might be the result of forced migrations due to famine or civil war. It might be the threat from an ideology, or from a threat to 'our' economy from another country. It is never due to a stated or unstated need to bolster 'our' economy at the expense of another state's. It is never about a faltering economic base, or to increase 'our' power. And it is never 'our' fault.

War and capitalism go hand-in-hand. War and interstate relations similarly go together. It is beyond the realm of logic to regard this in any other way. History is replete with examples. The present threat perceptions simply prove the point. Why? It is because capitalism is ultimately competition writ large. Individual capitalists are engaged in a constant battle for survival. You grow or you disappear. Capitalist conglomerates are equally engaged in struggle, one with the other. States are necessarily accomplices in this. Nicolai Bukharin (2003) all those years ago argued that capitalist competition can only go so far without there being a clash. At this point the state and its capacity for power, ideologically and militarily, assumes a position of ultimate significance.

This brings us back to the core business of this book. The world is witnessing the fall of an empire. The USA, arguably the most outstanding economic, political and military power that the world has seen, is beginning a slide that is unstoppable. Its economic power is still vast, but it is soon to be surpassed. Its political sway is already waning. Its most active, vocal and loyal allies are becoming fewer. Its last card, the colossal military machine, remains. Empires have a nasty habit of not reading the tea leaves. They do not leave the world stage willingly. The military force that the USA can and will project for many years to come is a constant reminder of why the doomsday clock is now just 100 seconds to midnight.

While the world watches this not to be lamented decline,

it also watches uneasily the ascendance of China as the new hegemon. Its economic might is growing to the point that it will overtake the USA. Its projection of 'soft power' across the region and the world is being portrayed by the USA as a threat. Its military budget is growing. It is not in the same league as that of the USA but is a substantial and lethal force. It maintains an authoritarian hold on power but is fully a capitalist economy.

Two forces appear set to clash at some point in the not-too-distant future. There has been economic war and the possibility of actual war is not to be discounted. The threat comes not directly from Beijing but from Washington. Two powers can be rivals but not co-hegemons. Capitalism cannot operate in this way and nor can states. It is in this understanding that we see, in microcosm, the larger, historical development and changes in entire economic and social periods. In the paradigm shift that sees the US's decline, then so too can we see the shift that brought capitalism to the fore and will see its ultimate demise. This element of Marxist theory, historical materialism, needs to be understood as it helps us understand the present and the future.

Chapter 2

Understanding the world

Can the world be understood? One can only imagine how many books of history have been published in the past century. What do these books tell us, not just about the past but the present and the future? What do they tell us about the motivations of people? All of this depends entirely on how the historian views his or her world. For some, history is about political developments. For others about social movements. For others it is about economic factors. The personal almost always intrudes in telling the story, of writing the history while still questing for objectivity. The result can often be confusion for the reader. What tends to happen is that someone takes a book from a shelf, reads it and an impression is formed. That historical impression seldom intrudes into the present and rarely into the future. And then there is historical materialism.

The previous chapter examined how capitalism so completely came to dominate the world. It explored its relationship with the state and how this duo shaped the world in such a way as to make the world more and more homogenous. Today two enormous powers, the United States and China, face each other and vie for supremacy. The rise of American power is historically rooted in the rise of capitalist power. So too is China's spectacular rise linked to the laws that govern capitalist history and development. It is a product of an historical process. This process is explained through the Marxist conception of history or historical materialism. Historical materialism is a part of a body of theoretical understanding and appreciations that constitute Marx's scientific approach.

There has been nothing about Marx or Marxism that has not been subjected to the most insistent and endless critique and criticism. Anti-Marxist theorists have sifted through every point of Marxist theory and have 'proven' time and again that the theory is flawed and has no validity. Oddly enough the process of finding fault with a theory that has been declared 'flawed' just goes on and on. What is interesting is that lines of 'Marxist' scholars and theorists have also queued up to find fault, to criticise, to point out where Marx went wrong, and to offer ways of 'salvaging' the theory. While it is important to know what is being said and to fight for your specific corner, this work is not a polemic. It does defend a Marxist perspective but the point of this chapter is not to wage battle against other 'Marxists'. Its purpose is quite different.

The chapter sets itself a range of tasks. It first outlines, in an abbreviated form, why Marxism can be legitimately called a science. It is here that the first steps at appreciating Marx's contribution to historical method will be presented. While the book does not engage in polemics, it is still necessary to consider some of the criticisms of this method before examining in any detail the idea of historical materialism and its utility and agency. This is done by closely looking at just what Marx meant and the most appropriate way into such a discussion is, oddly enough, through Marx. Consequently, there is a focus on Marx's brief outline of his materialist conception of history. Finally, the chapter examines the merits of historical materialism beyond the theoretical realm and as a means of explaining and shaping ideas in the more immediate world of the here and now.

Marxism as science

In his *Contribution to the Critique of Political Economy*, Marx (1918: 11-12) argued that social existence determines consciousness and that through social production people enter into sets of relationships that are independent of their own will. What Marx did was describe how society operated and how the class relationships of that society were central to how society developed. He showed that the aspirations of classes are necessarily antagonistic to one another. He also showed that these relations were transitory. He maintained that economic formations and society advanced in accordance with what he termed a materialist conception of history. The capitalist mode of production with its inherent contradictions and antagonisms is an integral part of this process because, 'the productive forces developing in the womb of bourgeois society create the material conditions for the solution of that antagonism' (Marx 1918: 13).

It is from this relatively unadorned description of how the world turns that the Marxist method of analysis develops. It has come to be regarded by some as a scientific approach to understanding phenomena and as 'pseudo-science' by others. The credentialing of Marxism as scientific is oddly enough sometimes downplayed or given peripheral importance by some Marxists. For some Marx's declaration that 'philosophers have only interpreted the world, in various ways; the point is to change it' (Marx and Engels 1964: 647) can override all other considerations, while for others, the appellation 'scientific' carries a comfortable and comforting degree of 'academic' prestige. Marxism describes contradictions. Here we see just one more. Marxism, however, is not simply a practice, and nor can it simply be a theory. It has become all but a cliché to speak of theory without practice as being sterile, and practice without theory being blind, but the point remains just as important as ever it was. There is or ought to be a dialectical unity between the two.

Can the claim that Marxism constitutes a scientific approach to understanding society and the world be validated? If it can, then the tangle in which the world now finds itself can be explained and approached with more than a hint of optimism. If it constitutes a scientific method of analysis, then the chaos of capitalism can be understood. In a philosophical sense, since 'materialism in general explains consciousness as the outcome of being, and not conversely, then materialism as applied to the social life of mankind has to explain social consciousness as the outcome of social being' (Lenin 1977b: 23). Marxist theory is built on the premise that this 'social' being comes from a largely economic base. Stephen Whitefield, in the *Oxford Concise Dictionary of Politics* (1996), outlines the concept of historical materialism, whereby 'social structures derive from economic structures, and that these structures are changed through class struggles...that human history develops as the result of contradictions, mainly among social cases'.

Jon Elster, in *An Introduction to Karl Marx*, describes what he sees as Marx's two-fold approach to understanding historical development. Each has a direct relevance. 'Marx had both an empirical theory of history and a speculative philosophy of history' (Elster 1995: 103). The first of these relates to historical materialism and its macrosociological view of analysis of social systems and economic formations at a global scale. The 'speculative' view is one that divides the history of the world into what Elster (1995: 3) describes as three separate stages: pre-class society, class-based society and post-class society. The historical epochs that have come to us as the basis of the development of historical and economic formations and therefore historical materialism include slave society, feudal, bourgeois and from there into a future socialist and ultimately communist formation. The importance of Elster's comments and those of many other observers is that they display the clearly scientific nature of Marx's work and analysis. Speculation becomes linked to observation and to a close study of economic history.

Lenin (1977c) described Marx's contributions to the study of historical materialism, his economic theories and the issues surrounding classes in society. These interrelated components form the basis of Marxist theory and its claim to the status of science. Primary among these is the concept of historical materialism.

Intimately related to this is the fundamental premise that class and class conflict remain central to understanding developments in society, and that economic issues drive political and societal responses. A materialist construction understands historical processes as being impelled by antagonistic relationships between classes, explains how social structures are shaped by economic factors, and sees class struggle as being framed by the labour process (Boucher 2012: 5).

Engels, it might be safely argued, was the first 'Marxist'. Among an exhaustive list of achievements, he presented an outline of the essential propositions that culminate in the theory of historical materialism. In doing so Engels staked an early claim to Marxism's scientific credentials and that it was a scientifically valid means of interpreting the world. Engels argued that:

> The materialist conception of history starts from the proposition that the production of the means to support human life and, next to production, the exchange of things produced, is the basis of all social structure; that in every society that has appeared in history, the manner in which wealth is distributed and society divided into classes or orders is dependent upon what is produced, how it is produced, and how the products are exchanged. From this point of view, the final causes of all social changes and political revolutions are to be sought, not in men's brains, not in men's better insights into eternal truth and justice, but in changes in the modes of production and exchange (1966: 50).

This, in a nutshell, goes to the heart of the whole 'science' debate that was to follow. It has been just one of the many nagging controversies that have accompanied Marxism pretty much since the *Manifesto of the Communist Party* was first published in 1848.

The heated debates surrounding Marxism's scientific mantle have often overshadowed what Marxists have been describing for generations. They deserve at least a cursory glance, but first we need to dig a little deeper into just what this science is and what it is for. In doing so, we can get a hint of why such heat has been generated in criticising and defending the claim.

Marx, as Terrell Carver (1991: 109-10) explains, believed that science was much more than a simple collation of facts, as important as this is. Science, for Marx, by necessity involved the development and propagation of theories. These theories were, and remain, related to causal agents that act upon the world: entities, relations and processes. It is in the process of these theories acting upon the world that Marxism unites philosophical inquiry with economic analysis. This is what is important. The materialist conception of history stresses the overarching importance of economics as a driver of political and societal development. This has also led to some of the more virulent criticisms of Marxist theorists, and the claims of 'economism' and 'determinism'. These criticisms never seem to lose currency, which is odd, as the theory has always been deeply immersed in philosophical enquiry. To arbitrarily separate the two seriously limits the theoretical underpinnings of Marxism itself. Engels (1976: 42) argued that investigative science and theory inevitably become intertwined. In a similar vein Albert Weisbord (1937) argued that scientific socialism originated as a method of analysis, as well as a body of conclusions, later becoming a combination of theory and practice. It becomes all but impossible to separate economic and political issues from those of philosophical considerations. In other words, ideas, like economics, exist and co-exist in historical time and space.

It is precisely because ideas exist in real time that they assume importance. It is because they are important that they are fought for so vigorously. If Marxism can be shown to be scientific, then it can claim, with a sense of authority, to have answers to some rather traumatic questions that threaten us all. If, however, it is not science, but an easy-to-be-dismissed 'pseudo-science', then Marxism can be belittled and relegated to a nether world of irrelevance.

Sides get taken

There are few things in the realm of ideas that so divide the world as Marxism. Its critics are legion. There are, naturally enough, obvious suspects; those with political and ideological axes to grind. After all Marxism stands in direct opposition to the *status quo*. In the blue corner is capitalism. In the red corner is socialism. That is how it must be. Ideas must be fought out but there are a whole range of theorists who proclaim a belief in Marxism, but then spend most of their waking moments engaged in polemics with other Marxists. This, while at times irritating, is hardly novel. Lenin, writing in 1913, wrote that, 'throughout the civilised world the teachings of Marx evoke the utmost hostility and hatred...and no other attitude is to be expected, for there can be no "impartial" social science in a society based on class struggle' 1977c: 44). Marxism, when those words were written, had yet to split around the question of war, nationalism and internationalism. The acrimony towards Marxist social science has not abated. What has changed is that Marxism has become more and more riven by crisis.

The crisis in Marxism has seen the emergence of warring tribes. The range of 'Marxisms' is wide indeed. Emmanuel Wallerstein (1986) described the emergence of a 'thousand Marxisms' in the post-World War II period. It is a sadly apt commentary. There are many Marxist schools of thought, Marxist analysis of just about everything in every area of physical or mental endeavour, and doubtless in areas yet to be imagined. Marxist critiques flourish, not only of capitalism, but of every permutation of every social issue, real or imagined, let alone critiques of other Marxist theories. The crisis largely grew out of the Stalinisation of Marxism in the years after the Russian Revolution. Marxist theory became stultified and many theorists, in seeking new visions, began hiving bits off the core of Marxism. It is not necessary to go into any of the sad details of the last century, but we have today a situation where there have been attempts to rescue Marx from Engels. As bizarre as it might seem, there is a body of thought, situated under the broad banner of Marxism, that depicts Engels as somehow being antagonistic to his inseparable co-thinker. So, it ought not to come as any surprise to learn that while most, if not all, 'Marxists' agree that they are dealing with science there is disputation as to its utility. Comments such as, 'theorists have interpreted Marxism in various ways; the point, however, is to change it' (Aronowitz 1990: 1), may be droll but convey a whole world of meaning and despair. This discussion will, however, be better served if we focus on the bigger debates and criticisms that have raged around the idea of Marxism as science.

The 'science' debate framed Marxist theory and has evoked wide disputation. More than a few careers grew and thrived, depending on the stridency of the denunciations of Marxism's claim to the status of science. It certainly did no harm to philosophers such as Karl Popper, whose critique of Marxism has often been lauded as something of a seminal work. Popper was particularly critical of what he termed historicism or, 'an approach to the social sciences which assumes that historical prediction is their principal aim, and which assumes that this aim is attainable by discovering the "rhythms" or the "patterns", the "laws" or the "trends" that underlie the evolution of history' (1985: 290 emphasis in the original).

Popper's propositions vigorously rejected the scientific claim of Marxism. To give him credit he did accept that Marxism identifies trends and tendencies that occur in social change and that these trends can neither be questioned nor denied. However, Popper argued that 'trends' are not 'laws', in language that strongly echoed Eduard Bernstein's earlier work (1975). Science, in Bernstein's estimation, was based on experience, while socialism's focus was on a future social system which, by definition, could not have an experiential basis. It is a view that was rigorously contested by Georgi Plekhanov (1976: 33) who, in the first years of the twentieth century, asserted that it was eminently realistic to suppose that a scientific study of the present allows an opportunity to 'foresee', with some degree of accuracy, what is likely to occur in the future. This, he maintained, was not the province of prophecy, or of arbitrary declarations, but on the basis of experience and the accumulation of knowledge.

The criticisms of Marxism often centre on what is described as his 'determinism'. It is an interesting claim and has been levelled so consistently and for so long that more than a few 'Marxists' have sought to distance themselves from those 'disagreeable' elements of the theory. The determinist criticism, in a simplified telling, is that history has a degree of inevitability about it. Night follows day, socialism will follow capitalism and as history decrees then so shall it be. John Rees and Anthony Giddens (1997) once publicly debated 'Marx and the modern world'. Rees' arguments to discount the 'determinist' tags were succinct and worth repeating here:

Marx would not have written that 'men make their own history albeit not in circumstances of their own choosing', indeed he would not have spent a lifetime organising among the working class, if he thought the whole project was inevitable or automatic. Lenin explicitly dismissed this kind of criticism. He didn't use the common term 'determinism' but talks of an 'objectivist' as someone who simply thinks that the structure of society will deliver a particular historical goal. He said:

'The objectivist speaks of the necessity of a given historical

44

process. The Marxist gives an exact picture of a given socio-economic formation and the antagonistic relations to which it gives rise. When demonstrating the necessity for a given series of facts the objectivist always runs the risk of becoming an apologist for these facts. The Marxist discloses the class contradictions and in doing so defines his standpoint. He does not limit himself to speaking of the necessity of a process but ascertains exactly what class determines this necessity' (Rees 1997).

Despite this, that all-too-often subjective creature the 'truth' has come to damn Marxism for its 'determinism' and precludes what the actors involved actually said. Engels, as an example, might be accepted as a reliable source. He stated rather categorically that:

According to the materialist conception of history, the ultimately determining element in history is the production and reproduction of real life. Other than this neither Marx nor I have ever asserted. Hence if somebody twists this into saying that the economic element is the only determining one, he transforms that proposition into a meaningless, abstract, senseless phrase (Engels 1999 emphasis in the original).

This interaction with 'real life' is fundamental to appreciating Marxist analysis and particularly as it pertains to contemporary economic realities and to the historical movement itself. To fully come to grips with this 'reality' is to explore the abstractions that are evident and to propose possible outcomes. The Marxist method shows that 'even the most abstract categories, despite their validity – precisely because of their abstractness – for all epochs, are nevertheless, in the specific character of this abstraction, themselves likewise a product of historic relations, and possess their full validity only for and within these relations' (Marx 1974: 105).

Like everything pertaining to the realm of ideas and ideologies, sides are taken, and denunciations and acclamations are made. Some are muted and others tend towards the hyperbolic, but it is unwise to think that sides will not be taken. Anthony Giddens points an accusatory finger and remarks that 'there is much in Marx that is mistaken, ambiguous or inconsistent; and in many respects...are plainly defective when looked at from the perspective of our century' (Giddens 1983: 1). A century earlier, Franz Mehring wrote of historical materialism's detractors arguing that 'historical materialism finishes off every arbitrary construction of history; it eliminates all bare formulas that try to treat the varied life of humanity all alike' (Mehring 1975: 17).

Anatole France wrote of a king of Persia who called for a detailed history of the world to be written. The history began as 500 volumes, but the king called for it to be made shorter. The process was repeated and repeated again. Eventually, on the king's deathbed, a final 'draft' was presented. Human history was reduced to one sentence; 'they were born, they suffered and died'. Life needs to be more than that, although we are left floundering in an apparent senseless and arbitrary world. 'In bourgeois hands, history is truly a "dismal science" – at best a chronicle of scandals, at worst a nightmare of ghastly failures' (Lorimer 1999: 200).

Marx, the one whose ideas we have been discussing, has until this point appeared but briefly. It is with Marx that the validation of Marxist social science must ultimately rest.

Historical materialism

Historical materialism, or in Marx's terminology the materialist conception of history, has been the subject of endless scrutiny and criticism. Anti-Marxists and more than the occasional Marxist have sought to either refute, diminish or obscure the concept. Marx, of course, was a prolific writer but he has been consistently rebuked for not giving a full and exhaustive coverage of this or that element of what came to be known as Marxism. Whether he is 'guilty' or not is hardly the point and nor does it diminish the overall theory and body of work. For the point of this discussion, he presented a remarkably concise statement that goes to the very essence of what historical materialism is all about, and what it seeks to do. It is high time that Marx should be called upon to take part in the discussion. The statement in question comes from *A Contribution to the Critique of Political Economy* first published in 1859 (1918: 11-13) and will be broken into its constituent parts in order for us to better review this contribution.

'In the social production which men carry on they enter into definite relations that are indispensable and independent of their will; these relations of production correspond to a definite stage of development of their powers of production.'

This often repeated phrase holds the key to much that motivated Marx. The relations of production are, necessarily, the socio-economic relationships that exist at any period of history. In bourgeois or capitalist society this means the rather unequal 'relationship' that permits private ownership by one class and the apparent dependence on that class by the working class. It is the working people and their collective endeavours that constitute the 'productive forces'. The individual and the collective of individuals cannot disengage from the world around them. This world has always been 'a work in progress' and people's engagement with it depends on the economic, social and political level of development that has been achieved.

'The sum total of these relations of production constitutes the economic structure of society – the real foundation, on which rise legal and political superstructures and to which correspond definite forms of

social consciousness.'

The rights and wrongs of the base/superstructure construction have been long debated. Some argue that politics drive economic outcomes, while the classical Marxist view maintains that the reverse is true. The 'base' is the economic foundation of any society. Political, social, legal and the whole range of state institutions form the superstructure. The superstructure and its state institutions are pivotal for the development of capitalism and for the maintenance of social order and at least a sense of harmony. Ideas and ideologies are developed and come to infuse the thinking of people to the extent that the population eventually accept the often-exploitative nature of that very society.

'The mode of production in material life determines the general character of the social, political, and spiritual processes of life. It is not the consciousness of men that determines their being, but, on the contrary, their social being determines their consciousness.'

The 'mode of production' includes both the labour of the worker (labour power) and the privately-owned plant, machinery, materials (means of production). There is a clear delineation at work between the public, social aspect of production and the private nature of ownership. This quickly came to frame consciousness by the relative place occupied in the production process. It becomes a difficult thing to imagine a world that appears to be so vastly different to the 'normal', 'natural' order as it is constantly presented to us.

'At a certain stage of their development, the material forces of production in society come in conflict with the existing relations of production, or – what is but a legal expression for the same thing – with the property relations within which they had been at work before. From forms of development of the forces of production these relations turn into their fetters. Then comes the period of social revolution.'

Capitalism exists in a terrain marked by contradiction and conflict. Each step in the development of capitalism has come as a result of attempts to resolve these contradictions. Inevitably the contradictory nature of class society must meet and seek resolution. The *status quo* of capitalist relations and the growth of the working class therefore must clash. The 'era' of social revolution in this case is a point at which the slowly evolving awareness within the working class reaches a point of critical mass.

'With the change of the economic foundation the entire immense superstructure is more or less rapidly transformed. In considering such transformations the distinction should always be made between the material transformation of the economic conditions of production which can be determined with the precision of natural science, and the legal, political, religious, aesthetic or philosophic – in short ideological forms in which men become conscious of this conflict and fight it out.'

Once again, the singular importance of the economic base upon which the institutional superstructure rests comes to the fore. With a fundamental change in economic motivation and direction comes a changed state. The state, after all, and its various institutions are dependent on this economic base. Such a transition and change in the economic base (and therefore the state) can never be uncomplicated. Too many have too much to win or lose depending on how change is perceived and how it is accomplished. The only thing that can be said for certain is that once this point is reached then change cannot be stopped.

'Just as our opinion of an individual is not based on what he thinks of himself, so can we not judge of such a period of transformation by its own consciousness; on the contrary, this consciousness must rather be explained from the contradictions of material life, from the existing conflict between the social productive forces of production and the relations of production.'

There is always a tendency for individuals and entire organisations to view events from the perspective of what would be 'best', 'neatest' and least 'messy'. The period 2019 and into 2020 was a time of intense social upheaval. Class consciousness began to rapidly re-emerge. Some dismissed this as exhibiting 'anarchic' tendencies. Others saw it as a 'revolutionary' moment. Still others as a series of unrelated spontaneous risings that would fail because of their very spontaneity. Some saw these actions as 'rehearsals' for global change. All might contain elements of truth. What is certain is that the tumult that swept the globe sat within the broad framework of Marx's view of the 'consciousness' that exists and which is being developed.

'No social order ever disappears before all the productive forces, for which there is room in it, have been developed; and new higher relations of production never appear before the material conditions of their existence have matured in the womb of the old society. Therefore, mankind always takes up only such problems as it can solve; since, looking at the matter more closely, we will always find that the problem itself arises only when the material conditions necessary for its solution already exist or are at least in the process of formation.'

These few sentences are of great significance. They relate directly to the proposition that objective conditions must exist for there to be fundamental and revolutionary change. It would seem that those conditions are very much in place. What does not yet exist are the subjective conditions that relate to the awareness, the consciousness of those whose task it is to effect change. This again brings us back to the power of the apparatus of state, whose task has been to limit the growth of this consciousness.

'In broad outlines we can designate the Asiatic, the ancient, the feudal, and the modern bourgeois methods of production as so many epochs in the progress of the economic formation of society.'

Classes come into conflict and changes occur. It is the same process within entire economic formations. The productive forces grow, the contradictions become acute, resolution cannot be achieved and a new, stronger and more progressive structure is born.

'The bourgeois relations of production are the last antagonistic form of the social process of production – antagonistic not in the sense of individual antagonisms, but of one arising from conditions surrounding the life of individuals in society; at the same time the productive forces developing in the womb of bourgeois society create the material conditions for the solution of that antagonism.'

A class-based society is necessarily antagonistic. Each class in society has a differing set of objectives. They can never be in harmony. Managing this class-based society has never been an easy task for capitalism and its state, but the inevitability of this becoming unmanageable is made clear by the fact that the working class, regardless of all claims to the contrary, just becomes bigger and broader. For the first time in history, this now global class constitutes half of the population of the planet. It exists because capitalism created it.

'This social formation constitutes, therefore, the closing chapter of the prehistoric stage of human society.'

Marx brought the short exposition to a close with the statement that 'the prehistory' of human society was coming to an end. This has a strong echo in the opening lines of the *Communist Manifesto* where Engels and Marx state, 'The history of all hitherto existing society is the history of class struggles' (Marx and Engels 1977: 35). To divide the history of human society into a 'prehistory' of class society and a yet to be born 'history' or conceivably 'post history' was, of course, a conscious decision and one worth considering.

Can Marxism be designated as science? The answer does

matter but not from any desire on the part of Marxists to be taken into some warm embrace or accreditation by academe. It matters because if it does constitute a scientific method of appreciating the world, then it has application and utility. Marx's contributions to an understanding of economics and philosophy are all but universally acknowledged. Its application for today and into the future is what matters. So, is it science? The definition of science that the prestigious Science Council offers states that, 'science is the pursuit and application of knowledge and understanding of the natural and social world following a systematic methodology based on evidence' (Science Council 2020). Marxism indisputably does just that.

Critics of Marxism still maintain that Marxism is less than science. Earlier in this discussion, Georgi Plekhanov's (1976: 33) defence of Marxism as science was cited. His assertion was that it was entirely reasonable to suppose that a scientific study of the present (and doubtless the past as well) allows an opportunity to make valid assumptions about what was likely to occur. This, he maintained, had nothing to do with 'prophecy' but was based on accumulated knowledge.

The science of Marxism and in this special case, the historical materialist method, needs to be able to be tested in practice. It becomes a question of utility. The current stage of the development of history, based on the two-fold process that is the focus of this work, requires elaboration. Capitalism, according to Marxist theory, is but one economic formation in the historical development of the world. Theory points to a changed and new formation that will emerge from the preceding formation. In microcosm, the struggles underway within capitalism and relating to which power will dominate the capitalist economy are a reflection of this historical materialist perspective. If this can be shown, then the case for Marxism as science is clearly proven.

Putting the theory to the test

The issue being confronted in this work, the rise of a rival capitalist hegemon within the shadow of the decline of an entire economic formation, has excited the imaginations of a great many. There are, naturally enough, some facts that need to be considered and some areas of wishful thinking to be discounted.

It hardly needs comment that China's economy is rapidly rising. The US Congressional Research Service (Morrison 2019) is among a range of observers who note this extraordinary growth since China first seriously embraced capitalism in the 1970s. 'China's growing global economic influence and the economic and trade policies it maintains have significant implications for the United States and hence are of major interest to Congress. While China is a large and growing market for US firms, its incomplete transition to a free-market economy has resulted in economic policies deemed harmful to US economic interests' (Morrison 2019: 1). What Morrison finds problematical is interesting. He is concerned that China has not 'transitioned' to a complete free-market economy, although close to 70 per cent of all Chinese industry is in the private sector. The fact that the US government as well as capital regards this in a relatively negative light is significant, although even if the figure stood at 100 per cent, the anxiety would be just as great. Threats to power, real or perceived, simply cannot be countenanced and nor can state and capital be simply separated.

There have been influential observers who have argued for a 'concert of Asia'. In particular, Hugh White (2012) has promoted the idea that there needs to be and that there can be an understanding between the two powers. There is an echo to Karl Kautsky's 'ultra-imperialist' theories in this. Even as White's thesis was being promoted, problems were beginning to surface. Koji Yoshino (2016) invokes the concept of 'national interest' when criticising White's position. While Japan recognises that 'stabilising' Sino-US relationships is worthwhile, other problems remain. These include border tensions and disputes between China and other states. It is also virtually impossible to imagine Japan willingly relinquishing its security treaty with the USA. This would likely lead to a serious re-armament of Japan that would go well beyond its already ambitious re-shaping of its military capacity. Sharing is hardly a likely scenario.

The above example is just one small indication of the differences between what might be called 'mainstream' or 'traditional' analyses and those articulated by Marxists. Robert Gilpin (1987: 10) voices the opinion that the state and capital are quite separate entities, and have separate origins and independent agendas. It is a view that allows for the schizophrenic argument that Chinese capitalism needs to be positively engaged with, while simultaneously seeking to limit or 'restrain' its political policies at home and its influence abroad. The state, capitalism, political ambition, power are all interconnected and ultimately inseparable. Andreas Bieler and Adam Morton (2018) describe a situation where state and market in capitalism attain the appearance of separation due to the particular way the social relations of production are organised around the private ownership of the means of production and wage labour. Their analysis focuses on Brazil, Russia, India and China (the BRICS economies). 'Analysing the emergence of the BRICS through the philosophy of internal relations makes clear that the rise cannot be an issue of different state policies, nor a binary issue of great power rivalry versus cooperation. The economic is always internally related to the political' (Bieler and Morton 2018: 161).

This is particularly well-illuminated when considering China. The changes in economic policies cannot be simply separated from a changing state structure. While those changes are occurring, there is also the issue of changes to class forces and their interactions. Once again this is interconnected with all other aspects of development.

China's rapid ascension into the ranks of global capitalism and its position of becoming rival and threat has come about not by some miracle but by the labour of hundreds of millions of Chinese workers, by the foreign investment from global capitalism including US capitalism, and by a concerted effort on the part of the Chinese bureaucracy and growing capitalist class. The world view of scholars such as Robert Gilpin, who assume an autonomy between state and capitalism, provides full and rich analyses of this or that aspect of life, but they all too frequently become impressionistic. The 'dots' are seldom joined. This is where Marx's method becomes so very pertinent.

Marx (1974) argued that what was essential was to make observations that move from the simple to the complex and that show the inter-relationship of all component parts:

> simple conceptions such as labour, division of labour, demand, exchange value, and conclude with state, international exchange and world market...The concrete is concrete because it is a combination of many determinations, i.e. a unity of diverse elements. In our thought it therefore appears as a process of synthesis, as a result, and not as a starting point, although it is the real starting point and, therefore, also the starting point of observation and conception (1974: 100-1).

Marx was not speaking of the development of a single economy, but it has direct relevance when considering developments in China. Here we can see the process unfold as he described. Labour becomes important, it is necessarily exploited, which results in profitability, which is reflected in capital growth and the development of state structures and institutions to augment that growth, which sees China taking its place in the broader world economy. The problem is not in the progression, but in the fact that the process begins with labour, and the development of a huge industrial working class whose aims must remain antagonistic to those of the new ruling class. The connectivity of these themes remains an essential element of Marxist analysis and method, whether they are represented in one country or across the globe. Marxism synthesises the components of capitalist relations, beginning with the role of labour and concluding with the development of globalisation.

A recent World Bank statement reported that, 'China's high growth based on resource-intensive manufacturing, exports, and low-paid labor has largely reached its limits and has led to economic, social, and environmental imbalances' (World Bank 2019). The Hong Kong based China Labour Bulletin (CLB) (2020) records protests, strikes and labour unrest in China. They rely on press reports and their own contact base in China and, as a consequence, they are largely understated as a result of some rather adept censorship measures. Even so, in 2019, CLB recorded more than 1700 strikes and worker protests; a rise of 36 per cent from 1250 reported cases in 2017. What becomes clear is that Chinese capitalism is riven with crisis and the contradictions that so haunt capitalism everywhere, and which validate the premise upon which Marxist theory and method is predicated.

If historical materialism and the Marxist method of analysis can clarify what is happening within economies and states, then it has the same capacity to analyse what is taking place on a global scale. It is, as Marx and Engels so eloquently put it, a case whereby, 'the bourgeoisie cannot exist without constantly revolutionising the instruments of production, and therefore the relations of production, and with them the whole relations of society' (1977: 38-9). Consequently, as Solomon and Rupert assert, historical materialism 'approaches the question of globalization not with puzzlement over dramatic changes in forms of accumulation, but fully expecting them' (2002: 284).

Georgi Lukacs writing in the 1920s in *A Defence of History and Class Consciousness* declared that:

> historical materialism eclipses all the methods that went before it, on the one hand, inasmuch as it conceives reality as a historical process, and on the other hand, inasmuch as it is in a position to understand the starting point of knowledge at any one time. Knowledge itself is understood to be just as much a product of the objective process of history (2000: 105).

We shall allow Hazel Smith, co-editor with Mark Rupert of *Historical Materialism and Globalization*, the final word:

> Historical materialism, like any other theory, can be judged by how well it satisfies certain criteria which include explanatory power, normative acceptability and, perhaps more controversially, emancipatory potential. By explanatory power, I mean the ability to illuminate aspects of human society that are not immediately available to us through observation. A satisfactory explanatory theory is governed by rules of logic and consistency with an appeal to verification...by reference to empirical research. Normative acceptability means that due consideration is given to the ethical implications of the theory. Emancipatory theory links the empirical and normative aspects of theorising to social practice whose intention is to bring about emancipation... through political change (Smith 2002: 276).

It is within this integrated and interlinked view of history, its progress and the development of political processes, linked as they are to economic factors, that the rise of China, the fall of the United States and the end of the economic formation of capitalism can be understood. It is also a more than useful tool in understanding the rather disturbing trend towards a resurgent nationalism, economic nationalism and the inherent threats that this poses.

Chapter 3

Power, nationalism and the dogs of war

There is no end to the round of questions and contradictions that the world throws at us. On the one hand it is abundantly clear that capitalism is a global system and has been engaged in a process of globalisation ever since its inception. On the other hand, governments and ruling classes in so many nation states are marching to the beat of nationalist drums. Surely this is contradictory and yes, it is. Globalisation is so obviously in the best interests of capital. It opens up vast markets, is efficient, is cost effective and allows for global production chains that certainly help reduce costs and bolster profit margins. While it does not and cannot make the inevitable threat of a falling rate of profit go away, it can, at least in the short term, keep the crisis at bay. It would seem to be logical from other angles as well. States are political representations of capitalism and capitalism is increasingly integrated across states and the entire globe. Surely co-operation would be better than antagonism, especially as the most powerful capitalist concerns are spread across numbers of nation states. That, however, is not how the world seems to turn. History is clear in this respect and the ruthless nature of capitalism is equally clear. Co-operation, for capitalism, is either anathema or a coded way of demanding submission of the weaker to the greater. You either grow or die, win or lose, and then when great power politics is added to the mix, there is trouble.

Regardless, however, of whether nationalism and economic nationalism are anachronisms in an age of obvious capitalist globalisation and economic integration, the fact of the matter is that both political nationalism and economic nationalism are very much alive and enjoying robust good health. This has serious implications for the world, for capitalism, for nation states and for the people who inhabit these same nation-state structures. This chapter, therefore, examines the rise of nationalist sentiment and how states are manipulating and promoting this regrettable rise. It also explores the rise in economic nationalism and the impact it might have on capitalist development. By implication this brings the discussion to the issue of imperialism and great power rivalry within a nationalist framework. These rivalries have, historically, ended badly with millions dead, as the inability of resolving the contradictions of capitalism have attested. Ultimately, what we are witnessing is the fall of empire, the fight for hegemony, and the inability of capitalism to alter the course of its historical development and demise.

Nationalism

A good place to begin in any discussion of nationalism is with Benedict Anderson and his *Imagined Communities* (2006). He insisted that the 'nation' is an imagined concept. Anderson argued that, 'it is imagined because the members of even the smallest nation will never know most of their fellow-members, meet them, or even hear of them, yet in the minds of each lives the image of their communion' (2006: 6). At the same time the very concept of nation can so easily evoke a deeply emotive and enduring appeal. He structured his theory around what he described as 'three paradoxes'. These are:

1. The objective modernity of nations...vs their subjective antiquity in the eyes of nationalists. 2. The formal universality of nationality...everyone can, should, will 'have' a nationality...vs the irremediable particularity of its manifestations [the claim by many nationalists to a 'unique' and specific 'identity' effectively conferred by blood as opposed to the reality of ethnically and

culturally diverse populations]. 3. The 'political' power of nationalisms vs their philosophical poverty and even incoherence (Anderson 2006: 5).

For many theorists the nation stands and maintains a claim to the bodies, minds and souls of people as a result of a shared history and shared cultural roots. If we were to fuse together the many definitions that abound, we would end up with something like, 'a nation is a stable community of people, connected by a common language, territory, history, and culture'. As Anderson described it, 'nationality...as well as nationalism, are cultural artefacts' (Anderson 2006: 4). What most definitions omit, but which is rather salient, is that these communities, be they 'real' or 'imagined', are framed around an economic and political structure and, in Marxist terminology, based on class relations and exploitative relationships. This divergence between bourgeois and Marxist interpretations becomes even more distinct when the rule of thumb definition of nationalism is brought into the equation. Nationalism, if we again distil the plethora of definitions, is simply 'loyalty and devotion to a nation, especially a sense of national consciousness'. People are exhorted, and have been for generations, to place a sense of primacy on 'their' specific nation. This can only lead to friction across borders. As Ernest Gellner put it, 'nationalism is not the awakening of nations to self-consciousness: it invents nations where they did not exist' (Gellner 1964: 169).

The nation and nationalism have proven to be most resilient phenomena and have been carefully and consciously engendered by capitalism and used to good effect. The use of emotive symbolism and the ethos of nationalism is a deliberate act of social control that is used to manipulate consciousness. Eric Hobsbawm noted that it is 'highly relevant to that comparatively recent historical innovation, the "nation", with its associated phenomena: nationalism, the nation-state, national symbols, histories and the rest. All these rest on exercises in social engineering' (2004: 13). This is counterposed by Liah Greenfeld who finds comfort in a structure that is at least in her opinion a positive thing describing it as:

> inherently egalitarian, nationalism has as one of its central cultural consequences an open – or class – system of stratification, which allows for social mobility, makes labor free...and dramatically expands the sphere of operation of market forces...Also, because of...investment in the dignity of the nation – that is, its prestige – which is necessarily assessed in relation to the status of other nations, nationalism implies international competition (2009: 23).

And so, just as beauty might be found in the eye of the beholder, so too nationalism is either a problem or a solution.

For a long time, there was a view that nationalism could be regarded as either progressive or regressive. This debate took up a lot of the left's time and energies. Right-wing nationalism was an obvious target. History clearly showed the post-WWII 'new left' that fascism and authoritarianism equated with a backward form of nationalist expression. This post-war period was also a time when the world (and the left, albeit at a remove) was engulfed and engaged in anti-colonial struggles and campaigns. Third World radicalism became the call-to-arms for the left in the West. Times, however, change and political realities resurface. Maintaining such a view, that one can separate nationalism into good and bad categories, is becoming increasingly difficult, given the shifts in political and economic development that have been accompanying capitalism as it sinks into deeper and deeper crisis.

Nationalism, at its most raw and unadorned, is, as Orwell described it, 'the habit of identifying oneself with a single nation or other unit, placing it beyond good and evil and recognising no other duty than that of advancing its interests' (cited in Williams 2017). Orwell was writing in the immediate aftermath of WWII and his views were clearly coloured by witnessing the worst possible endpoint of nationalist politics and policies. But surely life is different today? No, life unfortunately is not different. Overt expressions of nationalist sentiment recede and return with greater strength. Marxist theory promotes the view that economic issues drive political responses. The fall and rise of nationalism is but one proof of the theory. Global economic crisis runs parallel with nationalist reaction.

The period after WWII until the mid-1970s and the rapid rise in capitalist globalisation has often been described as the 'golden age' of capitalism. Things were moving along nicely. The constant fear that haunts capital, the fall of the rate of profit, had, for the moment, receded. The state loosened its ideological grip just a little or at least gave the impression of doing so. The people enjoyed some of the fruits of this intensely brief 'golden age'. The need to promote the sense of 'us' versus 'them' had become something of an anachronism. But this 'golden age' was little more than a pause. Crisis returned. A speed up in globalisation was unavoidable. Capitalism required that it be so. The small gains that had been made by the working class quickly evaporated. The welfare state began to be dismantled, manufacturing industries collapsed only to re-emerge in developing economies, wages stagnated, economies faltered. Someone had to be held responsible. The ever useful 'other' was once more resurrected, as it has always been, and nationalism resurfaced, bigger and brighter and more threatening than ever before. The problem, of course, with nationalism is that while Country A is fanning the flame, so too is Country B. Nationalism was a recipe for disaster in days gone by. The only difference today is that the stakes are that much higher.

The risks are higher in a number of ways. Previous experiences of nationalist approaches to resolving problems have led to the deaths of many millions. Major power rivalry is now at heights that mirror those preceding the two world wars, but this time around there is a difference. This is not just the degree of firepower that states possess, but the dangers of hegemon change and of the very future of capitalism itself. This work focuses specifically on the struggle between the USA and China. The USA, as the greater military force, has historically been the more belligerent. Its nuclear arsenal is vast, and it is adapting this arsenal with disturbing intent. In early 2020, the USA deployed a new 'low-yield' nuclear weapon. As Aaron Mehta, in *Defense News*, reported, 'a new nuclear warhead, requested, designed, and produced under the Trump administration, has been deployed aboard a nuclear submarine, the Pentagon confirmed...' (Mehta 2020). This is acutely alarming. For some time, there had been talk of developing such 'useable' nuclear weaponry and it was no secret that they were being produced, but to take that next step of deployment can only lead to responses from rival states.

Nationalism grows in climates of economic insecurity and fear. Individuals become fearful that jobs may disappear, that wages will not grow, that life is palpably becoming more difficult. They all too frequently and too easily fall prey to nationalist demagogues who repeat simplistic and irrational slogans about 'foreigners' stealing jobs and the great litany of irrationalities that we know so well. This fear has, in turn, been instilled in the broader population by the state itself with its nationalist symbolism that it invokes in difficult times. The state has the task of maintaining a sense of unity, community and oneness; a society where, according to the state, class is irrelevant but where our national identity is what holds us together. The global economy is in deep crisis. Capitalism is in deep crisis. Nation states reflect this crisis. Political expressions become more acutely nationalist and suspicious. Economic expressions of these fears make the present and future even more fearful as economic nationalism reasserts itself.

Economic nationalism

The trade war between the USA and China may have been technically launched by US president Donald Trump, but the decision was not an arbitrary one or based on a whim. It did not simply spring from the air, or from an idea that crossed the president's desk or imagination. James Dorn, in the *Beijing Review*, wrote that in:

> his closing remarks at the Third Strategic Economic Dialogue (SED) in Beijing in December 2007, US Treasury Secretary Henry Paulson stated that both China and the United States 'recognize the need to fight economic nationalism in our two nations'. Yet it is much easier for Congress to politicize US-China trade than to be patient and engage in the SED initiated by Secretary Paulson. It is also much easier to use China as a scapegoat (Dorn 2008: 13).

The date of this statement is significant. It comes before the Global Financial Crisis of 2008, before the Obama-inspired 'pivot to Asia' of 2011, and before the start of the trade war that began in 2018. China, free trade and its protectionist 'opposite' were fears that had been exercising the minds of many for a long time. Why? The answer is tied to the economic crisis of global capitalism and to the threat that the USA felt and feels from rivals to its hegemony.

This brings us to the worrying refrain that the world is 'returning' to policies of economic nationalism. What precisely are we talking about? George Macesich (1985) offers a rather straightforward perspective, that economic nationalism is about discriminating in favour of one's own nation and that this becomes a matter of state policy. Decades earlier, the idea was simplified into two propositions; that 'American Motors is better for the United States than British Motors and therefore deserves support' and 'what is good for the United States is good for American Motors' (Kahan 1967: 20). There are two obvious problems with such a view of the world. The first is that five, or ten, or 20 industrialised economies might simultaneously adopt the same idea with the resultant friction that must inevitably ensue. The second problem lies in an increasingly globalised and integrated set of capitalist relationships that collide with such an inward and regressive nationalist perspective

Economic nationalism is the antithesis of capitalist globalisation and yet it is growing in direct proportion to capitalism's globalisation and integration. Sam Pryke defines economic nationalism as 'the attempt to create, bolster and protect national economies in the context of world markets' (2012: 285). Pryke sees no essential problem arising from economic nationalism. History, however, can be a rather harsh teacher. Pryke's rather sanguine view of the world came in the immediate aftermath of the GFC. The gathering storm of protectionist policies had yet to crash upon any particular shore and so, 'contrary to much speculation, the financial crash of October 2008 and the subsequent recession have not seen a generalised rise in economic protectionism' (Pryke 2012: 290). What a difference a few short years can make. It would be wise to consider other more cautious views on economic nationalism.

There were clear indications that protectionist measures within national economies were being actively promoted well ahead of the eruption of the trade war. The World Trade Organisation (WTO) in 2016 pointed to a, 'relapse in G20 economies' efforts at containing protectionist pressures. Not only is the stockpile of trade-restrictive measures continuing to increase, but also more new trade restrictions were recorded' (WTO 2016: 4). A decade earlier, Ben Bernanke (2006), then Chairman of the US Federal Reserve, cautioned against such an economic shift and the negative consequences it might have for the global economy.

The move to protectionist policies, barriers and threats of trade war may give a false sense that they are somehow spontaneous acts. The fact is that they are the product of deliberate policy decisions by leading capitalist nation states. It is a calculated measure but one that is fraught with danger. The journey is certainly perilous. 'A trade war, initiated by the United States, would do serious damage to the global economy as protectionist actions escalate. Countries imposing tariffs and countries subject to tariffs would experience losses in economic welfare, while countries on the sidelines would experience collateral damage. If tariffs remain in place, losses in economic output would be permanent' (IHS 2020). There seems, from the US perspective, to be almost an echo of Cold War tactics and policy. Towards the end of the Cold War the USA engaged in a campaign of massive spending on its military with a view to 'bleeding' the economy of the USSR. It was a case of who has the biggest economic reserves. The USA today seems prepared to suffer economic losses in the hopes that their rivals will sustain even more crippling losses. It is a dangerous strategy.

In the period leading up to this precarious moment, voices were raised against what were such obviously negative policies. Former US Treasury Secretary Lawrence Summers (2016), for example, indicated an unease regarding perceptions that people have that 'open' economic policies in recent years are producing a political backlash. The former managing director of the International Monetary Fund (IMF), Christine Legarde, remarked that, 'I hope it is not a 1914 moment and I hope that we can be informed by history to actually address the negative impact of globalisation...because it has historically delivered massive benefits and it can continue to do so' (2016). She was referring specifically to Britain's decision to leave the European Union, but equally significant in this context have been nationalist sentiments affecting US-Russia relations, US-

China relations and the rise of nationalist political groupings across the globe. All of this seems to call into question the rather courageous call by Robert Gilpin (2000: 51) when he argues that economic efficiency and the ambitions of dominant nation states will determine the future power and prosperity of global capitalism. If Gilpin's thesis were to be carried to its logical or, possibly, illogical conclusion, then the world is in for some interesting, if dangerous, times.

Martin Wolf (2004: 37) describes the attempt by capitalist states to reverse the trend towards globalisation that occurred at the end of the nineteenth century. He makes the point that economic nationalism led directly to militarism and imperialism. Free trade was stifled and war was the ultimate and inevitable result. The motivations behind national states to enter into such a contradictory position is, in part, a response to economic downturn and also as a means of accommodating and ameliorating the fears and concerns of domestic populations that are increasingly facing difficult economic outcomes.

Nationalism, and in this context economic nationalism, pits one nation against another and by implication one worker against another There are implicit dangers for national economies and for the working class in such a perspective. Using the case of the post-communist period in Russia, David Szakonyi (2007) describes the potential, in the exercising of economic nationalism, to create both internal and external 'enemies' as a means of building a narrow national unity.

The promotion of nationalist perspectives echoes political and economic debates dating back a century when free trade and protectionist debates flourished in the lead up to World War I. What is fundamentally different in this twenty-first century version of the debate is that protectionism and economic nationalism are even less viable options. The economic costs are higher. The militarisation, and the rhetoric that accompanies this, gives cause for concern. Wolf's warnings were made in

2004. Much has happened since then and none of it bodes well. His reminder of events of a century ago, and the issues of war and imperialism, have special resonance for us today.

Imperialism in the twenty-first century

Surely things are not as they were at the beginning of the twentieth century? What is this talk of a 'return' to imperialist policies and of explicit danger? First, we need to take a look at just what constitutes imperialism and whether it can be considered a factor in this twenty-first century. James Petras states that 'imperialism can be understood as a policy or practice by which the government of a country increases its power by gaining control over other areas of the world' (Petras 2020: x). Petras is speaking not from the perspective of the historian but is observing conditions as they exist today. If we then weigh his words against those of earlier Marxist writers, we can see some obvious connections. There is Lenin's (1977e: 726-7) analysis of imperialism, which saw capital becoming more monopolistic, the rise of finance capital, the increasing importance of the export of capital and a division of the world between associations of capitalism. Yes, it is an analysis made a century ago, but its relevance is there for all to see. Then there is Nicolai Bukharin's (2003: 130-2) description of the state acting in the interests of national capital and argument that imperialism is, therefore, an expression of state power within an international context. Once again this does not sound all that dated. Finally, we can cite Leon Trotsky's (1996) assertion that capitalism had outgrown the restrictions of national boundaries and that imperialism was the proof that this was the case. Once more there is an immediacy to such an analysis, despite it being written over a hundred years ago. A pattern emerges and it tends to suggest that things have not changed in any significant way.

Capitalism and imperialism, in much the same way as capitalism and the state, are virtually inseparable concepts.

Capitalism and its deep crisis almost demands that imperialism remain a salient fact of life. Ellen Meiskins Wood (1998), for instance, noted that capitalism has been compelled to employ a new form of imperialism that becomes evident through financial control, and the manipulation of markets and debt.

Imperialism and capitalist expansion become the focus of Robert O'Brien. He makes the point that imperialism refers to 'a process of capitalist expansion and dominance emanating from the advanced industrial states' (2004: 53-4). Just as Trotsky outlined the connection between imperialism and a globalising capitalism, Fred Halliday (2002) describes five distinct themes that are pertinent to imperialism and to the development of capitalist globalisation. These include capitalism's historical tendency towards expansion, the militaristic nature of capitalist states throughout the twentieth century, [and certainly into the twenty-first century] the rise of global inequality, even as developing states acquire an industrial base, the growth in importance of institutions of capitalist domination in the form of the IMF and World Bank among others, and, finally, the seemingly irresistible rise of the world capitalist market.

What is most relevant in all this is the inseparable relationship that capitalism and imperialism enjoy. Capitalism expands. It must expand. It is invariably predatory and so imperialism becomes the very best fit to realise the aims and objectives of this expansionist economic reality. Gerard Dumenil and Domenique Levy capture the essence of imperialism and of its relationship to capital:

> by 'imperialism', we do not mean a particular stage of capitalism, but one of its constant features since its earliest stages (in particular, in the sphere of trade). Imperialism, itself, goes through various stages, but the common, continuous, trait that defines imperialism as such is the economic advantage taken by the most advanced and

dominating countries over less developed or vulnerable regions of the world...The crucial factor is to impose, within the dominated countries, a government prone to the development of economic relations favorable to the interest of dominating countries. This can be achieved by all means: collaboration with local ruling classes, subversion, or war...States are, indeed, crucial, both within dominating and dominated countries. Imperialism is not the fact of a single country, but of a group of countries. The nature of the relationships among these countries defines a central characteristic of imperialism at each of its stages (Dumenil and Levy 2004: 660-1).

Imperialism is not of itself hegemonic, although the United States has sought to maintain its total hold on political, economic and military power.

These definitions and observations of imperialism and of capitalism's expansion bring us almost inevitably to the question as to whether China is or is not an imperialist power. It is certainly an issue that hovers on the periphery of consciousness. China certainly exhibits some of the characteristics outlined above, but it must be remembered that since the 1970s and its 'opening up' to the West, its economy grew largely as a result of the advances made to it by US imperialism. American and international capitalism found a gigantic 'sweatshop' and conveyor belt. It became the West's factory. But then, as China's economy strengthened, so too has it found itself increasingly in the cross hairs of a nuclear-armed US desperate to maintain supremacy.

While it remains convenient to regard China as an imperialist power, there needs to be some serious caveats placed upon such a description. China is certainly a capitalist economy and, by definition, expansionary as all capitalist states are and ever have been. It certainly seeks to influence outcomes to suit its needs.

It uses 'soft power' to its advantage. Whether this is enough to successfully make the claim that it is an imperialist power is still questionable. It has a strong military capacity, and one that is growing rapidly. Its rival, the USA, is indisputably imperialist. It is expansionary, it dominates other states, governments and economies, and has always been prepared to use force to support its aims. The two states may share some similarities but around the question of militarism and brute force, there are very real differences.

The issue of whether China is imperialist remains contentious. It can certainly be argued that it exhibits some symptoms that are characteristic of an imperialist state, but equally it can be argued that it is not, at this stage of its development, an imperialist power as other Western states can be so designated. What happens over time is quite another matter. What is of greater importance in the immediate future is how China responds to measures that are put in place by the USA to constrain its growing influence and economic power. There are very real threats to peace that emanate from America's desire to enact policies that are euphemistically described as 'containing' China. What is certain is that there will be no sharing of any global economic pie.

To give any credence to the idea that America would consider a 'power sharing' relationship with its major rival is nothing less than engaging in a fantasy. The entire history of humanity since economics and economic relations came to dominate show this to be an unrealisable dream. Chris Hedges' statistics regarding war and peace (2003) were referred to earlier. It is worth repeating that the world has been at peace for just 8 per cent of the last 3400 years. Lenin (1977) reminded the world and reminds us today that, 'peaceful alliances prepare the ground for wars; the one conditions the other, producing alternating forms of peaceful and non-peaceful struggle on one and the same basis of imperialist connections and relations within world economics and world politics' (Lenin 1977: 724). Peace, under such conditions, is but a lull between wars.

The threat of war

Lenin's argument is one of those that divides opinion. For a great many people having lived through the golden age of capitalism in the post-WWII period, his words would seem impossibly pessimistic or simply historically incorrect. The great powers in the aftermath of the last world war may have snarled at one another across the 'iron curtain' but war between major political or economic entities has not occurred.

While Lenin was speaking of inter-imperialist wars and wars between major powers, it is worth considering, also, those 'other' wars and conflicts that just rolled on throughout the post-war years. Milton Leitenberg (2006: 9), for instance, sets the figure of 41 million dead from wars and conflicts between 1945-2000. For the most part, these conflicts can be categorised as 'proxy' wars that have been and are being waged by smaller powers to serve the interests of bigger players. Angola, East Timor, Mozambique, Georgia, Yugoslavia, the Congo, Darfur, Yemen, Syria, Ukraine, Libya...it's not difficult to get the picture.

The United States, as the principal imperialist power in the world, has had a hand in more than its share of military actions. There were 40 wars, large and small, that involved the USA in the twentieth century and another ten in this century. The USA has been engaged (mostly successfully) in exercises to effect regime change approximately 60 times in the last 100 years. Lenin's depiction might be wrong, or his view might not be all that cynical after all.

Hegemons like being hegemons. While this is probably trite, it does go to the centre of much of the United States' behaviour and bellicosity. As the pre-eminent imperialist power, it is hardly prepared to allow all that many dissident flowers to bloom. This becomes an acute issue for two reasons. The first is that capitalism has entered a particularly virulent period of crisis that bodes ill for the future of the economic formation. The second is that the United States is facing its own inevitable decline as economic paradigm. Either of these issues should be cause for concern, as each threaten the peace and well-being of the people on the planet. When the two are taken together, then the possibilities are horrendous. Each deserves just a moment's reflection.

A term that has gained currency in the past period to describe how things stand with capitalism is 'late capitalism'. It denotes a stage in capitalism's development beyond which there is no realisable future. More than a few theorists and observers have commented on this across the twentieth century and from a range of Marxism's perpetually warring tribes. Each, in turn, from Werner Sombat in the early twentieth century, to Theodor Adorno in the late 1960s, to Ernest Mandel in the early 1970s and Fredric Jameson in the 1980s, sought to analyse what was coming. While their propositions make interesting reading, the fact remains that Marxism has been predicated on the theoretical premise that capitalism is but one economic formation. What is clear for all to see in the twenty-first century is that capitalism is in deep and incurable crisis, whatever label one might like to attach to it.

The United States, it must be remembered, became the pre-eminent capitalist power only at the end of WWII. Capitalism's golden age coincided with the USA assuming complete supremacy, but it was also a time when the signs of capitalism's imminent decline were being seriously discussed and described by Marxist and non-Marxist economists alike. Their fears were soon to be realised. This placed enormous pressures on capitalism as a whole and on the USA in particular and lent a specific sense of brutality to how the USA viewed the world. No sooner had American capitalism become the dominant paradigm than it was compelled to fight to preserve this dominance.

Capitalism was once a progressive force. It has undeniably been an effective wealth-creating economic system. At the social and political level, it has been instrumental in revolutionising interactions between cultures and states. Marx (1977: 38) characterised capitalism as a progressive formation. While such a characterisation can be defended, and particularly from an historical perspective, it is difficult to attach anything like a progressive label to late capitalism. Bill Dunn points out that Marx, 'saw capitalism as a complex and contradictory social system. It created enormous material advances, yet because it did so for private profit, it did not necessarily produce any general social improvements' (2009: 76). Dunn is echoing Marx's assessment of the process of capitalist development. 'Accumulation of wealth at one pole is, therefore, at the same time accumulation of misery, agony of toil, slavery, ignorance, brutality, mental degradation, at the opposite pole' (Marx 1986a: 604).

David Held (2008: 111) paraphrases Marx when he states that capitalism's success has depended on the rapid growth of the productive forces of society. While this initially represented capitalism's progressive character, it was contradicted by the exploitative system of productive relations. Herein lies a contradiction that Marx maintained would ultimately bring capitalism to the point of destruction. Significantly it is at this point along capitalism's trajectory that American capitalism assumed dominance and it is at this same point of fundamental crisis that the monumental 'clash of capitalisms' between the USA and China can be observed.

If there is a clash of capitalisms and between capitalist rivals, and it is abundantly clear that this is the case, then how such a clash is resolved has serious implications for us all. Capitalism does not operate like a board game. Playing 'Monopoly' may be a good way to while away the hours, but when the stakes are a little higher, then the 'game' becomes a little rougher. Leon

Trotsky summed things up rather succinctly in 1914, and his words have particular resonance today. 'Our entire planet, its land and water areas...provide today the arena for a worldwide economy...This work has been accomplished by capitalism. But capitalism also compels the capitalist states to fight in order to subordinate this world economy to the profit interests of the respective national bourgeoisies' (Trotsky 1996). What happens when the fighting starts is a cause of fear for the world. What happens after the fighting ends determines the future for us all.

To speak of war being an ultimate and unavoidable consequence of capitalism and of capitalist rivalries appears to be an exercise of the deepest cynicism. Nobody in their right mind could consider, even for a moment, that war was a realistic option. At the same time, it is hardly a secret that the Pentagon and the White House concoct strategies and plans to wage 'winnable' wars that can and do involve nuclear weaponry. It would be naïve to assume that those who are in the United States' sights do not also engage in the same grotesque manoeuvres. It ought to be equally naïve to imagine that the imperialist powers in 1914 did not know what was at stake when they drove the world to war. Historians such as Christopher Clark (2014) can write of the world 'sleepwalking into war'. The reality was that the war was the result of capitalism's inability to resolve the contradictions of a globalising market and the nation-state, and of the question of power within the capitalist world economy. The leaders of the day went into that conflict with their eyes wide open. Today's world leaders are just as aware as their predecessors.

The point remains that nobody in their right mind could wish for war and especially the sort of war that nuclear-armed states might unleash. The people, the working class, have absolutely nothing to gain from such a scenario and yet an entire state apparatus exists with the aim of making people believe the lie that nation matters, that nationalism matters, that we have something in common with our leaders and our ruling class and that this separates us from that 'other'. Engels (2000), in his letter to Mehring, offered the view that ideological processes can and often are used to effectively mask what is the real class nature of society. What Marx and Engels described as 'false consciousness' was later adapted by Antonio Gramsci to become 'cultural hegemony'. Robert Cox (1993: 51) describes this as a situation arising from the ruling class seeming to offer concessions in a bargain for both acquiescence and ultimately acceptance of state power. Nobody would accept war as an option were it not for this acceptance of the status quo that the state has so carefully engendered.

The future certainly appears to be precarious. A great power looms on the horizon. Another, still greater, power seeks to control, contain and diminish its rival. One power seems to be on the wrong side of history. States and empires are not immutable things. Change comes and economic power shifts. Capitalism was not always the dominant and all-encompassing force in the world. History would suggest that it will not always be that paradigm. The United States has not always been, and nor will it remain, the dominant force in the capitalist world. America's rise as political entity, economic power and military force does show in microcosm how capitalism has risen.

Chapter 4

The rise of a capitalist giant

America stands as the most perfect metaphor for capitalism. Or should that be the other way around? If we trace capitalism's rise from the time of the industrial revolution, then there are some rather obvious comparisons to be made. Capitalism arose as the dominant force in the world from about 1760. The industrial revolution had achieved its revolutionary upheaval of economic and political relations by about 1840. The American War of Independence, the Revolutionary War, ran from 1765 until 1783. One event overlaps the other. It is obvious that capitalism did not miraculously begin in the USA when the British were driven out, but the nation was formed within a capitalist framework.

Capitalism has moved from being broadly regarded as progressive to reactionary. Capitalism transformed the world and revolutionised economic relations, relations between country and city, between states, and began the process that we now call globalisation. The problem, and this is now being proven on a daily basis, is that there are limits to capitalist expansion. The elastic can only stretch so far. Capitalism has nowhere to go. And so the life cycle of capitalism is coming to a crisis-riven conclusion.

The United States is at once capitalism in microcosm and capitalism writ large. Capitalism was revolutionary and so too was America born of revolution. It was expansive. It offered a semblance of hope and aspiration to millions. 'Give me your tired, your poor, your huddled masses yearning to breathe free', had not become a savage parody when first written in the 1880s by Emma Lazarus. Whether the words of her sonnet were used by the US state to show compassion, or to encourage a labour force to make capitalism strong, is neither here nor there. Capitalism and the United States had something to offer. A century on and the reverse is the case.

This chapter traces the journey of the United States from those early optimistic days, not quite to its apogee, although defining such a point is a little subjective. By the late 1800s, the USA had become a significant world economy and, through its war with Spain and acquisition of extra-territorial possessions, had assumed the mantle of imperialist power. The new idea that surrounded the birth of the new nation will be examined, as will its history of slavery. America's slave history has been the focus for many scholars in the most recent period. A common idea is that America, its capitalist growth and its social outlook is not simply a by-product of slavery, but that slavery was integral to the country's past and present. This theory will also be visited and critically assessed.

The USA, capitalism and democracy become interchangeable in the lexicon of some observers. Democracy as a means of promoting specific values and ideology will also be considered, as will the issue of 'American exceptionalism' as a motivating force within political debates and foreign policy. The United States' success as a developing capitalist state was, in the final analysis, the direct result of labour, the immigrant working class and the burgeoning of global capital.

The USA and the birth of an idea

The United States, just like capitalism, exists in a web of contradictions and paradoxes. The founding fathers of the USA, from the very first, wished to signal to the 'old world' that a new and better future was possible. The first 'official' words uttered were inspiring ones and yet the country's growth and its economic prosperity was predicated on the exploitation of labour. The new nation loudly proclaimed freedom to be a cornerstone and yet people lived as slaves. The good was mixed with the bad. Despite all these paradoxes and contradictions, it was seen by many in Europe as that 'better' option. It was regarded as a metaphor, an idea. It was also viewed as a social experiment, with its focus on democratic forms and structures. It was a new economic structure, sitting within the new economic order that was capitalism. Capitalism was burgeoning. A new capitalist state, without the baggage of a feudal past, was, in effect, capitalism in microcosm.

It is a rare thing for Marxists to have much to say in support of the United States. The USA epitomises capitalism, and in the twenty-first century it encapsulates all that is wrong with capitalism. Marxism represents an idea that stands in stark contrast to the barbarity of capitalism. Marx, however, was almost complimentary about the new nation born of a revolutionary war against Britain. This came, in part, from his assessment of capitalism and of its role in revolutionising society and the world. 'The bourgeoisie, during its rule of scarce one hundred years, has created more massive and more colossal productive forces than have all preceding generations together' (Marx and Engels 1977: 40). This same young capitalism, in Marx and Engels' estimation, 'has accomplished wonders far surpassing Egyptian pyramids, Roman aqueducts and Gothic cathedrals; it has conducted expeditions that put in the shade all former Exoduses of nations and crusades' (1977: 38). Marx's depiction (1975b: 195-201) of the introduction of steam and of the railways in relation to the transformations of India has often been used to describe an almost globalising 'mission' of capitalism. At the same time Marx was implacably hostile to capitalism, as it represented an intensely exploitative system. He famously stated that to, 'prevent any possible misunderstanding, a word. I paint the capitalist and the landlord in no sense *couleur de rose*' (1986a: 20).

While Marx saw things in America to admire, it was always with an eye to the contradictions that were revealed. The very fact that those 'huddled masses' chose to cross the Atlantic was itself caught up in contradiction. Robert Weiner (1980: 468) describes the situation whereby workers moved in large numbers from Europe and that this worked against potential European radicalisation. What was happening, however, was a rapid industrialisation and therefore proletarianisation of America and one that happened in an historically short period of time. The United States presented a puzzle to many observers. It appeared to be so very different in its economic and political development. It was an issue that Marx felt needed to be clarified. Marx's, 'view of history claimed not only (a) the universality of capitalist development but also (b) the inherent dependence of culture and politics on economics and society. America appeared to contradict both of these points... but Marx's materialism was historical or dialectical...Marx was convinced that what appeared to be difficulties would be resolved through America's subsequent historical development' (Weiner 1980: 467-8). By the early years of the twentieth century, this establishment of a working class, and a highly radicalised working class, had become yet another contradiction for capitalism.

The creation of a new nation, unencumbered by European history but sympathetic to the ideas of liberty, fraternity and equality, first espoused by the French Revolution, can be seen as constituting a revolutionary birth. It inspired many. It was inspiring from the point of view of capitalism's still innovative and outward-looking perspective. Many could not quite come to terms with the simple fact that America was, first and foremost, a growing capitalist economy, with all the upheavals and crises that go with capitalism. Engels was quick to point out the obvious, remarking that, 'as to those wise Americans who think their country exempt from the consequences of fully expanded capitalist production, they seem to live in blissful ignorance of the fact that sundry states, Massachusetts, New Jersey, Pennsylvania, Ohio, etc., have such an institution as a Labour

Bureau from the reports of which they might learn something to the contrary' (Engels 1886a). While few could be blind to the fact that the USA and its economy was being built on exploited labour, it was still perceived by large numbers of immigrants who came to feed the capitalist machine to be a better option than the 'old world'. Things have changed but it took time for the gloss to wear off.

While Marx and Engels might have recognised the promise that the new nation offered, they were acutely aware that its promise was being realised at a cost. The rise of this new and vibrant capitalist economy inevitably meant suffering as well as wealth creation. It came with all the inherent problems that are associated with such growth. The difference was in its speed. It did not have to first slough off the remnants of feudalism. Engels described it as being, 'the ideal of all bourgeois; a country rich, vast, expanding, with purely bourgeois institutions unleavened by feudal remnants or monarchical traditions and without a permanent and hereditary proletariat' (Engels 1886b). America was born as a capitalist economy, and with a sense of its destiny as a new state. The words of its founding fathers may sound today more than a little hypocritical but the *Declaration of Independence*, and its cry that, 'we hold these truths to be self-evident, that all men are created equal, that they are endowed by their Creator with certain unalienable Rights, that among these are Life, Liberty and the pursuit of Happiness' (National Archives 2019) had a clarity. True, the new nation's primary objective was to build capitalism, but it declared itself to be apart from the old tyrannies of Europe.

James P Cannon, American Marxist and founder of American Trotskyism, once commented that, 'when they said: "We hold these truths to be self-evident," they started something that opened up a new era of promise for all mankind' (Cannon 1951). He wrote of the birth of America as the 'first' American Revolution, and of the Civil War as its 'second'; a war that 'smashed the system of chattel slavery, unified the country and opened the way for its unobstructed industrial development' (Cannon 1951). The Civil War and the end of slavery was a source of great inspiration for many. Marx, in 1864, wrote to American president Abraham Lincoln congratulating the American people:

> upon your re-election by a large majority. If resistance to the Slave Power was the reserved watchword of your first election, the triumphant war cry of your re-election is Death to Slavery. From the commencement of the titanic American strife the workingmen of Europe felt instinctively that the star-spangled banner carried the destiny of their class. The contest for the territories which opened the dire epopee, was it not to decide whether the virgin soil of immense tracts should be wedded to the labor of the emigrant or prostituted by the tramp of the slave driver? (Marx 1865).

Looking back on that early history of the United States shows that the promise of America was at once both fulfilled and yet left its people and the world to wonder just what went wrong. Lincoln's *Gettysburg Address* remains perhaps the most inspiring and hopeful of speeches and yet its words sound so hopelessly hollow in this twenty-first century.

> Four score and seven years ago our fathers brought forth on this continent a new nation, conceived in Liberty, and dedicated to the proposition that all men are created equal... this nation, under God, shall have a new birth of freedom – and that government of the people, by the people, for the people, shall not perish from the earth (Abraham Lincoln Online 2020).

Something went terribly wrong. The beauty of the sentiments

expressed have little resonance with the America that we now recognise. Despite this, so many still cling to the notion that America is different, unique, is unlike any nation that has come before. The idea of 'American exceptionalism' has in large part infused the very psyche of the nation.

An 'exceptional' nation

Long before the American War of Independence, and long before the republic was formed, there existed the idea of an American destiny. James Ceaser (2012) is one among many who cite John Withrod's 'proclamation' in 1630 as his puritans were about to land, on the establishment of the 'city on the hill' and that the eyes of all people are on us (Winthrop, cited in Ceaser 2012: 7). This sense of creating something new and special was carried on and became imbued in the psyche of the nation, if indeed nations can be said to possess psyches. Alexis de Tocqeville (2009), writing in the early 1800s, exhorted all democratic nations to emulate the US example of establishing and forming its republic. It was, from the political standpoint, a rather unique experiment. As Godfrey Hodgson puts it, the, 'American Revolution did create the world's first large republic...it created a state based on a political ideology of republicanism' (Hodgson 2009: 36). In this sense it was a rather self-conscious act. Its founding fathers were well aware that history was looking over their shoulders. Those founding documents were also the product of a century of self-awareness of building that 'city on the hill'.

What is this 'exceptionalism' and is it a well-executed move by the state apparatus to inculcate a sense of unity? The early colonists, explains Deborah L Madsen, strongly felt themselves to be, 'charged with a special spiritual and political destiny: to create in the New World a church and a society that would provide the model for all the nations of Europe as they struggled to reform themselves' (Madsen 1998: 1-2). They saw in this the beginning of a 'redeemer' nation. Dreams and reality do not always coincide. Madsen describes how 'exceptionalism has always offered a mythological refuge from the chaos of history and the uncertainty of life'. In the process American history has been made a site of contention where there is a struggle to control and dominate the terms of national destiny...a struggle for appropriation, annexation, conquest and invasion (Madsen 1998: 166).

The 'dream gone wrong' view assumes greater clarity as the history of the United States unfolds. Hilde Eliassen Restad (2015: 3-6) offers a concise explanation of what exceptionalism is and, importantly, how it has been perceived. She breaks the idea into three related parts. Firstly, the USA is distinct from the Old World. This is not a question of geography but holds that the USA is 'better' than other nations, from the position that it is freer, more individualistic, more open and more dynamic than any other nation. Secondly, it has a special and unique role to play in the world. Here we return to the 'city on the hill' idea and the sense of a mission from God; a nation where 'no one is fit to be a master, and no one deserves to be a slave' (Bush 2005). The third pillar is that the United States will somehow manage to resist the laws of history. It will rise and not fall as other empires have risen and fallen. It is a view that is premised on the fact that it defeated the world's most powerful empire in Britain, that it conquered a continent and expanded its influence far beyond its borders. The end of the Cold War seemed to reinforce this rather grandiose view. And then along came China and threat perceptions began to seriously undermine this idea.

The concept of American exceptionalism may be discounted. It may be shown to be part of a deeper role that the state actively participates in to build a sense of unity. The fact is that this concept has enjoyed an astonishing strength and tenacity. It is hard to find an American leader, Republican or Democrat, who does not reference, in some way, the exceptionalism of the USA. Much has happened along the way, from the moment that

John Winthrop and his puritan colonists viewed Massachusetts Bay, to today. There has been a coupling of terms and ideas, of philosophy and economics, and a drawing of them all under the umbrella of 'America'. A word association game might be played. Democracy – America. Freedom – America. Capitalism – America. The first colonists who saw a 'city on the hill' were probably not thinking of establishing a capitalist megastructure on that same hill, but as Hodgson says, 'in recent decades, capitalism has taken its place on the podium as an aspect of American exceptionalism, almost equal with democracy' (Hodgson 2009: 99). He goes on to state that, 'one specific new element in the American belief system, from the last quarter of the twentieth century, was the elevation of American capitalism, alongside American freedom and American democracy in the pantheon of American exceptionalism' (2009: 160). We might pardon his slight equivocation, or coyness, when he describes the 'almost equal' status. Capitalism and America are virtually interchangeable terms. It becomes more difficult to forgive him his thoughts that American capitalism has only been 'elevated' to such heights from the 1970s. The actual process of 'Americanisation' of capitalism has been an ongoing thing. The USA had achieved a global position of dominance, politically and economically, far earlier than the 1970s.

The three elements that go to make up American exceptionalism, as described by Restad (2015), still serve to rally individual Americans and can unite people to rally to the banner, but there is a hollowness to the call. For some writers, such as Daniel Bell (1975), the end of exceptionalism came with the Vietnam War. Paul Kennedy (1989) in similar vein argues that by the end of Vietnam, the USA had reached its apex and had begun a slow descent. Something had clearly gone wrong.

What was it then that went wrong? It is called Capitalism. It is, after all, an economic system that is prone to inescapable contradictions and perpetually lives with crisis. It would be unrealistic to imagine that the United States could escape this. The development of America's economic base and of the ideological underpinnings of that base need to be explored. As Marx described American capitalism's stunning growth: 'the corresponding enslavement of the working class has developed more rapidly and shamelessly than in any other country' (Marx 1881). The figurative enslavement of the working class aligned perfectly with the way capitalism had developed everywhere. Literal enslavement is an issue that has been capturing the imagination of many American scholars. It requires some thought and analysis.

An economy built on slavery?

In 2019, the *New York Times Magazine* published a lengthy essay entitled *The 1619 Project*. It coincided with the 400th anniversary of the first African slaves to arrive in Virginia. The 'Project' has as its primary focus an intent to, 'reframe the country's history, understanding 1619 as our true founding, and placing the consequences of slavery and the contributions of black Americans at the very center of the story we tell ourselves about who we are' (Silverstein 2019). It immediately found itself at the centre of controversy. Nobody was denying the importance that slavery had in the development of early American capitalism. What is controversial is that, according to many scholars including Gordon Wood, Richard Carwadine, James McPherson and James Oates (Serwer 2019), the 'project' seeks to present American history primarily through the prism of race and racial conflict. It is a debate that is hardly likely to go away. It has ramifications for how twenty-first century issues in the USA are regarded and whether there is some inherent racism that all but affects the national DNA of the country, whatever that might be. It is a dubious theory. Slavery was important but the idea that it was all-encompassing and its aftermath all-consuming is all but impossible to support.

Slavery and the history of the United States go hand-in-hand. What has happened along the way has been to focus entirely on America's role. It is a period that stains US history but needs to be considered alongside a long and deeply unpleasant history and a history that is not unique to America. Slavery came to America courtesy of Britain and Spain. Paul Lovejoy (2012) explains how: 'slavery has been an important phenomenon throughout history...Africa has been intimately connected with this history, both as a major source of slaves for ancient civilizations, the Islamic world, India and the Americas, and as one of the principal areas where slavery was common. Indeed, in Africa slavery lasted well into the twentieth century' (Lovejoy 2012: 1). The infamy that was the slave era in America saw the arrival of 380,000 Africans. While this is a bleak statistic, it represents a fraction of the 10.7 million African slaves who were brought to the New World (Manning 1998: 119-20). We are looking at capitalism in its most raw and primitive form.

What then of slavery as a feature of American capitalism in its early period of development? Was it the springboard from which to launch an economic powerhouse? It did create wealth, but having said that, it was a clumsy and inefficient process of accumulation. Marx, in *Capital*, was quick to point out the avarice of capitalism's most primitive form of accumulation:

The discovery of gold and silver in America, the extirpation, enslavement and entombment in mines of the aboriginal population, the beginning of the conquest and looting of the East Indies, the turning of Africa into a warren for the commercial hunting of black-skins, signalised the rosy dawn of the era of capitalist production. These idyllic proceedings are the chief momenta of primitive accumulation. On their heels treads the commercial war of the European nations, with the globe for a theatre. It begins with the revolt of the Netherlands from Spain, assumes giant dimensions in England's Anti-Jacobin War, and is still going on in the opium wars against China, andc. (Marx 1986a: 703).

Capitalism is successful when private owners invest with a view to increasing capital flows. Physical capital is essential for this to occur. Roger Ransom and Richard Sutch (1988) show that 'slave capital' made up 44 per cent of total wealth in the South at the time of the Civil War, while 'physical capital' accounted for less than 10 per cent. As they state, 'slaves as assets crowded physical capital out of the portfolios of southern capitalists' (Ransom and Sutch 1988: 139). Just as capitalism concentrates wealth into fewer and fewer hands, so too was this being played out by the slave owning society of the South. By 1860 and the Civil War, there were fewer slave-owners in the South than in 1840. Slave-based economics, to put it in its bluntest form, was pricing people out of the market. Most whites in the South were not slaveholders.

American economist Karl W Smith argues that slavery served to weaken the development of US capitalism. He makes the point that the South had become a virtual one cash economy by the time the Civil War began and that at its height, cotton accounted for just 5 per cent of the entire US economy in 1860 (Smith 2019). None of this suggests that much wealth was not created and that many did not become fabulously rich, but the South was in effect curtailing economic development in the USA. Smith observes that, 'just before independence, the per-capita GDP of the South, adjusted for inflation, was $3,100 per year – compared with just $1,832 in New England. Over the next 60 years Southern per-capita GDP actually declined, to $2,521. British demand for cotton helped it to recover to $4,000 per person in 1860, but by then the comparable figure for New England was $5,337' (Smith 2019).

Capitalism was, in these years, a developing and expanding economic system. The North was becoming more and more attractive a destination for immigrants from Europe. The industrialisation was continuing at a rapid rate. As Smith remarks, 'slave labor was no match for canals, railroads, steel mills and shipyards. Slavery – and the parochial rent-seeking culture it promoted – inhibited the growth of capitalism in the South. Ultimately, it was Northern industrial might that ended that peculiar institution in the US once and for all' (Smith 2019). Slave society was bad for capitalism and it had very little support outside the states that were to form the Confederacy. Even there, it was by no means universally supported. Twenty-five per cent of Southerners held slaves which is a disturbing figure but belies the mythology of the support that slave society enjoyed and of the arguments that suggest a racism that is in the 'DNA' of America. If that were the case, then why did millions of Americans take up arms to defeat slavery? There was a high degree of consciousness about this, but consciousness can be constructed. It is what the state does. While this is true, the actions of Abraham Lincoln were remarkable.

Ultimately American capitalism required the end to slavery. It was more an economic question than any selfless act on the part of the North. This may sound a little cynical, but capitalism and its state is, above all else, about survival, growth and forward movement. The United States economy was on the march and nothing was about to get in its way.

The rise and rise of America

Much has been written about the development of capitalism in the United States. It is, when all is said and done, the dominant paradigm in the capitalist world. A certain mystique seems to hang in the air when discussing this development and in some of the analyses of capitalist development in America. This may be excused to some extent when one considers its seeming unassailable position of strength. A slightly peculiar logic infers that it must be 'different' which mingles with the mythology that has grown up around its claim to exceptionalism. The slave period is another strong factor in most, if not all, analyses of American capitalist development, as is its late entry into the global sphere of developed capitalist economies. However, the point to remember is that capitalism, in the end, behaves like capitalism. As Ernesto Screpanti puts it, 'capitalism is an economic system in which control of production and the allocation of real and financial resources are based on private ownership of the means of production:' (Screpanti 1999: 1). It is a simple statement of fact. Even more succinct was Rudolph Hilferding's 'capitalist development is the accumulation of capital' (Hilferding 1981: 302).

Those two explanations, or descriptors, of capitalism should serve us well when contemplating the rise of American capitalism in the nineteenth century. Capitalism, after all, 'is that stage in the development of commodity production at which not only the products of human labor, but human labor-power itself becomes a commodity' (Gaido, 2006: 32). The process of capitalist development, while possibly taking different paths and beginning at different points along the timeline of history, ultimately ends up at the same point. Charles Post correctly describes how, 'the realisation of the necessary conditions for capitalist production in the United States took place through the articulation, expanded reproduction and transformation of three forms of production, and through a process of political class struggle that culminated in the Civil War. Each of these forms of production – slavery, petty commodity production and capitalist manufacture...affected the capitalist development in the US' (Post 2011: 7).

Those specific forms of production necessarily affected America's economic development, but this does not alter the fact that US capitalism ultimately conforms to the 'norm' of capitalist progression. Each form could not remain as if locked in amber, but had to be exposed to and affected by the very laws that drive capitalism. While each cannot be dismissed as unimportant, they need to be weighed alongside one other feature that propelled America from a largely agrarian economy to a major industrial powerhouse in a very short period of time. That factor is the constant and impressive wave of migration into America. Capitalism cannot function without exploited labour. The continent drew workers in their millions to cross the Atlantic. They came for a variety of reasons, but the one which remains pivotal for the workers who boarded ships was a quest for a new life and one that would provide work. They knew that work was to be found in the New World. Capitalism was expanding and so too was its need for labour.

The migration of workers transformed the United States. From 1815 to 1880, millions arrived. Five million Germans, 4.5 million Irish, millions more from other European nations but all with the same fundamental need and one which was reciprocated by the burgeoning capitalist machine that America was becoming. And nor was it just the emigrant ships that fed the factories of America. In the post-Civil War period tens of thousands of black and white workers were drawn northward to become industrial workers. Capitalism demanded it.

Marx, in Volume II of *Capital* (1986b), described capital in its three forms – money capital, productive capital and commodity capital. He portrayed these forms as 'circuits' of capital. These forms are dependent upon one another and operate as a cycle. Money capital creates the foundation upon which productive capital can be developed. In short, goods are produced. These goods are translated into commodity capital. This, in turn, produces an increase in money capital. The centuries-old process of capitalist globalisation has seen this cycle replicated, at first on a national and increasingly on a global scale. None of this, however, can happen without labour. What is significant is that even as capitalist relations were internationalising, productive capital remained essentially bound by national borders. The expanding world market saw raw materials acquired globally, and commodities exported globally. Productive capital, however, remained based in individual nation states. Profit, as understood within a Marxist framework, is derived from surplus value (Engels 1959). If productive capital remained localised, then labour was similarly localised. It was intrinsically connected with the process of the 'sale' of labour power (*Capital Vol. 1* 1986a Chapter 25). Immigration and the transient nature of labour became a more obvious factor as capitalism became a more internationalised system. Workers were obliged to migrate to where productive capital resided. By so doing, modern America was formed and, in its formation, a new working class came into being.

American capitalism grew and prospered but was prey to all the ills and crises of capitalism, both at home and abroad. In the years of ascendancy, up until 1900, the American dream was repeatedly hit by a range of economic problems that came from being a part of an intensifying world market. Among a list, which is by no means exhaustive, are economic and financial crises and depressions that occurred in 1819, 1837, 1857, 1873 and 1893. American capitalism was certainly not exceptional. It was simply capitalism at work. As Seymour Lipset describes it, 'America has been the purest example of a society which has followed capitalist market norms, relatively unhindered by values derived from feudalism' (Lipset 1996: 154). His choice of the word 'pure' is used advisedly.

By the 1880s America had become a major player on the world capitalist stage. In a rather unexceptional but intensely significant manner it became a global influence and began to assume a character that was later to define it. America's rise to a position of power and influence in the world capitalism system came at a time when imperialism was dominating the consciousness and economic aspirations of capitalist powers. It was an easy fit for the USA to don the mantle of imperialist. It was no stranger to the ideas of conquest and expansion. It was a nation born of war, against Britain and its own indigenous population and had in the period leading to its first foray into imperialist adventures been engaged in a second war with Britain, and one against Mexico before the Spanish-American war changed US foreign policy for ever.

Empire building

It should not have come as a surprise to anybody watching in the late 1800s to see the expansion of US capitalism and its projection of power abroad. For starters it was the age of imperialism and the USA was a booming global capitalist player. Little phrases such as US isolationism have sometimes sounded out of place, but we need to remember that the US interpretation of isolation and anyone else's need not coincide. For American policymakers, isolationism has meant different things, depending on circumstance. It certainly meant that the USA would not be beholden to anyone else. It has also been used as legitimising the pursuit of US self-interest.

Foreign policy, domestic political needs and economic policy are inevitably interwoven. The rapidly rising US economy in the latter part of the nineteenth century had placed it in the forefront of global economies. By 1895 the USA had surpassed Britain's capacity in manufacturing output (Zakaria 1999: 46). Exports into the growing world market were assuming an intense degree of significance. Fareed Zakaria, writing from an essentially realist perspective, asks what, 'turns rich nations into "great powers"? Why, as states grow increasingly wealthy, do they build large armies, entangle themselves in politics beyond their borders, and seek international influence' (Zakaria 1999: 3)? Why indeed! A state grows 'wealthy' as a result of its relationship with capitalism. The state, it must be remembered, has a special task to facilitate the development of capitalism. Capitalism can only survive by pursuing a forward motion. To stand still is to be overtaken. Marx and Engels (1977: 39) famously observed that for capital not simply to survive, but to thrive, it was compelled to expand beyond the borders of the nation-state. They further noted that, 'the bourgeoisie has through its exploitation of the world market given a cosmopolitan character to production and consumption in every country. To the great chagrin of Reactionists, it has drawn from under the feet of industry the national ground on which it stood' (1977: 39). Trotsky similarly described the growing tendency towards globalisation in terms of 'the future development of world economy on the capitalistic basis means a ceaseless struggle for new and ever new fields of capitalist exploitation' (1973: 22-3).

Marx (1974: 539) also remarked on how capital must not only eliminate spatial boundaries in order to develop a world market, but that it also must seek to reduce time as a factor in this development, thereby promoting the most expansive market possible. The underlying motivation for this development of capitalism to become an increasingly global phenomenon is the expansion of capital accumulation, the quest for profit and the ever-growing need to at least maintain the level of profit. Expansion beyond the limitations of national borders can be achieved amicably, but force is never far away and never to be discounted.

While the American capitalist economy was becoming dominant, it was still a relatively moderate military power. Its potential for force projection was limited. This was not seen as a special drawback in the period of continental expansion of American capital but by 1883 it was deemed to be necessary to begin constructing a substantial naval force. In 1883 Congress approved a relatively modest naval shipbuilding programme which gained greater momentum with the Spanish-American war in 1898. It was the beginning of a long and uninterrupted growth in American military capability. Military endeavours are all too frequently made palatable to the local population by the use of the state apparatus. US military growth and imperialist designs were promoted by the careful use of interlocking arguments. The economy needed to grow ever stronger. New markets would ensure this. A strong military is something that the population can 'see' as an expression of a strong and respected nation. By the time William McKinley won his second presidential term, the USA had secured imperial victories, and had annexed Hawaii. Politics was used to serve the economic imperative.

While all this was taking place a paradoxical mingling of isolationism with imperialism was becoming obvious. The US economy had reached a point that demanded a break from the fetters that national boundaries imposed. At the same time the state happily lived with the Monroe Doctrine. Some regarded this as a non-interventionist set of policies that viewed European affairs as alien and irrelevant to the interests of America. At the same time, it was used to legitimise expansion and the projection of force. 'In the wars of the European powers, in matters relating to themselves, we have never taken part, nor does it comport with our policy, so to do. It is only when our rights are invaded, or seriously menaced that we resent injuries, or make preparations for our defense' (Yale Law School 2008). The document was suitably ambiguous enough to permit interference in neighbouring states, the annexation of Hawaii and the beginnings of American imperialist power.

The USA was able to justify this imperial design from a number of perspectives, not the least of which was how international relations and world capitalist relations were being conducted in the latter decades of the nineteenth century. In late 1884 the Berlin Conference was convened. Its work continued over 4 months. The 15 states represented at the conference resolved to regulate the 'business' of imperialism. Among the participating states at the conference was the United States of America. It was beginning to acquire limited imperial possessions in this period, fully in line with both its requirement to expand its capitalist base into more and more areas, and to manifest power in a world that was dominated by capitalist power. The world economy was becoming global. It was integrating, while at the same time the power of individual bourgeoisies and states was becoming enmeshed in growing rivalries that would ultimately lead to WWI.

Fareed Zakaria and scholars of various schools of international relations that dwell within the broad framework of Realism may attribute motivations of states to the acquisition of power and prestige. In part they are right but the twin-requirements of capital and state, of state and capital, must never be ignored. Capital must expand. American capitalism might well have been a dominant economic player by the late 1800s but around it were other contenders. The latter years of the nineteenth century and into the twenty-first were marked by imperialist expansion. The United States, using the Monroe Doctrine as a shield, saw its influence expand within its self-designated sphere of influence. Thus began a long and not always glorious tradition of exerting economic, military and political pressure on its near neighbours. War with Spain opened the door to limited imperialist sorties.

The brief war with Spain might have seen the end of one empire, but it heralded the beginning of another. The USA sided with Cuba in its campaign for independence from Spain. The USS Maine was sunk in Havana. The media fanned the flames of American nationalism and dudgeon with reports of Spanish atrocities. Congress passed a resolution giving the president the power to use force to aid Cuba. Spain immediately broke off diplomatic relations and simultaneously the USA blockaded Cuba. War ensued. The USA declared war on 25 April 1898. On 6 February 1899 at the signing of the Treaty of Paris, the USA had 'temporary' control over Cuba, while it also gained Guam and the Philippines. As the sun rose on a new century, so too did the sun rise on American global power.

Mention was made, a little earlier, of Hilde Eliassen Restad's description of the key features that go to make up the notion of American exceptionalism. She argues that there was a belief that America was 'different' inasmuch as it believed itself to be able to resist the laws of history. It would rise and not fall. Its power would maintain. The fact that America rose as others fell ought to have sounded a cautionary note, but it seems that it did not. The twentieth century saw the rise of American economic, cultural, social and political power. It appeared to vindicate those who spoke of its ability to resist history's cruel hand. In 1900, there were other powerful nation states and empires. As the century rolled by these empires clashed as empires do. Capitalist power became entrenched, but by the end of the twentieth century, America's reign, just like those of others before it, was being seriously threatened; just as it threatened and overcame other dominant states along the way, but its flame was burning bright as the twentieth century dawned and with it came *pax Americana*, even if there was very little *'pax'* about the American century.

Chapter 5

The American century

The twentieth century began amid heightened imperialist and capitalist rivalry. Capitalism had been rapidly integrating. Globalisation was intensifying. There was a clash of contradictions. Individual bourgeoisies fought to maintain power, even as capitalism had already broken from the confines of national borders. In a vain attempt to resolve the rivalries, if not the contradictions, capitalism plunged the world into war. It resolved nothing but did slow the tempo of globalisation, at least for a time. The new player, the United States, arrived on the world stage and into this new century as a formidable economic and political force. Its time was coming. It continued its rise throughout the century. Those who saw a special, exceptional US that would rise but not fall seemed to be vindicated. The contradictions that marked the birth of the twentieth century, however, remained unresolved as the century ended. Globalisation was again a dominating force. The more powerful nation states were again seeking to assert dominance. By millennium's end the insuperable strength and power of the USA was being seriously questioned. Capitalism is faltering and the dominant capitalist power is faltering along with it.

This chapter examines the new and risen power that was and remains the United States from about the turn of the twentieth century. The power and influence of the USA, over time, became all but complete. All aspects of economic and social life came to be dominated by America. The Cold-War period certainly assisted. The world was divided into two blocs and the comic-book hero Superman's none-too-subtle slogan of 'peace, justice and the American way' neatly summed up the thinking that lay behind US policy. America dominated economic relations across the 'free' world. The term democracy came to be a substitute for the American version of how states should manage political affairs. It became an unquestioned truth that if push came to shove then America would 'export' its values to other states. The dream of those who described an American exceptionalism in terms of a power that would rise but not fall remains alive, but it is increasingly just that; a dream. Deep cracks and fissures have emerged.

The economic rise of America to superpower status had largely been achieved by the beginning of the twentieth century. At the same time, the trajectory of this powerhouse of manufacturing and finance was still on an upward curve. It remained a dynamic and developing force. The USA followed the capitalist rule of maintaining forward motion and did so assiduously. The state and capital worked in harmony. Power was intensified. Economic power and military power are inseparable. World wars and the largely imagined Soviet threat permitted the USA to move from economic superpower to become a military power unparalleled in history. The existence of the Soviet Union was, for the USA, both an interesting problem and a blessing. The Cold War was able to be used to maintain political stability at home, while also being a useful means of promoting its 'values' abroad. It permitted an obscene arms race and cemented US global power.

Capitalism, however, is a troublesome thing. It is subject to endless contradictions and crises. Capitalist crisis became deeper and more enveloping. By the 1970s, the golden age of capitalist growth had come to an end and the rate of profit again began to fall. The crisis meant that there was a necessity to rapidly globalise to overcome or at least stall some of these problems. Nation-state became pitted against nation-state. The wheel of history was turning and the monolith that was the American Empire was beginning to be threatened. The end of the Cold War was seen by some as resolving the crisis with the beginning of a unipolar American period. The enveloping crisis of capitalism and the rise of China quickly made this theory redundant. The century ended as it began: in turmoil. The USA remains the dominant paradigm but is seriously challenged.

An economic superpower

The boom of American capitalism from the late nineteenth century and into the twentieth century was remarkable. From 1860-1910 the population of the United States had tripled to 91 million people. By 1910 America was the largest and most homogenous market in the world. By the time that WWI began it had become the world's largest industrial power (Kemp 2013: 16). It was, indeed, a remarkable trajectory but one marked by an often-ruthless level of exploitation of its massively growing working class, but then the two tend to go hand-in-hand.

These were years of rapid growth. GDP rose more quickly in the USA than in any other country. At the same time, between 1881-1900, 35,000 workers died annually in industrial accidents. There was a relentlessness in the way capitalism and the state operated. In the 20 years from 1890, the productivity of US steelworkers, as an example, rose by 300 per cent, while their wages grew by 50 per cent. Profits were soaring. Meyer Weinberg speaks of, 'another source of increased profits [that] came from the lengthened workday. By 1920, 85,000 US steel workers labored for 12 hours per day for 7 days a week. This number had risen from slightly over 45,000 nine years earlier' (Weinberg 2003: 159). America's economic power was being entrenched. There was nothing 'magical' about this, and nothing especially exceptional. As Adam Tooze remarks, 'America's own entry into modernity…was every bit as violent, unsettling and ambiguous as that of any of the other states in the world system' (Tooze 2015: 27).

Capitalism creates wealth. How many times have we

been reminded of this? However, that wealth comes from the exploitation of labour. It is hardly surprising to note that these same years were ones marked by a rise in class struggle. Workers engaged in protracted strike actions that were often brutally crushed. In 1892, a strike of steel workers in Pennsylvania (the Homestead strike) saw a gun battle between workers and strike-breakers. The strike was finally put down when the Governor of Pennsylvania sent 6000-armed state militia to ensure that the employers won the day. Today Chinese workers are similarly engaged in militant strike activity and are being met with virtually identical approaches from the Chinese state.

Capitalism creates wealth. It also, by necessity, builds a working class. The upsurge in militant activity during the early years of the twentieth century posed some real dilemmas for American capitalism. Strikes were erupting and the perspective of the ruling class needed to be re-appraised. Strike-breakers were the obvious solution and they were recruited. These were also times of relatively low unemployment, so strike-breakers were called in from quite far afield. James Cannon wrote that:

> American capitalism took hundreds of thousands of Negroes from the South, and exploiting their ignorance, and their poverty, and their fears, and their individual helplessness, herded them into the steel mills as strike-breakers...in the space of one generation, by its mistreatment, abuse and exploitation...this same capitalism succeeded in transforming them and their sons into one of the most militant detachments...(Cannon 1946).

Such a response, the brutal response that was so much a part of capitalist-labour relations in the USA at this time, could not go on without threatening capitalism and the *status quo*. The stakes were becoming a little too high. Capital and the state had already come to terms with such problems in Britain. In Britain the organisations of the working class had become integrated into the state, had become institutions of the state. The rise of the USA as economic superpower demanded that a similar 'peaceful' resolution be found. Capitalist society is framed by class relations and class interests that are ultimately opposed to one another. In order to preserve a sense of harmony and accord, the state must therefore limit any obvious manifestations of class antagonism. This task is made easier if the views of the working class can be aligned, or at least be made to appear to be aligned with those of the ruling class. An effective integration of the working class and of its organisations occurs. This integration into the structure of the state serves to both reduce overt expressions of class antagonism and to promote capitalist development.

This is not to suggest that labour unrest and militancy disappeared. Far from it, but its focus was able to be channelled away from becoming a threat to the economic system itself. The early decades of the twentieth century were dramatic ones for capitalism. They represented, in many ways, existential moments for capitalism. They were years of war and depression. Robert J Gordon (2016) refers to a 'special century' that ran from 1870-1970, where a 'singular rapid growth that will not be repeated' (2016: 3) was able to be observed. Gordon insists that while this growth was also evident in other countries, it was most evident in the USA. He is correct, but only inasmuch as America was burgeoning as capitalism burgeoned internationally. His description of American growth as a 'Great Leap Forward' needs to be considered in that light, as does the end of that 'special century' in 1970. It was from the 1970s that capitalism entered into a major crisis that led, in turn, to the rapidity of capitalist globalisation and the subsequent retreat by many nations into economic and political nationalism.

The period coinciding with the end of Gordon's 'special century' also coincided with a dramatic shift from industrial to finance capitalism. Richard Peet describes the situation whereby:

> over the last thirty years, capital has abstracted upwards, from production to finance; its sphere of operations has expanded outwards, to every nook and cranny of the globe; the speed of its movement has increased, to milliseconds; and its control has extended to include "everything." We now live in the era of global finance capitalism' (Peet 2011: 18).

What, then, has happened? The United States, as the world's economic superpower, led the way in innovation in capitalist relations. It became the most efficient producer of goods. Its manufacturing industries were the envy of the world. It was, indeed, industrial capitalism taken to the very highest degree imaginable. Industrial capitalism, as the name suggests, is that mode of production that is both labour and capital intensive and based on manufacture for domestic and export use. What happened was that capitalism grew, developed but was still beset and haunted by inescapable contradictions, the spectre of the tendency of the rate of profit to fall being at the forefront. This meant that capitalism was compelled to globalise, to seek new markets and centres for production. This rapid expansion of capitalist globalisation from the 1970s was accompanied by a dramatic shift in manufacturing from industrialised countries to the developing world. Western capitalism, and chiefly American capitalism, sought to ameliorate the growing crisis that had been presented by rapid economic downturn and a reduction in profit levels. Berch Berberoglu (2003: 97) describes how US capital reacted to the crisis it was facing by transferring production overseas but that this had the obvious effect of producing mass unemployment along with a general reduction in wages. The wages stagnation has remained a feature of all industrialised nations for the past several decades.

Industrial capitalism became an issue that affected the developing world and with it came a growth in the global working class. Capital, in the developed world, shifted focus to maximise profit. The result has been an explosion in finance capitalism. Money is circulated. Currencies become the basis of investment. Massive incomes are generated but little of this finds its way into the pockets of the working class. The United States became very much richer, or at least wealth grew. This wealth has been concentrated into fewer and fewer hands. Oxfam figures show that the world's richest 26 individuals control the same wealth as the poorest 3.8 billion people (Oxfam 2019). Not surprisingly, six of the ten wealthiest individuals on the planet are American. Credit Suisse (2015) research reveals that nearly three-quarters of the world's population have a per-capita wealth of less than $10,000. Conversely the richest 8 per cent of the population own 84.6 per cent of global wealth. The US Federal Reserve issued some quite telling figures in 2016. The total US 'household' wealth was an impressive $99 trillion. Had this been distributed evenly, then each household would have received $782,000 for the year. The median figure was $97,000. However, as the Fed figures show, 25 per cent of US households had a net value of zero (Board of Governors Federal Reserve 2016)!

America's meteoric rise as a capitalist superpower has been framed by the exploitation of labour, the innovative nature of its capitalists and the assiduous support of the state. It reached outward to secure total dominance. In this it was assisted by external influences, not the least of which were the two world wars. As has been observed, the US economy was already the dominant economy among capitalist nations in 1914. This position was significantly enhanced when the imperialist powers' vainglorious attempt to resolve the then crisis in the world economy led to war. The USA emerged as by far the most powerful economy. America was in a position to provide sizeable loans to Britain and France which provided the springboard for further economic power and growth in the post-war period. American influence was also felt in the political and diplomatic spheres in the period immediately after WWI.

The business of war

There were some rather significant events that took place in 1916. There was the battle of the Somme, the Irish Easter rebellion, the evacuation of Gallipoli, the battle of Verdun. There was another that captured fewer headlines and fewer column inches in the world's media. It was the year when, 'the combined output of the British Empire was overtaken by that of the United States of America. Henceforth, down to the beginning of the twenty-first century, American economic might would be the decisive factor in the shaping of the world order' (Tooze 2015: 13). American power was certainly enhanced by WWI, but America was already a major economic power prior to the war. Its power and ascendancy were certainly enhanced by WWI.

Wars are expensive things. While figures can be deceptive, it is widely acknowledged that America's war in Iraq, from 2003-2010, cost over a trillion dollars. This is a little more than the US military budget for one year, but then the USA is an extraordinarily powerful economy. WWI was similarly a very costly affair. Millions of lives were lost and the cost in dollars and cents for the allies, adjusted for inflation, ran to over $3.8 trillion. The warring sides were going broke as the fighting continued. In 1917, the USA made loans to Britain and France to the tune of just over $68 billion. War is costly but there are economic winners.

By war's end, the United States was by far and away the most dominant capitalist economy in the world. The imperialist powers had expended and destroyed populations and wealth. There was a nagging problem of what to do about the potential for revolutionary upheavals. The Russian Revolution remained a threat. Soon, however, this threat receded as the world Marxist movement became subdued, not by capitalist or imperialist intervention but by Stalinism. There were also other global dilemmas to contend with. After a very brief respite following the war, the world sank into economic depression. The same set of unresolved contradictions convulsed global capitalism. As had been the case just a generation earlier, the world was engulfed in war.

Again the USA supplied finance to assist the allies through the lend-lease scheme. Britain made its final repayment of a post-war loan of $31 billion (adjusted for inflation) in 2006. The USA emerged from WWII in a more than healthy economic position. Its power appeared unassailable and its influence enhanced not least by the introduction of the Marshall Plan to assist the re-building of Europe. When converted to current dollar values, the USA injected $135 billion into Europe. It was a winning system for the USA as it consolidated its position as a global economic and military superpower. Marshall Plan money had to be used to buy goods exclusively from the United States and transported to Europe on US merchant ships. The deal was doubly useful as the United States was able to ensure support for its foreign policy which was aimed at 'containment' of the USSR.

The war had seen the American domestic economy boom. During the war years the economy revived from the depression years. Seventeen million new jobs were created. Industrial production rose by 96 per cent. America was the only country in the world to expand the supply of consumer goods, despite rationing. Labour unrest was significantly reduced, as calls for national unity in the cause of the war were made and heeded (Goodwin 2001). Union leaders pledged to refrain from industrial action in order to support the war effort. The pledge was kept, but with a good deal of resentment. As soon as the war ended, there was a massive upsurge in labour unrest. There were a record number of strikes in 1946. As a consequence, Congress enacted the Taft-Hartley Act in 1947. It resulted in a massive reduction in the potential power of the union movement in the USA. Laws, once enacted, are often invoked and across time. In 1959, Eisenhower used the same law against steelworkers. In 2002, Bush was able to use it against West Coast Longshoremen. In 1965 the Democrats briefly sought to repeal some of the more punitive aspects of the law, but quietly abandoned the attempt.

Capitalism and labour have very different objectives, regardless of how things might be presented by the state. The immediate post-war years represented a brief 'golden age' for capitalism. In the United States there was also the very real chance that the working class was about to break out of the restrictive war-time conditions. A clash was imminent, and a clash of classes can be a tricky thing when placed alongside the quest for profit and global power. Hence the Taft-Hartley Act. Wyatt Wells (2003) outlines some of the more pertinent areas that the Act covered and how it:

> banned several 'unfair' union tactics such as jurisdictional strikes and secondary boycotts. It also gave the president the authority to order striking workers back to their jobs for a ninety-day 'cooling off' period if a labor dispute threatened national well-being. And it outlawed the 'closed shop,' under which companies agreed to hire only union members, and gave state governments the option of banning the 'union-shop,' under which a newly hired worker had to join the union with which his or her employer had a contract (Wells 2003: 19).

How language is used to convey or conceal meaning is often interesting. The phrase 'right to work' has, in a rather cynical fashion, long been associated with this anti-worker legislation.

The 'right' in this case squarely rests with those who do the hiring. The new law came into being at about the same time as the anti-communist McCarthy period in American history. Significantly, the Taft-Hartley laws required that union officials sign affidavits promising that they had no connections with any communist organisations.

America was by this time the undisputed leader of global capitalism. Profits in the post-war period were soaring. Living standards were rising and yet the ruthlessness that underpins capitalism and its development was there for all to see. It was not about to willingly accept any challenge, at home or abroad. An ideological offensive had begun. The politics and economics of the Cold War demanded that, even in the midst of plenty, little was about to be given away.

Cold War and ideology

The world has lived in the shadow of nuclear threat for decades. It was inextricably linked to the Cold War and the fear of mutual assured destruction. It became an almost acceptable truth that the world was caught in a battle of ideologies. There was the 'free world' and there was 'communist expansionism'. Yes, the world was faced with an intolerable arms race and one that came so very close to the end of human existence. How this came to be is significant. It shows in grotesque clarity how powerful ideology can be. An 'orthodox' view maintained in the West that the Soviet Union was ready at any moment to cross borders and 'export' revolution. They had to be stopped. The late William Rees-Mogg (2003) was still adamant, years after the collapse of the Soviet Union, that 'after the Second World War, the USA saved Europe from Soviet rule' (Rees-Mogg 2003). It is an emotive story but does not stand up to scrutiny. Reality suggests that there was never a Soviet 'threat' as has been so carefully crafted for so long. If this is so, then why was the Cold War launched and how did such an expensive venture secure the United States as global hegemon?

The USA emerged from World War II as the indisputable capitalist hegemon. The Cold War was a response by US capitalism to a range of ideological dilemmas that it faced, both domestically and internationally. The Cold War was, in this sense, a pre-emptive rather than reactive response to impending crisis. Hardt and Negri (2000: 176) argue that the USA, in response to rising class antagonisms, invoked a feeling of hostility towards communism to best suit its domestic agenda. Anti-communism became national policy and working-class movements in the USA became targets of this policy. The Cold War's formative moments, however, were not in the aftermath of World War II, but in the period immediately following the Russian Revolution which the Western powers sought, by armed intervention, to crush. Domestically the US state and capital was acutely aware of the potential for dissent and class awareness. The Russian Revolution was a worrying moment, as was the depression, just a few years further on. Enemies are handy. There are so many instances throughout history of the careful creation and nurturing of imagined enemies. In the international sphere, the USA was able to cement its place as leader and guide of the 'free world' by appearing to resolutely defend shared values and ideals. It all worked magnificently. The USSR clearly felt a degree of threat and obligingly fell into the 'game' of Cold War rhetoric.

The claim that the Soviet Union was not a threat is based on the trajectory of Soviet political and foreign policy from 1924 and the death of Lenin. Stalin acted very quickly to turn Marxism into a caricature. His great gift to the West was the theory of socialism in one country. It closed the door on the idea that revolution was about to be fomented by 'fraternal' parties around the world. Where revolutionary moments emerged, they were destroyed; not by imperialist power but by the policies of Moscow. Things reached a critical point at the end of WWII.

There were very real possibilities that Italy and France might take a socialist path. The communist-led resistance movements in those countries awaited orders from Moscow. The call was to disarm. Stalin wanted buffers, satellite states, not a socialist Europe.

The new world order that emerged after the war was dominated by US economic influence. Marshall Plan dollars spoke very loudly in European capitals. The military build-up by the USA and its ideological offensive ended up having the desired effect of seeing a heavily armed Soviet Union ever-ready to suppress dissent among its Eastern-bloc allies. The decades that followed were marked by increasing US influence. They were also decades of crisis, economically, politically and internationally.

The idea of untouchable, all powerful and all-pervasive American power was challenged. Vietnam stands as the greatest single cause of this challenge. Pure power was found to be incapable of subjugating peoples and nations. Anti-colonial movements around the world were proving troublesome, and yet the colossus that was the United States remained. The end of the Cold War came as a surprise to many. The USSR was collapsing; partly due to the economic drain that the Cold War was having and more specifically to the contradictions that Stalinism, bureaucratism and the theory of socialism in one country had imposed on it. The Soviet Union finally ceased to be on Christmas Day 1991, but clues were being given for some time. Charles Kegley (2008) cites Georgi Arbatov, senior adviser to Mikhail Gorbachev who, in 1987, had said that, 'we are going to do a terrible thing to you – we are going to deprive you of an enemy' (Kegley 2008: 108).

The 'enemy' that Arbatov was speaking of was the Soviet Union. While it had never really been a credible enemy or threat, the Marxist ideology that Stalinism had so maligned remains a singular threat to capitalism and its state. Anti-communism has been so entrenched in American political thinking that to remove an external threat must have been regarded as deeply problematic. As John Updike's character Harry Angstrom, in *Rabbit at Rest*, sardonically expressed things; 'without the Cold War, what is the point of being an American?' (Updike 1990). The Cold War had very strong domestic implications and was a useful tool for state and capitalist development in the United States. The greatest threat to capitalism, apart from its own interminable contradictions that hang over it, is the working class and an ideology that is anti-capitalist. Marxism, socialism, communism have always been seen as a threat, and rightly so.

Robert J McMahon (2003) outlines how the:

state required a population that was committed to this ideological war against communism. The vast budgetary demands and multiple military obligations that the Cold War imposed upon the American populace required a mobilized and committed citizenry. US leaders from Truman onwards laboured assiduously to forge a domestic consensus supportive of the nation's new role as the world's ever-vigilant guardian against any sign of communist-inspired instability or aggression. They managed to do so with consummate skill and success through the mid-1960s, aided by what seemed unmistakable evidence of Soviet and Chinese adventurism (McMahon 2003: 120).

The use of the phrase 'what seemed unmistakable evidence' can be viewed with a degree of cynicism. This is especially the case when the political perspective of Stalin is taken into account. His view of the world was predicated on the nationalist ideas promoted in the theory of socialism in one country. This was diametrically opposed to the more classical Marxist position of advocating permanent revolution. Stalin's control of the world socialist movement was a total control and had been so long before WWII. There was no fear of the dark hand of Moscow.

At the same time, it needs to be recognised that the Cold War, and in particular the American policy of anti-communism from the end of WWI, left an indelible imprint on the very psyche of the United States. McMahon comments that:

the federal government assumed vastly enhanced power and responsibility, the 'imperial presidency' took centre stage, a substantial increase in defence spending became a permanent feature of the federal budget, and a military-industrial complex took root within American society. The broad shifts in the country's post-1945 residential patterns and occupational structures are, in significant measure, a by-product of the Cold War as well. So, too, is the co-opting of scientific and technological innovations for military-related purposes and the concomitant transformation of many top universities into leading sites of government-sponsored research. Many specific domestic priorities were similarly shaped, and in some cases explicitly justified, by the Cold War: from Eisenhower's proposed interstate highway system, to increased federal spending on education, to space exploration (McMahon 2003: 117).

In other words, the perpetuation of a myth enabled the USA to militarise its society. By the end of WWII, the USA was the globe's supreme economic power and, with a monopoly of nuclear power, was an unassailable military power. The task of maintaining order and acquiescence at home was made simpler by first the creation of a 'threat' and loudly reminding the world that the USSR was rearming. Moscow's behaviour towards its 'fraternal' allies simply acted to seal the bargain.

Military superpower

'The United States has become what it was founded not to be. Established as a haven for those fleeing the abuse of power, it has attained and now wields nearly absolute power. It has become an empire' (Garrison 2004: 12). James Garrison made that comment, as he described it, not in judgement but as a simple statement of fact. It is a view that is shared by many. Whether the appellation is correct may be argued. What is unarguable is that the United States is a superpower. Its military capacity and reach are known to all. It has not only projected force across the globe but has been in an almost perpetual state of military engagement since the beginning of the twentieth century. It has lost vast numbers of soldiers in wars that were often hard to justify and expended trillions of dollars that are equally hard to justify. It appears, at first glance, to be a paradox. Why should a country that has been a major economic power from the beginning of the last century feel the need for such belligerence? The immediate answer to that question is tied up in the idea of imperialism as a means of maintaining control. It is also caught up in the idea that competitors for economic supremacy just cannot be tolerated. The USA is a capitalist power. Its state exists to facilitate capitalist development and power. It is a very short journey from keeping economic competitors in a weakened position to wielding military muscle to achieve your aims.

American military power has never been kept quietly on a shelf to gather dust. The champion of the free world has worked strenuously to make sure that its version of that free world remains in place. In every decade since the turn of the twentieth century, American troops have been engaged in wars to varying degrees of devastation. A truncated list of the involvement of the US military includes: the Philippine-American war, the Boxer Rebellion, the occupations of Nicaragua, Veracruz, Haiti and the Dominican Republic, WWI, the Russian Civil War, WWII, Korea, the Lebanon crisis, the Bay of Pigs, Vietnam, Bolivia, Cambodia,

South Zaire, Grenada, Panama, the Gulf War, the Somali Civil War, Bosnia, Afghanistan, Iraq, Libya and Yemen. We do not have to include all of the military adventures undertaken by the USA to appreciate the level of foreign intervention that has been undertaken.

As the years and decades rolled on, the size and destructive power of the military superpower's armoury developed. There was a quantitative shift and most certainly a qualitative change in the capacity and firepower that the USA was able to deploy. Its conventional weaponry appears limitless. The growth of its nuclear arsenal is yet another factor. The USA has spent $9.4 trillion in today's dollar values from the time it manufactured and used its first nuclear weapons at the close of WWII until 1996. Since 1945, the USA has produced 70,000 nuclear warheads, a figure greater than all other nuclear nations combined. Protecting the 'free world', or maintaining an empire, is a costly affair.

Reference was made earlier to the fact that since 1975 between 15-30 per cent of the US budget has been spent on the military (Hedges 2003). This has not been a static figure. The 2015 budget, for instance, saw the military receive 54 per cent of the nation's budget. Education and health each received 6 per cent (Institute for Policy Studies 2015). The total allocation of funds in 2019 amounted to $1.4 trillion dollars (Gould 2019). Economic good times may come and go. Budgetary restrictions and cutbacks may be enforced, but the bottomless pit that is military spending goes on unimpeded.

America, like all capitalist states, buys and sells. It exports and imports. The value of its exports last year was $1.7 trillion. More than $10 billion in export earnings came from the sale of military hardware. It is a lucrative market and one that is increasing. The military-industrial-complex is also a substantial employer. There are 1.6 million Americans employed supplying the military with the equipment it needs to supply its 1.4 million soldiers and its export markets (Reich 2010). Corporations such as Lockheed, Boeing, Raytheon, General Dynamics and many others would, in all likelihood, collapse were it not for US military contracts. Lockheed, for example, derives 86 per cent of its entire revenue from the military-industrial-complex (SIPRI 2018). In 2016 alone, there were 2408 contracts totalling a stunning $231 billion awarded to companies by the US Department of Defense (MIC 2020). The mutual advantage that state and capital have come to enjoy is clear for all to see. The state has a particular role to play in advancing capitalist relations. Many of the biggest corporations in the USA rely on these state contracts. It becomes a circular relationship.

It is hardly an exaggeration to say that for decades the USA has consciously become a militarised state and economy. Robert McMahon (2003) a little earlier described how militarisation had become a central component of the development of the modern American economy and of how anti-communist ideology had been used as a means of forging a sense of national unity. The military-industrial-complex, operating as an 'informal' alliance between capital and government, has become central to American capitalism.

A certain logic comes to dominate American economic and political thinking. As its rise to world hegemon continued, then so too did the need exist to maintain not only economic power but military power to overcome real or perceived threats. Friends and allies are permitted a degree of autonomy, provided that order and recognised norms of behaviour are not undermined. Coercive behaviours have been commonplace when dealing with 'less friendly' states and the threat of intervention has been made and carried out on numerous occasions. External threat perceptions that have so often been confected have also played into the hands of the state when looking to maintain a sense of harmony at home. The domestic population has long been encouraged to view 'their' country as exceptional in the world and a beacon of hope. The Marxist concept of false consciousness, whereby ideological processes are used to mask the reality of how a class-based society operates, rings clearly. The end result has been an acquiescent working class willingly accepting state power, even if this is at odds with its own real needs.

Achieving power, while an onerous task, is but the beginning. Holding and maintaining power becomes a little more problematic and especially so when considered against the perpetual state of crisis that surrounds capitalist development. Superpowers and empires are constantly at war; figuratively and literally. They can never rest. There is always a usurper in the wings. That is bad enough but with limitless rivers of cash, anything is possible. When we factor in economic crisis, downturn, falling rates of profit and pandemics, then the future is cloudy and uncertain. History, one might assume, should make the superpower, the empire, fearful. The USA, after all, is not the first global superpower and it is impossible not to imagine that the sun will set on America.

A real and ever-present danger

In 2008, the former United Nations chief weapons inspector Hans Blix offered some sage advice to those in power in the United States. In an interview with the American Broadcasting Company he said that, 'to lose an empire is not easy. The British did it, and they learned how. The French did it, and they learned how. Then the Russians did it – they have not quite learned how. And now I think the Americans should learn how to lose an empire' (Setrakian 2008). It is a comment well worth considering. Empires, paradigms, superpowers can never escape the march of history and events. Just as capitalism emerged from an earlier economic formation, so too do economic and military formations within capitalism have a limited time.

Blix spoke of the British, French and Russian empires and

of their decline and fall. Each saw its demise in the twentieth century. We might add the short and brutish Nazi empire to this list. The 1000-year Reich was a short-lived affair. The sun set on Britain's empire. Bloody upheavals in Indochina and Algeria saw French power slide away. The Stalinist regime in the Soviet Union folded its tent in 1991. The writing is on the wall for the USA, but it seems unlikely that Blix's advice that America should learn how to 'lose an empire' will be heeded. Power is never relinquished easily.

There is an undoubted rival to US economic supremacy. The rise of China, while disturbing for the American national bourgeoisie, cannot be seen to upset the global capitalist order. While a paradigm shift may well be occurring, this does not of itself signal a threat to the rule of capital. Regardless of that simple fact, the United States can be expected to cling to power, and given its military capacity that becomes an alarming scenario. Empires may be 'lost' but they don't run up white flags.

America's sliding economic power can hardly be surprising. It exists amid a crisis that cannot be escaped. It is the crisis of capitalism. What is surprising is that anybody should be surprised. Marx and Engels wrote of the disorder and crisis that capitalism engenders and of the contradictions that lead to economic crisis. Capitalism and the bourgeoisie, in seeking to manage these critical moments, react and respond by engaging in a relentless building up and tearing down. As the crisis deepened in the latter part of the twentieth century and the looming fall of profits drove capitalism to globalise, the result was the destruction of productive forces in the developed world and the creation of new forces in the developing world. Capital flows, as described by Beverley Silver (2006), are elements of a constant drive to maintain a high degree of profitability. The period since the economic crisis years of the 1970s is undoubtedly a period marked by stagnating profits, and a general decrease in wages across states. Dennis Smith (2006: 10) describes the dynamic of globalising capitalism, of the quest not simply for power but of the necessity to seek to maintain profitability as a means of survival. The very *raison d'etre* of capitalism as an economic formation is to expand but there are ultimately limits to this expansion. The elastic can only stretch so far.

Despite the most obvious problems, apologists for capitalism and, by default, America still cling to the belief that capitalism is the best imaginable system and portray it as an almost immutable force. Steve Forbes and Elizabeth Ames (2009) are particularly vigorous in their declarations that capitalism will not merely survive but will 'save us'. They assert that capitalism, and by implication the United States, is a moral system that promotes democracy and democratic values, is creative and that its most remarkable achievement lies in its ability to turn scarcity into abundance. Anatole Kaletsky (2010) is another who confidently points to capitalism's capacity to reinvent and reinvigorate itself, especially by using the experience of crisis. Capitalism is also said to be successful because it is self-correcting (Easterly 2008: 129). It is worth remembering that in the period since the beginning of the Great Depression until the eruption of the Covid-19 pandemic, there have been 17 significant recessions and crises that have affected global capitalism. The IMF reports that from 1970 to 2011 there were 147 banking crises, 217 currency crises and 67 sovereign debt crises (Claessens and Kose 2013: 27). While there is an understandable degree of overlap in these figures, they seem to show that capitalism's self-correcting capacities have, at best, been largely ineffective. The fallout of the economic catastrophe that is linked with the Covid-19 pandemic is still to be reckoned with.

Capitalism's crisis is a cruel fact of life that capitalism and capitalist states must live with. Sadly, it has such a devastating impact on those who have created the wealth that capitalism so earnestly wishes to maintain. It is never wise to make hard and fast declarations, but it is difficult to see a future that is particularly bright for capitalism and if it is not bright for capitalism, then the future is possibly bleaker for the USA as world hegemon and standard-bearer for capital. The American experience and its pre-eminent position is often said to rest on three pillars; economic strength, military might and the soft power of cultural dominance. While this is true, it needs to be borne in mind that economic factors determine political and social outcomes. Heer Jeet (2018) cites Jeffrey Sachs when describing the economic decline of the USA. In 1980 the US share of global income sat at 24.6 per cent. That fell to 19.1 per cent by 2011. The IMF projections were for this to continue to fall. By contrast China's share was 1.2 per cent in 1980, rising to 14.4 per cent in 2011 with the same IMF projections for continued rises. The figures may slow or speed up depending on the stage of the crisis at any moment, but the writing appears to be on the wall.

What happens next is the question that might keep many awake at night. Empires do not like relinquishing power and nor do entire economic formations. We can only expect that the USA will fight to maintain its power. Capitalism, too, will cling to its position. What happens? So many problems face the world, not the least of which is the ever-present issue of climate. War is always possible and especially so since the USA has committed so much to strengthening and adapting its military capabilities. A shift to blatant authoritarianism is possible in order to maintain capitalist rule. There is a clear shift in political thinking in many countries to accommodate what can only be described as fascistic elements of policy and programme. *Pax Americana* might be slipping away as the sun sets on yet another empire. Attention can only turn to another hemisphere and that ever-present rival for the mantle of capitalist and economic hegemon: China.

Chapter 6

China's long march

The relentless rise of China has been the source of fascination for observers and commentators. While the China that we know – the rival to the United States – is a fully functioning capitalist economy, it maintains political power via the agency of the Communist Party. Too many in government and the media roll out the communist epithet. It serves them well to do so. If China threatens the power and hegemony of America, then it is as well to portray it in as black, or in this case, as red a light as possible. The world is used to Cold War tactics and any rise on China's part can be dismissed as communist-inspired. There is also a degree of old-fashioned 'yellow-peril' racism at work. The two factors work in tandem. What to do about and with China occupies the minds of many. Smaller economies, long-time allies of the USA, move uneasily. Where to jump? Chinese trade is vital and yet the US alliance must not be questioned. It all goes to make for some rather schizophrenic posturing.

The Chinese story is a remarkable one. Its history is long. Any starting date for analysis is inevitably arbitrary. For our purposes, let us begin at around about the time of the Boxer Rebellion of 1900. It was by no means the most violent of uprisings or revolts against imperialist domination, but it has a special significance. It epitomised, in so many ways, the rising nationalism that was to dominate Chinese thinking. It came as the new century dawned. The preceding half century had seen the very worst that imperialism had to offer, with opium wars, the forced ceding of Hong Kong, the Tai-Ping rebellion with its 20 million deaths. It saw the unity of two empires and six powerful states come together to enforce the rule of force. It also immediately preceded the birth of the Chinese Republic and the monumental changes that lay ahead.

China's history in the first decades of the twentieth century was dominated by nationalist movements that struggled against feudalism, and against imperialist domination. Sun Yat-sen became the first leader of republican China in 1912 with the creation of the Kuomintang (KMT). Chiang Kai-shek later led the KMT. They were years of turmoil and violence. They were also years when Marxist ideology first arrived in China. Following the Russian Revolution, the CCP was formed. The Stalinisation of the Marxist movement led to a disastrous alliance between the CCP and KMT with thousands of communists being massacred.

Those same years were also marked by Japanese imperialist occupation and subsequent resistance by the Chinese. The history of China in the years leading up to 1949 and the coming to power of Mao Zedong is inextricably linked with the history of the CCP and its betrayals by Stalinism. By the time that Mao read his proclamation of the formation of the People's Republic, the CCP had become a caricature of a Marxist organisation. In order to appreciate the later developments of China since the 'opening up' from the 1970s, it is important to examine the political and economic developments that led to 1949 and beyond: the period of Maoism.

The fact that so many in the West are still happy to speak of China as being in some way a 'communist threat' is an absurdity. The path that the CCP took from first accepting the ideology of Stalinism could have one of two destinations. A social revolution was possible or a restoration of capitalism. It is clear which path was chosen.

Enter imperialism – exit Chinese imperial rule

The entry of capitalism and imperialism into China was marked by brutality. It also came with a certain air of inevitability. From the late eighteenth century the capitalist 'world economy' was beginning to take shape. To imagine that a country such as China, no matter what the Chinese might have desired, was ever going to be able to hold back this economic and military movement from the West was always an illusion.

Marx and Engels described the changes being wrought by the march of capital:

> The bourgeoisie has subjected the country to the rule of the towns. It has created enormous cities, has greatly increased the urban population as compared with the rural, and has thus rescued a considerable part of the population from the idiocy of rural life. Just as it has made the country dependent on the towns, so it has made barbarian and semi-barbarian countries dependent on the civilised ones, nations of peasants on nations of bourgeois, the East on the West (Marx and Engels 1977: 40).

The reference to 'barbarian and semi-barbarian countries' may jar on the ears of a twenty-first century listener. Despite that, the truth of those observations was never more evident than with capitalism's interventions into China. The first Opium War, a response to China's attempts to halt the importation of opium by Britain, was fought between 1839 and 1842. The simple fact that Britain could seek to legitimise both this trade and its war was astonishing. Britain invaded in order to crush any opposition to its interference in the economic development of China. The result was never really in doubt. The consequences were far reaching. In 1841 Hong Kong was ceded to Britain. Just 7 years later Marx and Engels, in the *Manifesto*, wrote that:

> The bourgeoisie, by the rapid improvement of all instruments of production, by the immensely facilitated means of communication, draws all, even the most barbarian, nations into civilisation. The cheap prices of commodities are the heavy artillery with which it batters down all Chinese walls,

with which it forces the barbarians' intensely obstinate hatred of foreigners to capitulate. It compels all nations, on pain of extinction, to adopt the bourgeois mode of production; it compels them to introduce what it calls civilisation into their midst, i.e., to become bourgeois themselves. In one word, it creates a world after its own image (1977: 40).

It is not all that surprising that the Chinese maintained a simmering discontent at the way they had been handled and poorly used by Britain. It provided rich soil for the propagation of nationalist seeds to thrive. The intrusion into Chinese life, economy and political regime that accompanied imperialism was a significant element in the fall of Imperial China. For over two thousand years emperors had ruled. The final dynasty, the Qing, came to power in the mid-1600s, but met with a force that far outstripped its own. China resolutely clung to a belief that it could reject modernisation. Stephen Platt, in *Imperial Twilight*, writes of the 'moment when China left its traditional past behind and was dragged forcibly into the world of European imperialism' (Platt 2018: xxiii). Platt is specifically commenting on the Opium War, when 'Great Britain unleashed its navy on a nearly defenceless China in order to advance the interests of its national drug dealers' (2018: xxiii). Chinese imperial power quickly moved into sharp decline as imperialism's force and economic might enveloped the country. Ultimately capitalism and imperialism created a 'world after its own image'. It is true that there were strong internal influences that led to the end of imperial rule in China, but the naked aggression of the West, and repeated rebellions which were often a response, in one form or another, to Western interference, ultimately led to the creation of the Republic in 1912 (Twitchett and Fairbank 1980, Spence 1990).

That the Qing dynasty was in deep peril should have come as no great surprise. Japan had been rearming and modernising its state and military as a precursor to its entry into the world of global imperialism. China made moves to reform and modernise its military capacity, but it was a reformed army that remained largely focused and engaged with maintaining the position and internal power of the Qing regime itself. A lesson was about to be learned. Armies are used by the state for external projections of force as well as the maintenance of domestic power. This was brought home with full force in the brief Sino-Japanese war of 1895. The defeat of China in that war further weakened the internal power of Zaitian, or the 'Guangxu Emperor'. The result was a further sharpening of the demands of nationalist and republican forces for the overthrow of the monarchy. Just 16 years on, the Kuomintang and Sun Yat-sen achieved just that.

Immediately preceding the revolution of 1911 that ushered in the Chinese Republic was the Boxer Rebellion. It was but one in a chain of rebellions. Motivations varied but a growing anti-foreigner sentiment was prominent in all cases. There had been a continued erosion of power and prestige within China that came with British and other Western powers' dominance. The Chinese state was becoming increasingly powerless in the face of this domination. Whereas it had been Britain that set the tone, it was not only British imperialism that was expressing an interest in China. Other European powers had secured interests in China, as did Japan and the USA. The Americans, in an attempt to secure a more lucrative access, but couched in diplomatic language, proposed an 'open door policy' in relation to the exploitation of China. The countries with interests in China were to have 'equal' access across the country. Its immediate degree of success was limited but it did have three major results. These were that there was a decided increase in US interest in the East Asia Region and there was a corresponding increase in anti-Western sentiment among the Chinese.

China had been, for millennia, nationalistic and isolationist. While religious motivations have been attributed to some of the risings, the fact remains that the underlying causes came from the friction engendered by foreign encroachment. The Boxer Rebellion sought to redress these problems. The Boxers were supported by the empress dowager Cixi. For the Qing rulers it seemed to be a case of one last throw of the dice. However, despite the numbers of Western troops not being especially great, the result was never really in doubt. A little over half a century earlier the Opium War saw British force overcome the Chinese regime. This time, there were armed contingents from Britain, France, Japan, Russia, Italy, Austria-Hungary, Germany and the United States. After all, the imperialist powers had much to gain or possibly lose, depending on the outcome.

The ramifications of this rebellion were far reaching. The Chinese regime was even further weakened. Significant reparations were paid to the foreign forces and the Qing dynasty eked out one more decade of constrained existence before the Xinhai Revolution was launched against imperial rule and the Chinese Republic came into being.

The arrival of a Chinese working class and the development of capitalism

The influence of imperialism into Chinese political and economic life followed, to a large extent, the path foreseen by Marx. There is a rather pertinent observation that needs consideration. Marx and Engels wrote of capitalism's inevitable expansion and of how older, pre-existing economic systems must be destroyed in order for capitalism to create new ones (Marx and Engels 1975: 200-1). It is an argument that most eloquently describes the effects of colonialism and imperialism in the nineteenth and early twentieth centuries. Imperialism, after all, is well described as the 'penetration and spread of the capitalist system into non-capitalist or primitive capitalist areas of the world' (Warren 1980: 3). Imperialism, in this context, is a step towards industrialisation and therefore the proletarianisation of the world.

China, at the time of imperialism's forced entry, was not, so to speak, in the market for a capitalist market. This, however, was irrelevant to the march of capitalist development. From the time of China's humiliating defeat in the Sino-Japan war and by the time the Boxer Rebellion had been crushed, there was no way forward for China but via the rule of capital. The revolution of 1911, the Xinhai Revolution, inspired by Sun Yat-sen and his 'Three Principles of the People', set in place a transformation of the Chinese economy, political system and society. The 'Three Principles' are described by George T Yu (1991) as encompassing a new vision of nationalism that became broader than a mere regionalist approach and drew on the experiences of Western nationalist movements. They also promoted the idea of democracy. Again, Western experience was seen as a broad guide to the future. The third element, described as 'people's livelihood', was central to the aims and aspirations of the Kuomintang in this revolution against the monarchy. It was a call to radically transform the Chinese economy. China was to be open to free trade and encourage foreign support and investment. In other words, the integration of China into the burgeoning capitalist world economy was being established.

What is rather telling is how the Western imperialist powers regarded and responded to the revolution. They had substantial investments in China but remained neutral throughout the struggle for power. The timeline for the transition was remarkably swift. In February 1912 the last emperor abdicated. In March a provisional constitution was declared. In April the government was moved to Beijing. The USA and Britain simply maintained relations with the new regime. For capital, it was a most satisfactory manoeuvre. The years immediately preceding the revolution had seen the beginning of significant infrastructure and economic development. Western economists and advisers were brought to China (Trescott 2010). Paul Trescott describes

China in 1900 as a country of 400 million people, almost entirely living in poverty and as farm labourers (2010: 2). He then goes on to show the rapidity of development in the period from 1900 when there was just 600km of rail lines in China and that by 1920 this figure had risen to well over 11,000km (2010: 6). The figure has an unmistakable echo to Marx's observation that the railways represent the arrival of modern industry (Marx 1975). While Marx was writing of India, the parallels are clear.

Capitalism can only develop, survive and prosper if it constructs an industrial working class. China had been almost exclusively a peasant economy when capitalism made its fateful entry. The growth of capitalism in China can best be reflected in the growth of its industrialised working class. In the 1890s, as the Qing dynasty was being nudged unceremoniously into history the working class was just 90,000. That figure rose appreciably in the period following the 1911 revolution. By 1914 there was a working class of 600,000, rising to 1 million by the 1920s and to 3 million by the 1930s (Deng 2011: 115). These are still small numbers for a country the size of China, but it gives an indication of the growing influence of capitalism.

There was a flood of Foreign Direct Investment (FDI) into China in the early years of the twentieth century that accompanied the establishment of manufacturing industries. Despite the limitations on investment that WWI imposed, there was a wave of industrialisation. Mining and manufacturing rose dramatically. Domestic Chinese investment in the period from 1911-25 was at a rate 11 times greater than that between 1840-1911. Industrial output grew rapidly from the time of the 1911 revolution (Ma 2008). It must be remembered that this growth comes from a very low starting point and the FDI flows were seriously interrupted by WWI, the depression and the internal disruptions, and incursions by Japanese imperialism.

Regardless of the size of the Chinese capitalist economy in these years, the point is that as it grew, then so too did the Chinese working class. The working class faced exactly the same problems as workers everywhere. Their labour was exploited, and their interests did not coincide with those of capital. This fledgling class was no less militant than the working class anywhere. As Mark Selden observes, there were four peak strike periods in the early republican period: 1898-9 with ten major strikes, 1904-6 with 15 actions, 1909-13 which saw 38 major strikes and 1917-19 with 46 strikes (Selden 1995: 72). These industrial disputes indicate the growing importance of capitalism to the Chinese economy as it moved beyond imperial rule. It is also a clear indicator of the antagonisms that are inevitable in a system that is based on class exploitation.

While the increase in militant activity in China was important, it is a reflection of what was taking place around the world. The periods of upheaval in China, for instance, are mirrored globally, and especially in the United States. The years 1899-99 saw a wave of strikes across the USA, Australia and in Russia. The 1904-6 period saw major industrial disruptions and strike activity in Britain and the USA. It was also the time of the 1905 Russian Revolution. The next upsurge in Chinese working-class action was between the years 1909-13, which coincided with more working-class actions around the world. This time there were major strikes in Britain, Ireland, New Zealand and again the USA. Not surprisingly the period between 1917-19 saw massive unrest. The imperialist war and the Russian Revolution acted as a catalyst for militant working-class action everywhere. In China, strike activity reached a highpoint in this period which coincided with the May 4 Movement.

Global events were beginning to have a far-reaching effect on the thinking of many in China. The end of the Qing dynasty, the creation of the new republic and the growing struggle against imperialist presence were necessarily influenced by what was happening abroad. It was the time of the Russian Revolution. Its impact was intensely felt. In China, all of these influences came together with the May 4 Movement. As Rana Mitter outlines the moment, 'the atmosphere and political mood that emerged around 1919, are at the centre of a set of ideas that have shaped China's momentous twentieth century' (2004: 12). The student protests quickly broadened to include merchants and, importantly, the working class. A general strike was called in Shanghai. The May 4 Movement played a decisive role in the formation, just 2 years later, of the CCP.

The CCP, Marxism and Stalinism

The establishment of the CCP proved to be the most decisive moment in China's modern history. The fact that the party was created was, of itself, not surprising. In the years immediately following the Russian Revolution, communist parties were formed in a great many countries. They became component parts of the Third International, or Comintern. Each party was originally perceived as a section of a world party. It was an idea that became distorted as Marxism became increasingly Stalinised from the mid-1920s. This same Stalinisation of Marxism and of the international communist movement was to have a lasting effect on the development of modern China.

While Chinese capitalism was in an early stage of development, it nevertheless exhibited all of the features of capitalism. An industrial working class was being produced and it was in and around this working class that the ideas of Marxism developed. The founding congress of the CCP was held in Shanghai. The 13 delegates, representing just 50 members, envisioned a time when they would challenge capitalism and begin to build a socialist state. Much attention has been given to the fact that Mao's revolution was primarily a peasant-led guerrilla campaign. Still more has been said that this was a departure from a classical Marxist perspective. Marxism maintains that revolution comes from an organised working class. Put bluntly it suggests that the revolution moves from the city to the countryside. Mao's revolution was an inversion of that theoretical precept. How this came to be is worth considering.

The political and programmatic basis upon which the CCP was established was quite unequivocal. It was to be a party rooted firmly in the theories of Marxism. As Stuart Schram describes it, 'the Chinese Communist Party came into existence 6 years before Mao even began his experiment with the pattern of revolution through guerrilla warfare in the countryside... the "Chinese road" to power' (1981: 410). Schram's comment is rather telling. The 6 years were ones that came to define how the CCP viewed the world. The party also had a lasting effect on how China's development unfolded until its ascendance as a leading capitalist economy and direct rival to the USA for global hegemony.

The CCP, like all fledgling communist parties around the world at this time, was formed as a Marxist political organisation. It had much in common with those other newly-formed parties. They also came to share a negative feature that parodied their original aspirations. The Stalinisation of the world Marxist movement was completed in a very short space of time. Central to the problems that Stalinisation brought to the world movement was the concept of building socialism in one country. The logic of a world movement under such conditions becomes difficult to sustain. The movement was given the task of working for the greater good of the Soviet Union and not in any real sense to be engaged with fomenting world revolution. The impact on national sections of the 'world party' is not difficult to imagine. In the case of China, the demand to follow the dictates of Stalin had particularly tragic outcomes. Having set the Stalinist train in motion, it has become all but impossible for many to find a way of stopping it. Writing in 2015, Lin Jianhua is still able to maintain that 'most of today's national communist parties were set up and run with the guidance and assistance of the Comintern, and the origins of almost all of today's important theoretical and practical issues can be traced back to the Comintern' (2015: 25). It is a remarkable statement, given the history of Stalinist leadership offered to the world communist movement in those fateful years. Revolutionary moments came and went. Historical possibilities were lost. All had a common denominator in the leadership presented by the Stalinised Comintern. The CCP and the Chinese working class suffered particularly badly.

The tiny group of Chinese who formed the CCP were quickly rewarded in their work. The party grew. Its influence spread. Stuart Schram spoke of a 6-year period. By 1927, at the end of that period, terrible crimes had been committed. The KMT had entered into negotiations with Russia soon after the revolution. By the time that Stalin's grip on Soviet power had been completed, a virtual 'unity ticket' between the CCP and the KMT had been effected. Why this occurred is of lasting significance. Stalin, rather than the CCP, considered it necessary for the CCP to move into such a union with the KMT. His logic was based on the notion that China was still a backward economy with a relatively low level of capitalist development. Therefore, it was deemed necessary to place the CCP at the disposal of the Chinese nationalists in order for this capitalist development to mature. The CCP acquiesced. The result was what has come to be known as the Shanghai massacre of April 1927. The KMT leadership knew all too well that a growing, militant and armed workers' movement would be a growing threat. With the cover that the Comintern offered, they quickly set about 'removing' the problem. Exact figures of those executed at the time and across the coming months are difficult to produce. Generally accepted figures (Jowett 2013, Harrison 1972) acknowledge that more than 10,000 CCP members and supporters were executed in a period of 20 days from April 12, when the KMT moved against the communists, and that ongoing purges resulted in the deaths of 300,000 more.

At the end of Schram's 6 years, the CCP had been decimated; its leadership destroyed either at the hands of the KMT, or Stalin's intrigues, depending on where the blame may be placed directly. Even so, Schram can say that, 'in one respect, the tactics imposed by Stalin on the Chinese Communist Party went too far, while in another respect, they did not go far enough' (1981: 413). How far is too far? As Lynda Shaffer states, 'Stalin had abandoned any semblance of internationalism and used the Comintern's influence to lead the Chinese Communist Party into the obviously ill-fated alliance with Chiang Kai-shek and to keep it there even after such a course was clearly suicidal' (Shaffer 1981: 33).

The remnants of the CCP, with Mao at the helm, performed a remarkable conjuring act. They did not break with Stalin and the Comintern but came up with a theory that turned Marxism in China forever on its head. No longer was the CCP to be a party based on and in the working class, but rather, it came to espouse a revolutionary road via the peasantry and guerrilla warfare.

The turbulent decades

Things for China moved from bad to worse. The disaster of the CCP's alignment with the KMT changed how the CCP regarded the world. After the improbable 'United Front' tactic had collapsed, the CCP and KMT began a long and protracted armed struggle: the Civil War, which was to last from 1927 until the Japanese invasion in 1937, only to resume once WWII ended. The next phase of hostilities between the communists and nationalist KMT continued until the successful routing of the KMT and the creation of the People's Republic in 1949. Statistics vary as to the extent of the casualties that resulted from that period of civil war and Japanese occupation. Accuracy would hardly make the appreciation any more or less acceptable. According to Rudolph Rummel (2017), the total in all wars, civil wars and uprisings from 1900-49 stands at about 9 million dead. He breaks these figures down to include 3 million in the Sino-Japanese war between 1937-45 and another 1.3 million from CCP/KMT battles between 1927-37 and from 1945-9.

The campaigns, the 'Long March' and the struggle against Japan are well recorded and documented from the point of view of each of the warring parties. There is, however, something that has particular interest that needs brief discussion. It is all to do with the economy, that great engine that prompts political and social development and change. China was, of course, economically a backward country at the turn of the twentieth century. This fact played a part in Stalin's thinking about the need to see the KMT lead and promote capitalist development before any serious thought could be given to fomenting socialist revolution. There is a particular irony here. The 1917 Revolution had also been conducted in an economically backward nation. However, the Bolsheviks worked in and among the working class to obvious advantage. They did not see revolution coming through armed struggle, but rather the promotion and prosecution of a political struggle. For Stalin, and his Chinese comrades, what had been good for the goose was, in this case, hardly fit for the gander.

The Chinese economy, one would think, after decades of war, dislocation, occupation and revolution, should have been barely alive. However, as Chi-Ming Hou (1963: 597) shows, economic infrastructure and output continued to rise, albeit in a sometimes uneven manner. From 1900-37, the reach of the railways grew by 10 per cent annually. Iron production grew at an annual rate of 10 per cent, coal at 8 per cent and cotton at 12 per cent. It is obvious that the working class, although tragically betrayed, remained a force and a growing force and that the capacity of China's economic growth remained considerable. What did happen, however, was that capital became heavily concentrated in the hands of government and especially in the period immediately prior to Japanese invasion. By 1942, 70 per cent of Chinese capital was under state control.

These figures can by no means be taken to show that China was anything but a peasant-based society. Capitalism, however, was becoming more and more entrenched and along with it an industrial working class was being produced. The period leading up to the Sino-Japanese war was marked by the means of production being largely in the hands of foreign capitalists. Chinese workers suffered much the same treatment as had their British counterparts a century earlier with poor wages, no security, little medical care and exploitative employers (Chesneaux and Kagan 1983: 70). The workday was rarely less than 10 hours and often more than 12 and nightshifts imposed in order to maximise already healthy rates of profit were the norm. These working conditions were not isolated to China in the 1920s and 1930s. We must remember that in the early 1920s American steelworkers were regularly working 7 days a week on 12-hour shifts (Weinberg 2003: 159). Chinese workers, in this respect, were achieving a parity, of sorts, with their international class-brothers.

The years after the 1927 massacres at the hands of the KMT, until the Sino-Japanese war, were marked by a steady and persistent militancy on the part of the working class. There was a spike in strike activity in the period immediately preceding the war, largely predicated on anti-foreign sentiment (Chesneaux and Kagan 1983: 79). Even during the war period strike activity continued, including in the occupied areas of China. Some of these actions were inspired by communist cells but many were spontaneous reactions to how the workers were being treated. There are contradictory ideas that spring from such data. There was still, despite the best intentions of the KMT, communist activity among the urban working class and a degree of class consciousness that existed beyond the direct influence of the CCP. The working class, as a potentially revolutionary class, has for decades now in the West seen its organisations become virtual instruments of the state. Trade unions and political parties of social democracy have been integrated into the state as a deliberate strategy (Trotsky 1972, Mann 1973, Smith 2014). This had not occurred in China. Regardless of this, Mao's 'long march', figurative as much as literal, was away from the working class as a revolutionary class and towards the peasantry. For Mao it was a matter of basing his future on the peasantry. He invoked an image that saw the peasants as a clean slate. 'A clean sheet of paper has no blotches, and so the newest and most beautiful words can be written on it' (cited in Gregor and Chang 1978: 321).

The imagery of Mao might be poetic, but it remains intensely contradictory and especially so, given the dual fact of Marxism's clear idea of the path forward and the realities being presented in China throughout those turbulent years. There would seem no other option but for revolutionary change in China. Jean Chesneaux and Richard C Kagan describe the situation in China whereby, 'any involvement of the labor movement with political struggles could be effected only by means of revolutionary strategy. There existed in China no open road towards labor reform of a social-democratic type, founded upon reciprocal recognition by the capitalist system and the labor movement of each other's supposed interests. This kind of reformism had no meaning in China' (Chesneaux and Kagan 1983: 81). They argue that there was no economic, social or political basis to allow for such a path. If, then, the only way forward for China was through revolutionary movement, then the nagging question remains as to why it had to be so contrary to Marxist theory. Admittedly the disastrous alliance with the KMT that had been forced upon the CCP and its aftermath played a role, but it would seem logical, even obvious, to set about rebuilding urban structures rather than engage in such a protracted civil war. It was and remains an alien position for a Marxist party to engage with. To understand why things moved the way they did it is necessary to look at how Maoism developed and why.

Maoism or Marxism with Chinese characteristics?

After WWII and the defeat of the Japanese, the civil war resumed with the final outcome being Mao's proclamation of the establishment of the People's Republic on 1 October 1949. The protracted war was over. The People's Republic of China (PRC) was born. Mao's credentials appeared to be impeccable. Under his leadership, China was now liberated. It was certainly the stuff of legend and the historic nature of that moment cannot be underestimated. China changed and with it the world. Ideologically it gave the world what has been described by some admirers as a 'creative adaptation' of Marxism. More than 70 years later, China is still asserting that it is building socialism with Chinese characteristics. To make sense of any of this, we must first come to grips with this 'creative' adaptation of Marxism. Who was Mao and was Maoism in any real way connected to Marxism?

At its simplest telling, Marxism is centred on the idea of a class struggle between capitalism and the bourgeoisie on the one hand and the working class on the other. The class antagonisms and the contradictions within capitalism are such that these two forces inevitably clash. Revolution and socialism are the result. The revolution is based on the working class and is international. It cannot be limited to a nationalist movement, no matter how progressive the claims might be. Mao, on the other hand, built his version of Marxism on a distinctly national programme, with the peasantry rather than the working class as the revolutionary subject. Admittedly the working-class movement was limited at this time but, as has been described, it was becoming an important class-conscious force.

Mao's attitude to theory and Marxist theory in particular is rather telling. Donald Lowe (1966) wrote of Mao's shifting and always tempestuous relationship with issues of theory. Lowe spoke of the period between 1927-35 where Mao all but ignored the idea of Marx's method of political and class analysis. Mao never fully accepted the duality of theory and practice. The period between 1935-40 did, however, see him, as Lowe described, attempting to provide a 'veneer' for his limited theoretical practice (1966: 113). The period 1940-9 produced nothing of any import regarding theoretical observations. This is relevant inasmuch as Marxism is and has always been a coming together of theory and practice. Each informs the other. But then Mao was never a Marxist in the strictest sense of the term.

When Mao joined the CCP he had no identifiable Marxist theory upon which to draw. This is not of itself a criticism. Marxist understanding is not an innate quality. One does not suddenly appear upon the earth fully formed. It is something that must be learned and nurtured. The problem was that he seemed loathe to either learn or nurture any such ideological appreciation. A James Gregor and Maria Hsia Chang (1978: 308) make the point that he had read 'part' of the Communist Manifesto at the time of his joining the party. Politically and theoretically he was called more to the ideas of the KMT. 'Mao stated explicitly that he recognized the ideas that inspired the peasants to revolutionary activity were the ideas of Sun Yat-sen and not those of Karl Marx' (Gregor 2019: 85). Gregor describes Mao's Marxism as 'odd'. Its 'oddness' springs from his insistence that, 'the ideology he publicly served was the Three Principles of the People of Sun Yat-sen. While his speeches and essays were dotted with Marxist allusions, he consistently maintained that he sought to realize the "bourgeois democratic" revolution of the founder of the Kuomintang. Over the years he consistently reaffirmed his commitment' (Gregor 2019: 86). Those 'Three Principles' were, of themselves, laudable enough for a movement that was nationalist and reforming but were hardly the stuff of Marxist theory or practice. A little earlier

Sun's principles were briefly discussed. To reiterate, they revolved around the promotion of a nationalist perspective that owed much to Western nationalist movements, to the promotion of a Western view of democracy, and a major transformation of the economy and an opening of that economy to the world.

The fact that China has, in recent decades, wholeheartedly endorsed an open, outwardly projecting capitalism would appear to show that Mao's vision is, in fact, being realised. Gregor cites Mao's works to show how his commitment to Sun Yat-sen's ideas was reaffirmed across many years with the Central Committee of the CCP declaring, as late as 1945, that it '"solemnly declared" that the Party was fighting for the "complete realization" of Sun's doctrine' (Gregor 2019: 86). Theory, for Mao, was a malleable substance and Marxism was whatever it needed to be to best suit the conditions at hand. This becomes abundantly clear in relation to his 'Sinification' of Marxism. Stuart Schram cites Mao:

A communist is a Marxist internationalist, but Marxism must take on a national form before it can be applied. There is no such thing as abstract Marxism, but only concrete Marxism. What we call Marxism is Marxism that has taken on a national form, that is, Marxism applied to the concrete struggle in the concrete conditions prevailing in China, and not Marxism abstractly used. If a Chinese communist, who is a part of the great Chinese people, bound to his people by his very flesh and blood, talks of Marxism apart from Chinese peculiarities, this Marxism is merely an empty abstraction. Consequently, the Sinification of Marxism – that is to say, making certain that in all of its manifestations it is imbued with Chinese peculiarities, using it according to these peculiarities – becomes a problem that must be understood and solved by the whole party without delay (Schram 2002: 324).

Maoism is still equated in the minds of many with Marxism. This is despite the very obvious differences and departures from Marxism that are apparent in so much of the 'theory' of Mao. It is of little profit for us to dwell on the Maoist road to power, or to focus on the simplistic sloganising; political power comes from the barrel of a gun, imperialism is a paper tiger, oppose bookism, and all the rest. The point is that Mao, the historical figure, was able, through military force, to unite China and establish a new order. The fact that the 'Marxist' Mao never entirely renounced the ideology of the KMT is highly significant. The new order that was instituted in 1949, while never able to be called socialist, did manage to introduce major reforms and undoubtedly benefited the people. Having said that it needs to be remembered that his nationalist and eclectically personalised form of power led to the deaths of millions.

The first half of the twentieth century had been for China a violent and tumultuous time. The 1949 revolution first sought to retreat into an intensely nationalist semi-autarkic, self-sufficiency mode of economic life. By 1978, China began to actively court capitalist economics and had begun to establish itself as a capitalist economy in the fullest sense of the term. Those years, from 1949 until 1978, require thought.

Results – 1949-78

The years following the revolution of 1949 shaped the China that we see before us today. There were many things to be admired but also many that were not. For all of its failings, the revolution did represent the hopes and aspirations of hundreds of millions of workers, peasants and intellectuals throughout the country. Its impact was profound, both from a global and national perspective. Mao carefully focused on developing a sense of Chinese nationalism that was based on the state as a means of capturing the minds of the people. The 'old ways' of imperialist oppression were over. Something new and essentially Chinese was being constructed. It was, as Shameer Modongai (2016) portrays it, a socialist-oriented state nationalism. In this his intensely nationalist view of the world was very much in line with Stalin's 'Russification' of Marxism and the pursuit of a national form of socialism. It was not all that difficult a task for Mao to adopt such a mantle. The Stalinisation of the CCP had been accomplished from the earliest days of the formation of the party.

The revolution offered sweeping social reforms. Inequality was targeted through land reforms. They were conducted quickly, but not without serious loss of life. It is estimated that between 200,000 and 2 million died (Roberts 2011). Private ownership of land in this overwhelmingly peasant country was finally abolished in 1958 under conditions that were not entirely dissimilar to the tactics employed by Stalin's collectivisation in the USSR. The state-controlled commune system was unpopular with many but was nevertheless stringently implemented.

Other social reforms enacted by the PRC that dramatically changed the lives of the Chinese people included the Marriage Law which gave women unheard of freedom in a traditionally conservative nation, and enormously successful literacy and health campaigns. These and other social measures served to promote a feeling of national unity, a cornerstone of China's political and social development. Such measures legitimised the rule of the CCP that became essential for its economic shifts across the decades.

The social reforms coincided with important economic changes. The economy was quickly brought under state ownership; a nationalisation of property relations was conducted. By 1953, the CCP had succeeded in stabilising the economy and so embarked on its first 'Five Year Plan'. The Chinese followed the Soviet model in this respect. The first Five Year Plan was largely a successful undertaking. Heavy industries flourished, factories were built and both industrial output and national income grew at impressive rates. Despite this, the leadership of the CCP was uneasy. There remained an imbalance between industrial and agricultural advance. The centralised focus was deemed to be the cause. Mao shifted course, calling instead for a more decentralised approach with the population being exhorted to produce a 'great leap' in all areas of the economy. The devastations wrought by the Great Leap Forward need not become the focus for attention here. It has been thoroughly documented. The entire period, however, from 1949 until the opening of the Chinese economy to capitalism, did see the economy, industrial output and growth in GDP rise steadily, often seemingly despite the crises that were inflicted upon the country by the CCP. Dwight Perkins (1983) offers a range of statistical evidence indicating this continued rise in all aspects of the Chinese economy. What remained a concern for these proponents of building socialism in a single country was that they remained far behind their capitalist rivals in all areas. This in part explains the motivation for such a remarkable change of tack after the first Five Year Plan. Mao's motivation for this abrupt about face can be traced to the fortieth anniversary of the Russian Revolution and Khrushchev's declaration that in 15 years the USSR would exceed the USA as an industrial power. Mao quickly made his own claim that China would similarly overtake Britain's capacity in a 15-year period (Mao 1957).

The result of that policy debacle was an immense human tragedy. Quantifying the casualties has been difficult. Jung Chang and Jon Halliday's (2005) estimate that 38 million died is regarded as being as accurate a reckoning as possible. The recklessness of this endeavour is an indication not so much of Mao's personal shortcomings, but of a major issue that is represented by China's Stalinist and nationalist programme. Socialism, according to Marxist theory, follows capitalism and must be more productive, and offer more than the formation it is replacing. Capitalism, by the time that Mao had come to power, had already become a globalised entity. To imagine that socialism could be constructed within the confines of a single state was and remains a ludicrous proposition. For Mao and for Stalin before him it was a case of 'catching up' with the West. Each specified a particular country that they were 'competing' against. The race was, however, never going to end well. The opposition was a global force. The revolution was necessary and totally justified. What it achieved was important. What it could never produce was a socialist state. At best it was a state in transition; no longer feudal, out of the grasp of capitalism and possibly, just possibly, given the right conditions and a different political perspective, part of an international revolution. This transitional period was one that caught and held the imagination of classical Marxists for a long time. Which way would the cards fall? For all its rhetoric and its various campaigns, China, in much the same way as the USSR, became increasingly dominated by a bureaucratic mindset. While this was possibly more pronounced in the USSR, and within the Communist Party of the Soviet Union, the same impacts were felt in China. Ernest Raiklin writes that while the bureaucracy was recruited largely from among the peasantry, 'the bureaucracy was becoming less concerned with the interests of the latter and more with its own at the expense of the peasantry...and not only was the bureaucracy losing its ties with the people. It was also gradually becoming differentiated within itself into various horizontal and vertical strata, each with its own agenda, and in this repeating the Soviet experience' (Raiklin 2013: 4).

This tendency towards bureaucratisation of the state and party is intrinsically bound up with the ideology that gave it birth; that of a nationalist form of socialism. Socialism, in a Marxist understanding of the term, is a momentous step forward. The achievement of socialism is seen to represent an end to class differences. Socialism in this sense becomes 'classless' and consequently the requirement of a strong state apparatus becomes redundant. Despite any claims that socialism has been built, the state remained and remains a strong and often repressive institution. Mao seemed to recognise the debilitating nature of the bureaucracy, or possibly that the working people of China were recognising this same fact, but his Great Proletarian Cultural Revolution appeared to be a reaction against bureaucratic deformations within society. Raiklin effectively expresses the view that it was a response by the leading bureaucratic echelons to 'paper over' the problems:

> The Great Proletarian Cultural Revolution was an attempt by the top party bureaucracy using the young and idealistic Chinese intellectuals (students) to provide 'correct' answers to these questions. The goal was to prove to the masses that the 'socialist' road to equality and brotherhood had not been deserted by the CPC; that rising inequalities and social divisions were not the norm for a peasant country searching for its way to modernity but simply aberrations; and that the culprits were various bureaucrats and intellectuals ideologically close to them who had lost their 'socialist' way (Raiklin 2013: 5).

The Cultural Revolution, it must be remembered, technically only came to an end in 1976. The movement had among its aims the removal of the bureaucrats and yet, less than 2 years later, in late 1978, the dramatic shift to capitalist restoration began with the promotion of 'socialist market forces' and 'socialism with Chinese characteristics'. Did such a shift emerge from the ether? Was it spontaneous or was it almost destined to be, given the politics of nationalism rather than Marxism, of building socialism in one country rather than an internationalist perspective?

The question was asked a little earlier as to how the cards would fall. We have the experience of history upon which to draw. In *The Revolution Betrayed*, first published in 1937, Trotsky (2004) depicted two possible paths that the USSR might traverse. The first was that a new social revolution might overthrow the ruling bureaucracy and therefore return the party and country to a socialist perspective, or that the bureaucracy would prevail, and a restoration of capitalist relations would ensue. We can see how things panned out in the former USSR. While the paths of the USSR and China might not be identical, the rapidity of capitalist restoration in China from the end of the 'Cultural Revolution' has been seamless, but not in the least surprising.

Chapter 7

China's rapid march to the market

Carl E Walter and Fraser JT Howie, in *Red Capitalism* (2012), make the claim that China remains a communist country. Such a premise is based on the continued existence and rule by the CCP and the rhetoric that party leaders use to maintain a sense of legitimacy. It is a claim that is made by many authors, academics, analysts and politicians around the world. Fraser and Howie add flesh to their argument by explaining that the Chinese state can and does make direct interventions in the running of the economy, including directly supporting struggling industries. It is an interesting thesis but enormously unsatisfactory. The USA is not a 'communist' regime and nor are any of the other major capitalist economies and yet all have a record of ensuring that capitalism survives. They all have intervened in various ways to makes sure that order maintains. John Bellamy Foster makes the obvious point that 'in the Great Financial Crisis of 2007-9, the big banks and corporations were almost all bailed out' (2019: 12). Not to do so would have brought the entire system crashing down.

It is important to understand why such confusion surrounds China and its rise. Just what is China today? Solving that riddle has been presented as a Herculean task but it should not really be all that difficult. This chapter goes some way to solving that riddle. China's position in the world, as the major rival to the USA for global economic hegemony, was assisted by the policies enacted in the Mao period from 1949. In this sense the notion of 'Mao' and 'post-Mao' needs to be re-examined. Many differentiate completely between the two periods, presenting them as polar opposites. While economic structures have significantly changed, it can be shown that there was an almost inevitability about the transition to capitalism. Appreciating Mao's legacy is important.

China's meteoric rise in the past 4 decades has been explained in a range of ways. For many it is attributable to 'state capitalism' in action. This idea, like so many, has a comforting simplicity to it, but is not satisfactory. Whether China is a state capitalist regime or not becomes a focus for this chapter. It will be shown that China is not state capitalist but a capitalist economy. After all, 60 per cent of GDP, 80 per cent of urban employment and 90 per cent of all new jobs are the product of the private sector. Private capitalists account for 70 per cent of all investment and 90 per cent of exports, not to mention the 66 per cent of all economic growth in the country.

Western observers and proponents of the capitalist ethos are quick to point out China's success in lifting so many millions out of poverty and it is a laudable fact. It is also a fact that inequality has been growing alongside the capitalist economic miracle. Capitalism, of course, is expansionary. Just as Western capitalism expanded into China, then so too has Chinese investment flowed outwards and with the capital expansion and outflow of capital comes foreign policy implications for China and its rivals, especially the rival that matters most: the United States. Marx and Engels in the *Communist Manifesto* presciently wrote of the globalising nature of capitalism and how capitalism effectively replicates itself across the world (Marx 1977: 71). What we are left with and which is affirmed in this chapter is that Chinese capitalism can best be regarded not as 'state' or 'hybrid' or 'Confucian' capitalism, and certainly not 'socialism with Chinese characteristics', but simply capitalism. It is in this appreciation that we can see the looming struggle between the USA and China for dominance of the crumbling capitalist economy.

Capital's debt to Mao

To suggest that capitalist development in China owes a debt to Maoism or Stalinism seems at first glance to be absurd. Maoism and Stalinism, despite their grotesque misrepresentations of Marxism or socialism, were in a very different camp to that of capitalism. There might be a logic to that argument, but the trajectory of modern Chinese history seems to destroy that logic. Something truly dramatic happened along the way from Mao's 'iron rice bowl' view of the world to Deng Xiaoping's famous 1992 declaration that 'to get rich is glorious'. Both men were CCP leaders. Deng had found himself in trouble during the Cultural Revolution as a 'capitalist roader' but he and Mao had resolved their differences by 1973. This was of course just a year after Mao had opened the door to the West with Nixon's visit in 1972. It is not a mere set of coincidences that sees Mao at the centre of each of these moments and hardly a random act of chance that capitalism was reintroduced with such a flourish just a few short years later.

A little earlier Trotsky's idea of the two paths open to the USSR and its bureaucratic control was described. He spoke of a society in transition. His prediction was, if anything, too optimistic. For there to have been a new social revolution to rid the country of its bureaucratic leadership, to reform the party and to theoretically re-arm the working class, was always fraught with difficulty. Those who control things, be they a class or a bureaucratic elite, will always be reluctant to step aside for the greater good. If truth be told, the writing was on the wall for the USSR by the time that Trotsky made his statement. The same can be said for China.

The Cultural Revolution was inevitably winding down when US president Nixon made his historic visit to China. Was this just another eclectic turn by Mao, was it a means of weakening the USSR, or were other factors at play? Certainly the Sino-Soviet angle is important but as Jeffrey Bader comments, 'at the core of opening up to China was a decision by Nixon and Mao Zedong to put to the side the issues of values and ideology that had kept us apart...and to concentrate instead on common interests' (Bader 2012). Bader, of course, is remarking on events from an American perspective. He sees an important, even crucial, element in the exchange as being economic. This is undoubtedly the case, but it was a mutually advantageous arrangement and one that was overseen by Mao. 'The element in the relationship that is recognizable...is the economic. The US business community has been the anchor of US-China relations for the last 30 years, as we have built up an annual trade relationship of over $500 billion, with huge US investments in China and growing Chinese investment here' (Bader 2012).

The meeting between Mao and Nixon came a year before what was to herald the major shift towards the re-establishment of capitalism in China. The disgraced 'capitalist roader' Deng Xiaoping was brought in from the cold by Mao. Mao's logic might have been a spur of the moment reaction, or it might have been a considered action aimed at strengthening China's position following the *rapprochement* with the USA. Whatever the motivations, the end result is there for all to see. Deng had been a member of the CCP from the early days and shared many things with Mao, not the least a general disdain for Marxism, despite what the party might have said.

Deng recognised a need, however, to mask what was a total abrogation of Marxism. He set up a theoretical argument, proclaiming that what he was doing was fully in line with Marxist thinking. He did what so many had done before him; cherry-picked selected phrases from the body of Marx and Engels' work. He used Engels' *The Principles of Communism* (1969) to 'prove' that private property could only be abolished when certain conditions had been met. He likewise quoted the *Manifesto* to further establish this idea and went on to remind people of the period of the New Economic Policy that had been introduced in the Soviet Union in the very early days after the revolution. The arguments were spurious, but when one controls the apparatus of state, things become a whole lot easier to sell. His theoretical exposition was lauded by the party. The *People's Daily* expressed the view that:

> regarding relations between the market economy and governmental interference, China's general designer of the Reform and Opening-up Deng Xiaoping had a very deep insight. In his South Tour Speeches 20 years ago, he said firmly and confidently, 'Planning and market forces are not the essential difference between socialism and capitalism. A planned economy is not the definition of socialism, because there is planning under capitalism; the market economy happens under socialism, too. Planning and market forces are both ways of controlling economic activity' (*People's Daily*: 2012).

Deep insights aside, Deng moved effortlessly from 'theoretical' expositions to the all-too-familiar aphorisms. Catherine H Keyser quotes Deng in this regard when she writes that '"it does not matter if a cat is black or white so long as it catches the mouse'; it no longer matters if an economic policy is capitalist or socialist, in other words, as long as it results in economic growth' (1984). And so, with a witty quip, all theory and practice was thereby jettisoned. China's next long march was well and truly under way. Deng's cat, whether it be the black or the white one, has, in the ensuing years, been rather busy. Capitalism in China has triumphed.

Is there such a thing as Chinese capitalism?

It is one thing to say that capitalism has triumphed in China, but what does that really mean? There are differing opinions as to just what is meant by capitalism in China. Branko Milanovic

(2019) mounts an argument that there are two distinct capitalist formations; a Western capitalism based on liberal, meritocratic structures and another pursued by more autocratic states, and here he specifies China as a capitalism that is state-led, political and authoritarian. His choice of language seems to imply that there is a 'good' capitalism based on merit and a 'bad' capitalism; ruthless and authoritarian. There might be some comfort to know that exploitation in the West is better than exploitation in the East! Milanovic's theory does, however, fit snugly with those who see China's success as being based on a 'state capitalist' model. Colin Hay (2020) outlines what might be described as an orthodox approach in contemplating capitalist development, the 'varieties of capitalism' thesis, before differentiating himself with another perspective arguing that while capitalism might be seen to 'vary' it does not 'come in varieties'.

A Marxist view of the world can only be appreciated in relationship to how it interprets capitalism. Capitalism and its development is predicated on the appropriation of surplus value as already outlined, and this surplus can only be achieved through an intrinsically exploitative class arrangement. Capitalist society is based on the reality that there is an economic base upon which rests a political and social superstructure. The state, as facilitator of the dominant economic ideology, is rooted in class and class divisions. Ultimately there is one capitalism that essentially conforms to that pattern. It adapts to change and exists in real time and in real historical moments but inexorably moves towards a model that is universal.

What then of the arguments that abound that regard China as a 'state capitalist' structure? We first need to discern what is meant by state capitalism. It is a term that was frequently used to explain the economic behaviours of states such as the former USSR and now China. There are any number of definitions but they all essentially accept that state capitalism does not entirely conform to the norms of capitalist development. In particular, the definitions maintain that state capitalism is an economic system where the state undertakes the primary economic role, where the means of production are organised as state-owned enterprises, or at least where they are dominated by the state and operate as profit-making entities. Originally these definitions were used to describe existing capitalist states. It has been a term that has been in use since the late nineteenth century. Does it have any currency today, and specifically, does it explain Chinese capitalism in the twenty-first century?

When the Soviet Union was first designated to be state capitalist in the period that coincided with the Stalinisation of the country, Trotsky wrote:

We often seek salvation from unfamiliar phenomena in familiar terms. An attempt has been made to conceal the enigma of the Soviet regime by calling it 'state capitalism.' This term has the advantage that nobody knows exactly what it means. The term 'state capitalism' originally arose to designate all the phenomena which arise when a bourgeois state takes direct charge of the means of transport or of industrial enterprises' (Trotsky 2004: 185).

Something of a conundrum or a riddle emerges. If, as Trotsky explained, state capitalism comes into being when a bourgeois state assumes control of capitalist economic structures, then how can a state that is clearly not bourgeois assume control of capitalism from the private capitalists where none exist? When China began its march towards capitalism, there were no private capitalists. We are told, *ad nauseum*, that China is 'communist' and that it is led by a 'communist party'. We are then expected to accept that this same communist state was and is simultaneously a bourgeois one. It is time to put the riddles to one side and look, instead, at reality.

The Chinese economy and its rising capitalism owe much

to the state and to the CCP. That is abundantly clear. Without the sponsorship of such an organisation the transition from 'socialism' to capitalism would have been a much bumpier affair. However, as a report by the World Economic Forum in 2019 showed, fully 60 per cent of China's GDP, 80 per cent of its urban employment and 90 per cent of all new jobs are the product of the private sector. Private capitalists account for 70 per cent of all investment and 90 per cent of exports, not to mention the 66 per cent of all economic growth in the country (Guluzade 2019). Rainer Zitelmann argues that:

> These figures should cause anyone who cites China's economic miracle as evidence of the superiority of 'state capitalism' to stop and think again...Capitalism is based on the twin pillars of free market principles and private enterprise...In truth, China is a mixed system that combines capitalism and socialism – just like every country in the world. This is equally true of the United States and European countries, all of which blend – in different proportions – capitalist and socialist elements in their economic systems' (Zitelmann 2019).

Leaving aside Zitelmann's rather cavalier use of the word 'socialism' to describe government regulatory activities, the point is still clearly made. Chinese capitalism is, at the end of the day, not especially different from any other capitalism. It has developed in a different historical moment and from a different form of state, but its destination is the same.

The development of capitalism is inseparable from that of the state. This has already been discussed at some length. What is important to remember is that a primary role of the state is to facilitate the development of the economic order that underpins that very state. As China made the transition from a state with some claim to represent the interests of working people to a fully functioning capitalist economy, then so too did its state structures enter into a transitionary phase to best accommodate that very transition. This no more makes China 'state capitalist' than any other nation-state that facilitates capitalism. It remains a fact that the Chinese state controls sections of the economy, although this has significantly shrunk since its 'opening up' from the 1970s. By the same token, those Western economies that were seen as bastions of the welfare state set about a rigorous process of privatisation. This was to further enhance the profitability of capital, especially in the period since the crisis years of the 1970s, the collapse of the Bretton Woods monetary order in 1971, and the re-emergence of the spectre of the falling rate of profit.

Capitalism exists only if it grows. Growth and expansion must include credit. The small proprietor borrows with the expectation of being able to service the debt and so expand to become a bigger proprietor, thereby profiting from his or her endeavours, and so it goes. States behave in a similar fashion. Credit, however, if not managed, quickly becomes debt. If the expected profits do not eventualise then the individual capitalist, the capitalist economy and state slides rapidly into crisis. This crisis was at the centre of global unease in the early 1970s. Nothing that has been attempted since that moment has eased the crisis. Debt continued to grow while new markets were created. Incidentally, total global debt at the end of 2019 stood at $255 trillion, up by $87 trillion from the time of the 2008 Global Financial Crisis (Roberts 2020). The implications of the Covid-19 effect are still to be considered.

The period from the early 1970s changed the face of the global economy. In an attempt to maintain profitability, capital was compelled to globalise at a remarkable pace. China's desire to embrace a capitalist future was naturally enhanced by this very crisis in capitalism. Capital flowed to China. Industries quickly established themselves. China was seen as almost a saviour of capitalism. Its transition period may have begun slowly and with great care and caution (Guthrie 2000) but by the early 1990s it had become a substantial borrower from the World Bank and by 1993 had become the single biggest recipient of FDI (Lardy 1995). Along with the flow of capital came the establishment of a vast array of multinational companies. China offered much to capitalism as it assumed the title of 'workshop of the world'. The past decades of capitalist development in China have seen its economy grow, in dollar terms, from $113 billion dollars in 1972, when Nixon made his famous visit, to over $21.4 trillion in 2020. While the figures are spectacular and tell a story, the simple fact remains that none of this could have been even remotely conceivable without that one indispensable factor that keeps capitalism alive: the working class.

China and the working class

The literature surrounding China's rise as a capitalist power is extensive. The scope of that research becomes just a little less intense when considering the importance of the working class in the development of capitalism. While this might be irritating, it is not entirely surprising. We are told, often enough, that the working class just about anywhere, but especially in the developed world, is less than relevant. However, the fact is that the working class, rather than shrinking, is growing at an astonishing rate, is a global issue and is directly linked to capitalism's own globalisation.

The global working class at the end of the twentieth century was estimated to be more than two billion people with the same number again occupied in closely related areas (Harman 1999: 615). Today 60 per cent of the working class is to be found outside the industrialised world (Harman 2010: 337). In this context, Beverley Silver's (2006) work describing the link between capital flows and the growth of the working class in developing nations becomes particularly relevant. Putting an accurate figure on the size of China's working class is not altogether as simple as it might appear. Figures point to a middle class of 110 million and a working class of 623 million. Defining class is, however, always a tricky concept. Class identification is so often a subjective thing. However, 623 million is more than enough to contemplate. It is a class whose numbers have swelled alongside China's growing capitalism. Class and capitalism are inseparable.

Capitalism requires a reproduction of itself. It must move forward. Like a shark it must maintain constant movement or die. One vital element of this ability to maintain its existence and its reproduction springs from the fact that the working class exists and grows in relation to capitalism. Profits are derived, after all, from surplus value. Surplus value comes from the labour of the working class. The working class, in one form or another, is responsible for everything that has been produced on this planet. Michael Lebowitz (2004) argues that capitalism's ability to 'keep going', or to reproduce itself, is due in large part to the acquiescence of the working class. He speaks of a dependency that workers are taught to feel for capitalism. They come to believe that capitalism meets their needs and that the worker needs capitalism.

> As long as workers have not broken with the idea that capital is necessary, a state under their control will act to facilitate the conditions for the reproduction of capital... Capitalism produces the working class it needs. It produces workers who look upon it as necessary...A system where the reproduction of capital is necessary for the reproduction of wage laborers. What keeps capitalism going? Wage laborers' (Lebowitz 2004: 24).

The Chinese working class has grown and changed since the restoration of capitalism. It has become a little more difficult to sell the idea to Chinese workers that they have all that much in common with their employers. Capitalism requires an acquiescent workforce. It would seem logical to imagine that China, as a state that is governed by a communist party and still clinging to the notion that it somehow represents socialism and therefore the interests of the working class, ought to have a happy, content and positive working class. The past few decades have seen this class become more restive. Ngai Pun (2019) observes that features, long apparent in Western capitalist societies, have been replicated in China. Specifically, she speaks of the process of proletarianisation that turns agricultural workers, voluntarily or not, into an industrialised working class. What goes with such a transformation is the inevitable alienation of the working class from the production process and ultimately from society at large. Pun describes the rapid growth in collective activity with which the Chinese working class has engaged. She cites official statistics that show an annual increase in strike activity of about 20 per cent, which coincided with the growth of the private sector. She uses an oft-repeated paraphrasing of Marx, but certainly a relevant one when she states that, 'a specter is haunting China—not global capital, but of a new working class' (Pun 2019).

The work of the China Labour Bulletin (2020) has already been discussed. The chronicling of worker protests, strikes and unrest over recent years, despite the repressive nature of the state, ought to finally debunk the arguments of those such as Goran Therborn (2012) and his ilk that claim that the working class is no longer a central force by which to effect change. The working class is in fact bigger than ever it was and with a potential power that remains a constant threat to capital. It was precisely that fear that was a key element in the West's capital flow to China. It was not merely a suitable place with a low-wage workforce. It certainly was but with the controlling hand of the CCP and the social capital it had developed over decades, it must have appeared as a dream solution. Low wages, high productivity and a rigidly controlled labour force. What could possibly go wrong? Something did go wrong. It was something called capitalism. Capitalism is exploitative. It must wring as much profit as it can from the working class. This can only lead to resentment and resistance.

The resentment of the Chinese working class to the exploitation that goes hand-in-hand with capitalist development mirrors that of any other capitalist state. It was described earlier (Trotsky 1972, Mann 1973, Smith 2014) how the organisations of the working class are first legitimised and then integrated into the state apparatus. In the case of China, this has taken a notionally different form. The organisations in China have long been part of the state. For Chinese workers to give vent to this resentment, they are forced to move beyond these state-sponsored organisations. This is, however, not all that different when one considers the wide-spread industrial actions of 2019 across much of the Western world. In these cases, the workers also began to bypass their 'traditional' institutions.

The dangers of a potentially revolutionary force, in the form of the working class, are real and always present. Capitalism lives with these dangers and has employed enormous resources over decades to keep a 'lid' on things. It is China's authoritarian form of government that made it such a prize for capitalism. It allowed for quick progress, behind a veritable firewall that kept its workers in check. There have been outbreaks and cracks in that same wall, but Chinese capitalist growth has been, nevertheless, astonishing.

The two parties to China's new capitalist enterprise, the Chinese leadership and Western capitalism, both had much to gain from the new arrangements. China was about to jettison its 'socialist' baggage and fulfil Deng's dream of the glory of wealth (at least for some). Capitalism was just possibly going to bail itself out and push through the crisis that so bedevilled it.

China was given every support that capitalism can give: good trade deals, abundant capital flows and all the rest. The only problem was that China proved to be too successful. It gave flesh to Marx's comment at the birth of modern capitalism that, 'the country that is more developed industrially only shows, to the less developed, the image of its own future' (Marx 1986b: 19). China saw that future and has embraced it.

Capitalism, for all its power, seems unable to learn from the past. It is foolish to assume that capitalism can long reside within the borders of a nation-state. Chinese capitalism in a very short space of time began the process of 'breaking out' that its mentor states had already accomplished. As its capitalism grew and expanded, then so too did its state seek to facilitate this forward movement. How could it be otherwise? China, by following the very pattern established by the other leading capitalist powers, and especially the United States, soon became not so much an ally and partner, but a rival. Sometimes this can be expressed by economic measures and sometimes in terms of foreign policy.

Capitalism dwells in a world that is marked by contradiction and crisis. China, for global capitalism and especially for the United States, presents as another contradiction. What began as a potential workshop for the world quickly became a centre for global capitalism and a rising capitalist entity in its own right. US capital flooded China. US corporations set up shop. Chinese capitalist enterprises also grew. Herein lies the contradiction for capitalism. Chinese capitalism is, after all, ultimately capitalism. It grows and breaks free from national borders. It has to. China then quickly became a rival and a threat to other capitalist states. Why anybody is surprised is in itself surprising. Capitalism does what it must do and what it has always done.

Chinese capitalism – a global player

Chinese capitalism was boosted in its early post-Mao period by encouragement from advanced capitalist states and by flows of capital into the country. The period from 1984-9 saw FDI into China of $2.3 billion. By 1995-9, that figure had risen to $40.6 billion (Tseng and Zebregs 2002). China was undoubtedly 'open for business' and business was open to China. Capital beat a path to China. In a very short space of time, China began to play a prominent role in FDI outflows to the world. In 2018 the total FDI from China had reached a total of $137 billion. While the corresponding figure for the USA was far greater at $342 billion, the trajectory of Chinese development is obvious. The logic of capitalism is there for all to see. From 2005-19, foreign investment by China, in the form of private capital and investment and through state-owned enterprises, had reached a cumulative $2 trillion dollars (American Enterprise Institute 2020). This growth has understandably slowed, due to economic problems that have engulfed the capitalist world and the United States' efforts at curtailing the rise of Chinese capitalism, but China remains the second largest global economy. This feat has been achieved in an astonishingly short period of time. It does show a mix of state-sponsored and private operations, but again, the overall direction is clear to all.

The growth of FDI across the globe is, of course, an indication of an increasing integration of global capitalism. Economic activity had traditionally been conducted between individual states representing national forms of capitalism, but increasingly this is taking place between transnational corporations as well as states. In this context, Chinese corporations essentially conform to the pattern. FDI outflows have become the effective means for financing industrial production outside the industrialised states. Brooks and Hill (2003) provide global figures showing the growth of FDI outflows from $53.7 billion in 1980 to $1.2 trillion in 2000. They also indicate that FDI grew at a rate of 500 per cent in the decade from 1990-2000, whereas total global trade grew at less than 200 per cent. While the GFC resulted in a contraction in the rates of growth, the general tendency of integration beyond state controls remains unchanged.

David Shambaugh (2012) outlines the rise of China's multinational corporations, showing that 12 companies made it onto Forbes 500 list in 2001 and that just 10 years later a Chinese company had risen to number three on that same list. Shambaugh points out that the bulk of these Chinese enterprises are still state-owned. He uses these figures to show that Chinese capitalism is still not 'free'. The fact remains that regardless of who is technically in charge, these companies operate within the capitalist world market. What is also of note is that the Forbes Global list of the world's largest public companies for 2020 has Chinese firms occupying five of the top ten places (Murphy, Tucker, Coyne and Touryalai 2020).

The momentum of Chinese economic development has an inevitability about it when considered from the perspective of capitalist processes. This is further enhanced when state policy is taken into consideration. As Ping Deng remarks, China 'will actively encourage its firms to invest overseas in order to sharpen their competitive edge and help make the country a key part of the global economy. This is evident in the speech made by then-President Jiang Zemin at *Fortune* magazine's 1999 Shanghai Forum and in the recently initiated "Go Abroad" strategy' (2004: 15). It certainly has become a 'key' part of that global economy.

An article appeared in the McKinsey Quarterly at the time of the GFC of 2008. It observed that, 'China's companies are on the cusp of a major foreign expansion. They have a great potential to reach beyond their home market, but to succeed they must overcome their inexperience' (Dietze, Orr, King 2008: 8). The article opened with a rather telling comment. 'Chinese companies are seeking opportunities abroad. They will have to acclimatise to new surroundings – just as the foreign companies that entered China did' (2008: 1). The McKinsey Quarterly, whose motto seems to say it all, 'learn fast and prosper', is geared towards an audience of businessmen and women. Like the economic system it represents, it has no other allegiance but to capital. For them, China in 2008 was an opportunity and certainly not a problem. China, in 2008, was affected by the GFC but far less critically than other competing states.

It was only in more recent times that a layering of emphasis on the role played by the CCP, the Chinese government and state has come to dominate debate. This coincides with the threat perceptions emanating from the USA, with the continued rise of China, especially through its combination of trade and foreign policy as seen from its 'Belt and Road Initiative' that was launched in 2013. The question was asked by *China Power* (2016), a publication of the Center for Strategic and International Studies, does China dominate global investment? While no definitive answer was offered, the paper did comment that, 'Overseas investment offers China an opportunity to not just bolster its own economy, but also leverage its economic strength to increase its influence abroad. Driven in part by Beijing's "Going Global" strategy that encourages investment in foreign markets, Chinese firms have actively expanded their overseas footprint in recent years and explored investment opportunities in a range of sectors' (China Power 2016).

This 'overseas footprint', that is synonymous with globalised capitalist relations, is the trigger for Chinese growth and a simultaneous trigger for Western concerns. The global market is a finite one. While capitalism owes no allegiance to national borders, nation states remain strong players and exert real power. This is the state of affairs that has accompanied all capitalist growth and national rivalries. China's wholehearted adoption of capitalism has seen its economy leapfrog others until today it is second only to the United States. In 2019 its GDP stood at more than $14 trillion (IMF 2019). By contrast the GDP of the USA was $21 trillion.

Marxist theory is consistent in expressing the idea that

economics drives social and political responses. It argues that there is an economic base upon which rests political and social institutions. The Chinese economic 'miracle' has, with the support of the state, meant that Chinese capitalism has necessarily moved beyond its national borders. Equally inevitably this has meant a changed focus for China relating to issues of foreign policy.

Foreign policy and Chinese capitalism

The state does what it must in order to advance capitalist interests at home and abroad. Foreign policy then becomes an expression of capitalist relations. Can this be any different for a state such as China? Foreign policy so often reflects the way a nation views itself as much as how it wishes to be viewed by others. One enduring feature that symbolises China's development and particularly from the beginning of the last century has been its sense of nationalism. This was, after all, the kernel of Sun Yat-sen's theory, a theory so thoroughly embraced by the 'Marxist' Mao and his heirs. As China moved further away from any pretence at socialism and embraced a capitalist ethos, it combined the twin elements of nationalism and the drive towards globalisation. The fact that these two are intensely contradictory remains and will plague China as it has done all other powerful economies for the last century.

China's foreign policy considerations are often portrayed, by other states, in threatening tones. It is hardly surprising, given the intensity of interstate rivalry that exists. For its part, China's official perspective in relation to foreign policy has been promoted in an eight-point 'philosophy'. Briefly this states that China will not seek hegemony, will not play power politics or influence other countries' internal affairs, will treat all states equally, will treat international issues on individual merit, will rely on the United Nations Charter, will advocate for peaceful negotiations to resolve international conflicts, will oppose terrorism and weapons proliferation, and will respect the diversity of civilisation (Washington Times 2007). This is certainly a benign list and more than a few observers might see it as being open to interpretation, but then this is the case for all nation states and their stated aims and objectives regarding national security. Thomas Kane succinctly describes China's, and for that matter all nation states', fundamental foreign policy considerations when he says, 'China, in short, is determined to secure its own independence, and will seek power over all outside entities which could have power over it' (Kane 2001: 45).

This fact, of ensuring that power can be exercised and projected, has come to dominate thinking within China and also by its actual and potential adversaries. The Chinese military is enormous and has enormous capacity. It is second only to the United States in its military budget, spending $261 billion in 2019, which was 14 per cent of total global military spending (Tian et al, 2020). An obvious military capacity serves two purposes. On the one hand it signals to the world and its rivals that China is more than capable of defending its 'interests' and on the other hand it becomes a powerful internal symbol of strength and prestige for domestic use in fanning the flames of nationalism. Whether that growing military capacity will ever be tested is largely out of China's immediate control. It is, however, deeply connected with that other and all-too-often interconnected aspect of foreign policy: economic policy. Its connection flows from the simple fact that economic activity underwrites all other social, political and in this case military components of state activity. China's foreign policy activities are designed to promote China's position in the world. Its Belt and Road Initiative (BRI) exemplifies this.

The Xinhua News Agency in 2015 wrote of BRI expressing the view that its aim is to 'promote orderly and free flow of economic factors, highly efficient allocation of resources and deep integration of markets by enhancing connectivity of Asian, European and African continents and their adjacent seas...It is open to all countries and international and regional organizations for engagement and honors mutual respect and market operation to seek common prosperity' (Xinhua 2015). The BRI has been the subject of intense debate and criticism from rival economies. The Xinhua statement was surprisingly open in outlining an underlying motivation for the initiative: 'China will fully leverage the comparative advantages of its various regions and further open up for more interaction and cooperation both at home and internationally' (Xinhua 2015).

Two years after that statement, a major international gathering was held in Beijing: the BRI Forum. A statement issued from that meeting stressed that the BRI:

> seeks to expand maritime routes and land infrastructure networks connecting China with Asia, Africa and Europe, boosting trade and economic growth...The initiative...aims to eradicate poverty, create jobs, address the consequences of international financial crises, promote sustainable development, and advance market-based industrial transformation and economic diversification. This is a long-term project which, for years to come, will give China a key role in guiding and supporting cultural, economic, political, and trade developments around the world' (Belt and Road Initiative Forum 2017).

Again, China is clear on how it projects its interests and how the initiative would promote those interests. There are obvious economic gains to be made for China and equally obvious is the potential to place itself at the centre of developing world political, social, and economic developments as well as playing a mutually advantageous role in Europe and beyond. This strategy has brought the wrath of the United States and its allies down upon it. The fact of the matter is that China is advancing what it deems to be in its own best interests, economically as well as politically. Chinese officials would be quick to point out that they are acting in China's 'national interests' and this brings us to the core of the friction that is so evident in US-Sino relations.

Any nation state, in its dealings with the world, ends up echoing sentiments uttered by other nation states. That tricky catchphrase 'acting in the national interest' is a case in point. The national interest of one state may very well be at variance with the national interest of another, but that is how things go when dealing with nationalist entities. If it is true, as we were warned so long ago by Samuel Johnson, that patriotism is the last refuge of the scoundrel and, by Oscar Wilde, that patriotism is the virtue of the vicious, then what are we to make of the national interest?

The problem is that these interests are inevitably 'sold' using such benign and inoffensive language. Who can take offence at Xiaodi Ye's comment that, 'generally, China's national interests – which mainly include defending sovereignty and territorial integrity, maintaining internal stability and political rules, sustaining economic growth, and securing China's status as a great power – have remained fairly consistent over the past few decades' (Ye 2019: 77)? For its part, the stated national interest of the United States is to protect the homeland, the American people, and the American way of life; promote American prosperity; preserve peace through strength; and advance American influence (White House 2017). Supporters and critics will find plenty to agree with or to rail against in such statements. Pierre Lemieux, writing for the right-wing libertarian organisation the Library of Economics and Liberty, remarks that:

at worst, the concept of national interest is a tool of tyranny because it justifies imposing the preferences of some individuals on others. Under the excuse of the national interest, protectionist wars and even real wars have been waged, and minorities allegedly not national enough have been oppressed. The national interest is used against both foreigners and fellow citizens (Lemieux 2018).

None of this makes any of us sleep any easier. Capitalism remains in intense crisis. The very future of the economic system has never been more problematic. This sits alongside the decline of the USA as the undisputed economic hegemon and the rise of China. The two giants seem destined to clash. What happens will determine the future for us all.

Chapter 8

The clash of the titans

Inevitably the nation states of the United States and China must be compared and contrasted. It is important, in doing so, not to damn each equally and, at the same time, not to regard one as being in any way 'superior' to the other. It is not about choosing one over the other or throwing up one's hands and saying there is nothing to choose between them. For many observers, and especially those on the left, there is a tendency to suggest that the USA, as the primary imperialist power on the planet, is by definition the enemy and therefore the enemy of my enemy is my friend. For others it has been a case of portraying China's rise as the rise of a new imperialist power and therefore a sense of moral equivalence or relativism has crept into the debate. While the argument that China is imperialist has been strongly and persistently presented by many, it is not entirely satisfactory. Where the 'imperialist' argument unravels is around the question of intimidation, the threat and actual use of force. For all of its sins, China has not exhibited these questionable traits. This might come to pass at some point in the future, but in the here and now, China's behaviour on the world stage is very unlike that of the United States. What we do have is an intense rivalry between the two major capitalist states and there can never be room for two leaders.

Pecking orders decree that there must be both pecker and pecked. Sharing simply does not come into it. While it is a simplistic analogy, it remains a brutal fact of history that a hegemon cannot and will not happily co-exist with other would-be hegemons. The stakes in the farmyard power-play are limited. The stakes in the struggle for global economic and political power know no limits. The global struggle for pecking rights has fallout for just about everyone and not just the protagonists.

It has been shown that China is, regardless of how some might wish it to be, a capitalist power with all the baggage that goes with that term. At the same time things should never be painted in black or white. China's road to capitalism has been unique unto itself. The destination is ultimately the same but history, historical moments in time, ideological forces, outside influences all have an impact on that journey. Capitalism has been developing as a global entity for hundreds of years. China's arrival has been a very recent one and as such is seen by many as having a distinctly 'Chinese' appearance. China does exhibit many of the same characteristics as its rival for economic supremacy, the United States, and yet brings its own distinct history and timeframe to bear. The two are the same and yet different. This chapter examines some of the similarities and differences. In doing so, it becomes important to explore the aims and motivations that drive the rival economies and what it is that propels each player along a path that appears to be almost pre-determined.

The practices of each country, their domestic and foreign policy actions, have already been discussed at some length. It is necessary now to see and appreciate how they play out in real time as each country vies with the other. Some of this has an historical perspective; how China and the USA have traditionally perceived the world and their place in it. By so doing, we are better placed to see how the future is likely to unfold. While the two have similar aims and objectives, the mechanisms by which their goals might be achieved do vary in important ways. The USA has long been a state that projects force, either implicitly or explicitly. It has never shied away from the use of force to gain advantage. China, for its part, has not been incursionary. It is a strong military power and is growing in strength but seems content to use economic levers to achieve its long-term aspirations. This difference will be considered as the chapter unfolds.

What is abundantly clear is that the future of billions of people is being decided by the clash, figurative and literal, between the USA and China. Pecking orders do not allow for sharing. There can only be one hegemon. This is especially so when the clash takes place between two powers who share the economic vision in the same economic structure. This again brings the discussion back to ideas that were raised earlier. There are those who seek to find some common ground, some shared platform that would allow a peaceful co-existence of the two economic superpowers. Such an approach is not new and reflects theoretical manoeuvres undertaken in the period leading up to WWI. Just as Kautsky's 'ultra-imperialism' thesis was an impossible dream, then so too are the arguments that would see China and the USA 'play nicely'.

The day-to-day reality that the world is witness to is one of tension and ever more heightened tension. The USA, in its endeavours to 'contain' China, has resorted to military postures through its 'pivot to Asia' strategy, to trade wars and further threats of war. Cold War conditions exist but without anything like an ideological cover for those conditions. There is a dangerous degree of pushing and shoving that is being reciprocated. A cold war can so easily escalate into a much warmer affair. Historians have too often fallen back on the trite and fallacious 'sleepwalking' description of the path to WWI. It is clear from the vantage point of the present that there is no 'sleepwalking' in the dangerous preparations being made for that final showdown between one superpower with a proven track record of belligerent and adventurous use of force and another who sees its 'interests' increasingly threatened.

The two capitalist rivals: the same but different
There are certain self-evident truths about this twenty-first

century. The world is dominated by two rival economic powers, the United States and China. The United States, while remaining in deep denial, is in steady decline. China is not waiting meekly in the wings but is making a grand entrance as the next rising star. The two nations have vastly different historical and ideological backgrounds but remain linked by one identical capitalist ethos. Politically and socially they are poles apart. They are so much the same and yet so different. These two giants inevitably seem set to clash. All manner of plausible reasons have been and will continue to be confected as to why the clash will occur and yet the real overarching reason is so simple. Each desires to bestride the global economy like a latter-day colossus. It is what unites them, and not what separates them, that finally acts as the great point of friction.

Samuel Huntington (1997) wrote authoritatively on what he described as the clash of civilisations. He based many of his arguments on the premise that, in the post-Cold War era, the fundamental source of conflict would be found not in ideological or political difference, nor around economic questions, but rather through issues that he broadly defined as cultural. So much of the discourse surrounding China and how to deal with it has followed this proposition of Huntington's. It is the cultural differences, a rather different world view, a specifically Chinese 'way' of perceiving history that are promoted by our political leaders and media. By promoting 'difference' it is so much easier to vilify and demonise, to discover a reason to be distrustful and to take what are really unnecessary sides. Huntington's scholarship was vastly significant for decades, but in defining the causes of future conflicts as being predicated on 'cultural' difference, he was fundamentally mistaken.

Graham Alison outlines what he sees as Chinese leader Xi Jinping's 'vision' for China as one that 'combines prosperity and power...it captures the intense yearning of a billion Chinese: to be rich, to be powerful, and to be respected. Xi exudes supreme confidence that in his lifetime China can realize all three by sustaining its economic miracle, fostering a patriotic citizenry, and bowing to no other power in world affairs' (Alison 2017: 92). There is, in such a description, a remarkable similarity with how the United States has traditionally seen itself and its place in the world. Alison makes the point that both the United States and China share a sense of exceptionalism. It could hardly be any other way. Much has already been said of the concept of American exceptionalism. The Chinese, while not using the same language, do mirror that same sense of occupying a special place in the world. The promotion of an intensely nationalist world view on the part of both nations has certainly played a role.

To accept the Huntington thesis that culture separates and has the capacity to heighten the potential for conflict is to deny what appears to be a logical expression of Marxist theory; that despite the uneven rate of development, the end point of capitalist development remains the same. The journey that China has undertaken in the past century has ostensibly been a different one to that undertaken by the USA and yet the leaderships of each nation, regardless of cultural, political or historical differences, appreciate and recognise the motivations and aspirations of the other without recourse to cultural awareness programmes. It is not culture that separates these two giants. What drives them apart, what makes enemies of the two, are the very similarities of economic aspiration. Those aspirations drive political and foreign policy agendas.

The perception that each nation has about their role in the world impels one state to seek to maintain supremacy and the other to assume supremacy. This is perhaps crudely put but the fact remains that the strength of each economy, relative to the other, is what is motivating foreign policy and, worryingly, military doctrine. Statistics can so often be manipulated or interpreted to suit particular needs, but in May

2020 the International Comparison Program (ICP), a statistical organisation partnered by many financial institutions and guided by the World Bank, announced that at least technically China has overtaken the USA as a financial and economic power. Jeffrey Frenkel (2020) writes that, 'for the first time, the ICP finds that China's total real (inflation-adjusted) income is slightly larger than that of the USA. In purchasing power parity terms China's 2017 GDP was $196.617 trillion, whereas the US's stood at $19.519 trillion' (Frenkel 2020). GDP figures can be misleading and especially when population differentials are considered, but it is a statistic that appears to be behind at least some of the United States' posturing and trade war policies in the most recent past.

If, then, the causes of friction are economic, what is to be done? The simple answer, given the driving compulsion of capitalist power, is very little. The 'game' that is being played has only one rule and that is win, by whatever means. Winning is all and there is no 'runner-up' prize. China may maintain a degree of state control of its economy. It may be an authoritarian regime and a one-party state, but this does not fundamentally alter the fact that Chinese capitalism is, at the end of the day, simply capitalism. The United States might allow for internal criticism and be a more 'open' society, but the real differences between these two players is in how each manoeuvres its pieces on the board.

Aims and motivations and practices of each

What the United States and China want from this most dangerous game is abundantly clear. Economic and political power, the ability to frame international policy to its perceived advantage, to manipulate other economies and to bask in the sunshine and glory of something very much akin to 'empire'. Such are the prizes that motivate each of the players. And ironically, while this goes on, global capitalism continues to do what it has been doing all along. It integrates, crosses and denies borders, eschews nationalities and gets on with the business in hand. This remains the great contradiction that faces the world. On the one hand is the power of an international capitalist reality that exists beyond the nation-state and on the other a nation-state system of governance that administers capitalism.

The aims and motivations of China and the United States remain clear. In many ways they are virtually indistinguishable, one from the other. One state aims to remain the recognised economic superpower. The other aims to become that superpower. It is not ego that drives them. It is not a mission with a view to achieving a place in history. The motivation lies in a rather different direction. It is best understood if considered alongside the logic of a Marxist view of the world and of its development. The state, the economy and capitalist development are intrinsically connected. Marxist theory is clear in its assertion that the economy acts as a base upon which the various institutions of the state rest. The economy maintains a position of primacy. China and the United States in their strivings to assume a dominant position confirm this theoretical perspective.

The economy drives social activity. The state acts to support the development of the economic base. Marx and Engels, in *The German Ideology* (1964: 36), outlined how the state evolves in a manner that reflects different social, political and economic necessities. Bob Jessop (1990: 39), writing a century and a half later, echoes that view, commenting that shifts in state intervention in an economy are determined by historical and economic necessities. This is most clearly observed in times of economic crisis and, as is the case with China, when the economic structures are being fast-tracked. Ultimately it is a simple case of the state advantaging class and capitalist interests. While this has been broadly discussed, Chris Harman's (1991) critique of the relationship between state and capital, or more precisely the role of the state in assisting the development of capitalism, remains pertinent.

While the aims and aspirations of the contending global giants essentially remain in concert, it is in the practices of the two states that differences emerge. It is hardly contentious to say that the United States' economic and associated foreign policy actions have been rather 'muscular'.

Thomas Lum et al (2008) observe that 'economics and diplomacy are the central, mutually reinforcing components of China's growing soft power...Trade, investment, and aid, particularly that which involves gaining access to raw materials for China's development, are behind much of the PRC's recent inroads throughout the developing world' (2008: 2). The document then goes on to describe how the United States and China:

> share the same vital national interests of security and prosperity, although each has a particular additional interest, and each defines its interests somewhat differently. Each seeks freedom from fear and want and to preserve its territorial integrity. For the United States, its particular interest lies in value preservation and projection of those values. Many Americans view the spread of democracy and free markets as enhancing national security and often seek improvements in human rights as part of their negotiating goals. China has a particular existential interest in regime preservation or the survival of the Chinese Communist Party as the sole ruler of China. This dovetails back into the Chinese vital interest of economic prosperity (Lum et al 2008: 6).

This work is part of a report for the US Congress. What becomes increasingly evident as the report unfolds is the acknowledgement of important differences in approach. 'The tool kit of US hard and soft power includes the military, diplomacy, and culture' (2008: 16). The authors place these 'tools' in order and it is hardly surprising that the military sits at the top of the list.

Lum and his associates completed their report in 2008. The following decade was an enormously busy one and one packed with developments, none of which boded well for the world. In 2012 US president Obama announced his 'pivot to Asia' strategy as a means to 'contain' China. In 2014 China began its programme to build artificial islands in the South China Sea. The United States, largely as a result of its foreign policy adventures in the Middle East under the guise of a 'war on terror', continued to become estranged from many states. It's spending on foreign aid typically stands at about 1 per cent of its total budget. This 'largesse' has not always been without strings being firmly attached. By contrast its spending on the military has been between 15-30 per cent of the total budget of the country (Hedges 2003). China's military budget is the second highest after the USA but military spending, as a percentage of its total budget, is much lower. Its foreign aid budget is also lower in dollar figures. Then there is the much vaunted and equally criticised BRI that is injecting vast amounts of money into overseas projects. This is not without rather similar sorts of strings that tied earlier US aid packages.

Many critics of Chinese economic and foreign policy in recent years have pointed to a desire on the part of the Chinese government to exert influence on other states. There is doubtless much truth in this, and it tends to reflect a similar set of behaviours exhibited by the USA over the past century. There is, however, a none-too-subtle difference in the manner that China has gone about its task. The United States' track record when it comes to foreign military interventions is in quite a different league. The military – force projection, threat and repeated use of military power to gain advantage – puts the United States into a clearly defined position of imperialist power *par excellence*. This is simply not the case with China. What might occur over time remains to be seen but without the benefit of the seer's eye, the facts seem to indicate that China is far less threatening to world peace.

The busy decade since Thomas Lum's Report to Congress has seen a much harsher interaction between these two capitalist giants. Where once, optimistic voices were being raised that co-operation between the rising and falling players could be an option, there is today a stark reality that we are witnessing the beginnings of a winner-take-all process. Even so, there are still those who wish to see the two 'play nicely'.

Co-operation or confrontation

Marcus Noland, of the Peterson Institute for International Economics (PIIE), wrote in 1996 that maintaining and promoting good relations between China and the USA was crucial to the well-being of the world economy. He was hopeful that the potential admission of China into the WTO would assist in this process because, as he remarked, 'trade disputes between China and the USA are resolved almost exclusively in public, acrimonious bilateral negotiations' (Noland 1996). Just 5 years later China did become a member of the WTO. The acrimony that he described has, if anything, become worse.

Worsening relationships between the two giants bodes ill for the global economy. It is with such an appreciation that the Center for Strategic and International Studies (CSIS) released its *Parallel Perspectives on the Global Economic Order: A US-China Essay Collection* in 2017. In that collection, William Reinsch recommends, among other things, that all should acknowledge and accept the role that China has to play in global leadership and that disputes and differences between China and the USA be resolved in multilateral settings. He concludes with the desire that 'the two countries work harder to address their particular grievances in order to ensure that the political concerns do not grow and take control of the policy process' (Reinsch 2017: 45). Regardless of the wishes and recommendations of highly regarded institutions like the CSIS and others, political concerns have continued to grow, with the policy process becoming ensnared in a spiral that threatens us all.

What appears to be happening, despite the very best of advice, is a process that has long been the subject of Marxist theoretical writings. At the beginning of the last century the world economy and its major players were moving towards a clash based on economic issues and control of global markets. Many hoped and presented most plausible arguments for a theoretical position that saw these major economic powers co-existing in relative harmony. The theory was briefly introduced earlier in this discussion. It was Karl Kautsky's theory of 'ultra-imperialism'. Kautsky (1914), in the period immediately before WWI, suggested that what would happen after the war would be that the capitalist states would come together to reorganise the world into a far more cooperative system, not altogether unlike the idea of a massive cartel. The world would be peacefully divided, war and conflict would disappear and everything in the economic garden would be rosy.

While the Kautsky thesis was quickly proven by history to be false, it is a recurring hope that what is inevitable might be swept aside and that a rosy future might yet dawn. It remains a truth, albeit an often-uncomfortable truth, that economic realities drive social, political and military responses. At the same time economic power is achieved and maintained by political and increasingly by military means. This all runs in parallel with the inevitability of the state supporting the development of capitalist relations abroad. The potential difficulties become immediately apparent.

These very real concerns re-focus the attention of many to ways and means of making things right and stable. At one end of the spectrum is the perspective of John Mearsheimer (2003), whose argument remains that every passing of the baton from one power to another has led and will always lead to war. While this has a decided air of truth to it, there are many who wish it to be otherwise, without fundamentally altering the mechanisms and the economic structures that lead to Mearsheimer's brutal conclusions. Hugh White (2014) has addressed himself to the question of what to do about China's rise and how to accommodate what is, in reality, almost a *fait accompli*. White argues that such an 'inevitable' outcome as described by Mearsheimer, is to 'underestimate people's ability to recognise their own best interests, and to compromise and cooperate with others to promote them' (White 2012: 126). White appreciates the dangers the world faces in the rivalry between the USA and China. His prescription to resolve the looming crisis is to 'share' the spoils. 'The best way for America to respond to China's growing power is to agree with China to share the leadership of Asia...a new world order in which China's authority and influence grows enough to satisfy the Chinese, and America's role remains large enough to ensure that China's power is not misused' (White 2012: 126).

Hugh White's wish has not been realised. Since the publication of his book, *The China Choice: why we should share power* in 2012, any possibility for power sharing possibilities have receded. Power, in the immediate thinking of many, is synonymous with political power or the projection of military might. States are seen as threats by other states and are presented as such. What underlies all of this is, of course, economic power and the domination of capital and it is ultimately this coming together of state and capital that promotes threat and counter threat, be it real or perceived.

If economic issues become obscured from the thoughts and considerations of scholars, then the class nature of the states that play such pivotal roles is even less visible. There is an assumption that the rule of capital is an immutable one. It is at the heart of John Mearsheimer's theory. Power, in such a 'classless' view of the world, is played out solely by states. The strong devour the weak and the state remains somehow a hermetically sealed unit with one will and one consciousness. What remains an unstated, unobserved and ignored fact is that each capitalist state is comprised of antagonistic classes. There is always the possibility, and that possibility can easily become a probability, that the hidden class nature of these states might just change the whole course of events. It is a reality that must remain beyond the level of conscious thought for those who seek economic, social, political and military power. And while this fact remains masked from view, the struggle for supremacy goes on. The reports produced by organisations like the PIIE or CSIS, among so many, from just a decade or two ago, all shared a desire that the economic superpowers might be able to understand each other. To put it crudely, they hoped that the US and China might 'play nicely'. Those hopes have been dashed. Today we live in the shadow of trade wars and worse. The times are dangerous ones.

What might happen?

So if there is little or no possibility that the USA and China are likely to 'share' the world and if each is being driven to either maintain a position of total dominance or assume such a position, then what does the future hold? Already there is the reality of a trade war with a very real possibility that it will not merely continue but intensify. The difficulties that this poses to a global economy that is already looking exceedingly fragile must be keeping many a capitalist awake at night and apprehensive during the day.

If John Mearsheimer's take on things is true, then we can expect a war between the two great economic powers. It is, in his estimation, unavoidable. While he would not thank anybody for saying so, he has more than a little in common with some notable Marxists. Vladimir Lenin, in replying to Kautsky's 'ultra-imperialism' thesis argued that any alliance between the great powers was little more than a truce that would lay the groundwork for future wars that would seek to resolve the problem of hegemony (Lenin 1977: 724).

A number of possible broad scenarios present themselves as we look to the future of the rivalry between the two powers. The USA may forestall the rise of China through trade war, military threat and through a grand coalition of allied economies. The USA may continue to weaken its international ascendancy, continue its economic slide and become more demoralised domestically due to internal ruptures and economic dislocations, thereby forfeiting its position of dominance. China might continue to rise and make profitable use of its abundant soft power capabilities, thereby rendering it less vulnerable to economic attacks from the USA. Economic dislocations not directly related to US pressure might seriously weaken China's capacity for continued rapid growth. Political unrest, the class nature of society, both in China and the USA, might effectively make all of the above scenarios inaccurate. There may be peace, or war, but the *status quo* is unlikely to be maintained for long. Each of these scenarios deserve brief attention.

The first of these, the 'containment' approach, has been given much rein in recent years. Then US president Barack Obama first gave substantial voice to America's desire in this regard with his 'pivot to Asia' strategy. Georg Loffmann (2016) describes its overall intent as an attempt to maintain American hegemony through a combination of cooperative engagement and restraint. This strategy was understandably seen as a threat by China. The USA pledged to shift the great majority of its military capacity to the Indo-Pacific region. This rather provocative measure was seen to be in tandem with the US-sponsored economic-based Trans-Pacific Partnership that included the majority of economies in the region with the notable exception of China.

Military threat combined with 'grand alliance' economic pressures failed to deliver the desired results. Trade war policies became the tactic of choice for the Trump administration. It is a strategy that is fraught with economic danger to both sides and to other nations caught in the crossfire as economic nationalism is engendered.

This potential for economic and political fallout for third parties is all too real. The situation for Australia is a case in point. A fierce debate has been underway concerning how best to 'deal' with China. Australia's economic security lies with China as its biggest trading partner, but this relationship is seriously being undermined in the relentless US campaign against China. US Republican Senator Rick Scott, of the Homeland Security and Armed Services Senate Committee, in 2020 bluntly demanded that Australia should more actively unite with America in its new cold war against China. The Covid-19 pandemic had already seen Chinese students unable to resume studies in Australia or for those still in that country, queue for food parcels because Australia had left them unable to earn money to support their studies. Education is a multi-billion dollar industry in Australia. Beijing has warned its students to be wary about studying in Australia. Other trade war actions had earlier been announced. This is but one example from one country that is being adversely affected by US foreign policy decisions that have the unrealisable aim of 'rescuing' the US economy and hegemonic position.

The failures on the part of the USA to stem the flow of economic decline present, in the thoughts of some, the chance of a continued slide, possibly leading to an American 'forfeiture' of hegemony remains. The continued decline of US economic power is hardly a controversial premise. Robert Gordon in *The Rise and Fall of American Growth* (2016) describes how the USA has entered a period of permanent stagnation that has led to growing social inequality and poverty. The post-war growth period, the 'golden age', was in Gordon's estimation an aberration. However, the power and influence that the United States still wields is such that its decline, although terminal and while continuing to gather pace, will be a protracted affair. In any case, there is little evidence to suggest that the American ruling class will leave the field easily or voluntarily.

Much of the discourse on China's rise to dominance has been predicated on its potential for continued unhindered rise. The rise has continued despite some rather significant events. Its economy has been struggling, it has faced a serious backlash from the USA and the global economy has been such that no state has avoided the repercussions and the onset of the global pandemic of 2020. Before the worst of these crises affected it, China was being seen as the almost inevitable leader in global economic terms and for this to be achieved in a very short time. Arvind Subramanian (2011) confidently stated that this would be a fact by 2030. 'Broadly speaking, economic dominance is the ability of a state to use economic means to get other countries to do what it wants or to prevent them from forcing it to do what it does not want' (Subramanian 2011: 67). Things were certainly moving in that direction. The USA began to react to this, and the other crises of economy began to assert themselves. The optimistic timeline for Chinese ascendancy might be re-configured, but there seems little to suggest that its rise will be hindered by outside influences. The economy may stall, as it appears to be doing, but the general trajectory would still seem to be evident.

The global economy is in dire straits and only the more starry-eyed of optimists would envisage anything like a return to 'better' days in either the short or long term. Something akin to stability that registers an economic pulse but little else is probably the best that can be hoped for. Given such a reality then it is correct to assume that China's economic growth will stall, just as it has been slowing for the past few years. This, of itself, does not mean that its journey to economic ascendancy will falter. The reason is really very simple and is not an indication of a superiority in ideas, strategies or even will on the part of the Chinese government, state and capital. On the contrary, there is no shortage of will. The Chinese economy will continue to struggle, but there is still forward momentum, a momentum that its adversary, the USA, does not enjoy, and nor has it enjoyed for quite some time. Economic malaise will continue to hurt both players. This, and the growing inequality and injustice invoked by capitalism in crisis, might have consequences for both the United States and China.

The very idea that economic progress for China, or the capacity for the United States to re-establish equilibrium and recapture the economic high ground, could not only be disrupted but threatened by working-class response to growing social inequality would have sounded absurd just a few short years ago. Events stemming from a deep-rooted crisis in capitalism that spilled over into global protests and strike activities in 2019 make such a scenario a little less fantastic. Wealth is accumulating into fewer and fewer hands. The working class is slowly beginning to realise that it has something in common with the working class internationally and less with the ruling class nationally. Capital continues to integrate on a global scale and yet nation-state political structures have become increasingly nationalistic and inward looking. The potential for serious dislocations in both China and the USA cannot be discounted. However, given the authoritarian nature of China and the growing sense of authoritarianism that is being seen in the USA, a working class-led crisis might not be an immediate threat. This leaves just one possible threat: the threat of war.

Mearsheimer's predictions of a paradigm shift through war look increasingly to be the most logical option for the powers involved. We have disturbing bits and pieces of evidence upon which to draw this conclusion. There is the production and now deployment of low yield nuclear weapons being undertaken by the US military. There is the stated US military doctrine of a shift away from the 'war on terror' and a renewed focus on preparing to confront global 'great power' rivalries. There is the 'doomsday' clock of the Bulletin of Atomic scientists with the hands now closer to midnight than at any other time in history. One side in this potential conflict is doing a lot of pushing. The other seems more than willing to shove back. Much might be dismissed as the normal 'huffing and puffing' that goes with such rivalries, but the stakes are increasingly high in this Cold War without ideology.

War and Peace

If John Mearsheimer's portrayal of the future were in another age, then it would be bleak, but the bulk of humanity might get to live their lives relatively untouched by the events of history. Wars, however, have become more and more disastrous for the innocent millions and hundreds of millions. This time around we are looking at something far more threatening and fearful and presented to us in language that is at once Orwellian while simultaneously cold and clinical. A headline in *Foreign Affairs* magazine cut very much to the chase. The magazine devoted an entire issue to the question of nuclear conflict. The article in question is titled: 'If You Want Peace, Prepare for Nuclear War: a strategy for the new great-power rivalry' (Colby 2018). It would be nice to think that Elbridge Colby was offering us a warning to pull back from some apocalyptic abyss, but that was not his intent. Colby, incidentally, was one of the principal authors of a paper published by the Pentagon earlier in the same year that explained that the 'war on terror' was effectively over and that the US military was recommitting to the concept of great-power competition and confrontation.

The US-inspired trade war is pushing the world towards a new cold war. The Cold War was, of course, framed by ideology.

Any new versions are less ideological and more economic in nature. The stakes remain high and especially so given the fragility of the global economy and America's place in that global economy. Interestingly, Colby's article appeared just days before the USA announced that it would be withdrawing from the Intermediate-Range Nuclear Forces Treaty that prohibited Washington and Moscow from developing short and medium-range missiles. Increasingly it would appear that the unthinkable is being thought and given consideration.

The new thinking, as articulated by Colby, acknowledges that the 'risks of nuclear brinkmanship may be enormous, but so is the payoff from gaining a nuclear advantage over an opponent' (Colby 2018: 29). To make sure that nobody was uncertain, he went on to argue the point that a future confrontation could easily include the use of nuclear weapons. People like Elbridge Colby do not dwell in a world of conspiracy theorists. They devise policy and advise the leaders of the world's most powerful arsenal. Given the size and destructive power of the two nations, it is of no great purpose to run comparisons. Some statistics are, just the same, of interest. The United States has over 5000 nuclear warheads at its disposal (this does not include the low yield weapons on the production at present). China has 250 such warheads. The Chinese military is numerically greater (2 million as opposed to 1.35 million). The relative firepower of their respective conventional armies is not entirely clear, but each is certainly lethal.

Vast resources, human and materiel, are expended by each state with the same ultimate purpose. That purpose for one state is to ensure it remains the unchallengeable power on the planet and for the other, to both defend its place and to make sure that a new world order will dawn with it as that one unconquerable power. Why are these states risking annihilation, and why are they willing to expend so much wealth, inevitably at the expense of the welfare of their own people? It is to ensure that their power remains, and that the world remains a suitable set of markets for 'their' capitalism. It is this thinking that drove nations to war and is so very likely to drive nations once more to war. It also reflects a huge contradiction that has marked capitalist development for more than a century. It is the contradiction between a globalised and globalising economy and a powerful set of nation states.

What is taking place in the rivalry between the USA and China has a disturbing echo from developments that shaped the world at the turn of the twentieth century. There had been an intensification of globalisation of the world capitalist economy which found a reaction in a rise in nationalist response. The ultimately vain attempt to resolve this contradiction, between a globalising and increasingly integrated capitalism and the power of individual nation states, led inevitably to the carnage of WWI. The march of globalisation was briefly halted by the intense nationalism and economic nationalism that ensued, but it was but a brief delay. Today, the very same conditions are in evidence and the same, equally vain attempts to maintain power and influence are being played out.

There is, however, a fundamental difference this time around. In the lead up to 1914 the prize was there for all to see. Global influence, access to markets and the possibility to develop new capitalist enterprises and an almost endless supply of labour to secure an almost endless supply of profits. The prize, as insane as that now seems, was deemed to be worth the risk of war.

The situation is very different in the twenty-first century. The contradiction is the same, but the prize is a far more dubious one. Capitalism has always been riven by crisis, but that crisis has reached a point that can only be described as existential. Capitalism has reached into every corner of the world. Markets are more and more developed. The drive for cheap labour resources goes on but with each wave of capitalist penetration, another contradiction, between labour and capital, intensifies.

Compounding the problem is the destruction that capitalism has wrought on the planet. Climate change and capitalism can never be reconciled. Pandemics, unlike the wild assertions of some politicians, are not 'once in a century' phenomena but are linked to climate change. The prize, then, is a dubious one. The winner will quite probably take all, but the 'all' might include a global economy that has no more elasticity, an earth scarred from war, a hostile planet devastated by climate disruption and the ever-present threat of deadly pandemics.

Chapter 9

Capitalism's long road to...where?

Ever since it first made its appearance there have been critiques of capitalism. There are just two sides, two arguments. Capitalism is either a wealth-creating system that brings people out of poverty, promotes democratic values and offers a chance for all to survive and thrive, or it is an exploitative, all-devouring system that enriches the few at the expense of the many. The pro-capitalist argument is more and more difficult to sustain. The anti-capitalist argument has often been derided. After all the state supports capitalism and the state includes all of the instruments that can persuade and mould opinion.

Chief among the anti-capitalist critiques is that of Marxism. It has been criticising capitalism in an organised fashion since the middle of the nineteenth century. Today there is a plethora of Marxist critiques and each vie with the other for space in the arena where the battle of ideas is contested. This hardly helps to clarify an anti-capitalist perspective. Capitalism, for its part, appears to have weathered all the storms, and there have been more than a few storms. In the eyes of so many, capitalism has become an almost immutable thing. 'There was capitalism, there is capitalism and there will be capitalism.' Marxists have been foreseeing the end of capitalism now for a very long time.

The premise upon which the end of capitalism claim is made by Marxists is essentially based on the theoretical concept known as historical materialism. This was given some scope earlier in this book and was used to promote the idea of Marxism as a science. It is hardly necessary to expand on that earlier exposition, but it is worth remembering that our present economic formation is but one in a series and that there is no rational or convincing argument to suggest that capitalism is in any way immortal. Capitalism, as we understand it, became the dominant force only in the eighteenth century. In historical terms this is a very short span of time. To say that we are witnessing what are the final stages of this all-encompassing economic system needs more than a little justification.

This chapter goes some small way in supporting that claim. It does so by following some interconnected issues that affect capitalism. It is a simple and undeniable fact that capitalism is in crisis, but then it has always been in crisis. Crisis is what has motivated it to develop and to expand. Things are quite different today. The period between each cycle of crisis is becoming shorter. The system never quite recovers before the next crisis hits. Crisis is all part of the set of contradictions that capitalism is forced to confront on a daily basis. Some of these contradictions and the increasingly sharp nature of them are also examined.

A feature of capitalist reality is its need to expand. This has propelled it from a localised set of relationships, to national and then global connections. Along the way the small have been eliminated by the large, the weak by the strong, and the globe, as a marketplace, has shrunk. Today there is virtually nowhere left for capital to explore, to consume, to exploit. It is what impels the USA to seek total submission from rivals and which compels China to seek to displace America. There is nothing personal in this acrimonious approach. It is simply how things are.

Such a realisation brings the discussion to a central plank of Marxist theory: the idea of historical formations expanding and being overtaken by new and more efficient formations. This case has already been argued but warrants another examination as it seems that capitalism's possibility for forward movement is very nearly at an end. The ramifications for us all in such a scenario need to be acknowledged. There is extraordinary wealth on the planet, but insecurity, poverty, inequality and anxiety are features of daily life for billions of people. There appears to be no possible chance that capitalism, or capitalist states, can reverse these trends. If that were not enough, the destructive nature of capitalist expansion has put the very survival of the planet at risk.

Such is the prize that the two capitalist giants strive to gain. The chapter brings this into focus. Nothing short of a fundamental re-ordering of society can clean up the mess in which the world finds itself. Too many Marxists have glibly set out a prescriptive formula for the future. The future is bleak but there is no magic wand that can be waved to take away the pain. There is one simple point that needs to be borne in mind. There can be no continuation of the present. That can only end badly. Time is running out for capitalism and those seeking the prize of power in this capitalist dystopia will be left holding a poisoned chalice.

A world of contradictions and crisis

The battle for the prize of being the leading power in the capitalist world would be worth waging if the contradictions that bedevil capitalism could be overcome. For the last couple of centuries, capitalist development has been achieved not by resolving these contradictions and crises but by forestalling them, by dodging them and hoping for the best. There was a certain elasticity to this development but there can only be so much stretch. The contradiction between the growth of a globalised capitalism and the need for a strong nation-state has already been discussed, but equally pressing are the intense points of conflict that include a general tendency for profit levels to fall, the growth of an almost inevitably antagonistic working class, the concentration of wealth into fewer hands, and the spectacular rise in importance of finance capitalism. These are all linked, all pose existential problems for the economic system and none of them are able to be resolved.

Estaban Maito (2014), in a study of 14 capitalist economies

over time, points to the fact that there has been a general global reduction in the overall rate of profit. This has been a telling factor in the increased speed of globalisation from the 1970s. New markets and new centres of production with lower-cost wage regimes were necessary. It was a major consideration in the courting of China, by the West and especially the USA, in the 1970s. This imperative led to capital flows from the developed states to the developing economies and as new centres of production were established then so too did a massive growth of an industrial working class occur (Harman 1999, Silver 2006). A growing working class can so easily see a replication of many of the problems that necessitated the move to developing states in the first place. When organised workforces begin to make economic demands then profits again begin to slide.

Capitalism also inevitably results in the accumulation of wealth into fewer and fewer hands, which hardly makes for a secure or content population. The people experience, on a daily basis, the growth of inequality that pervades and diminishes their lives. There are few more telling statistics than those offered by successive Oxfam reports (2014, 2016, 2019) showing the concentration of capital into increasingly fewer hands, while poverty and insecurity continue to grow exponentially. This brings us to the financialisation of capital, which has become the hallmark of economic development in the past several decades, but which has assumed a remarkable pace in the most recent history.

Costas Lapavitsas (2009: 142-6) focuses on finance capitalism in describing crisis points in capitalism. He describes the significance of financialisation in tracing the trajectory of the current problems that confront capitalism. Richard Peet outlines the significance of finance capitalism in the twenty-first century, arguing that:

The main difference between Hilferding's [an Austrian

Marxist and theoretician of the early nineteenth century] finance capital and today's global finance capitalism is a greater abstraction of capital from its original productive base, the faster speed at which money moves across wider spaces into more places, the level, intensity and frequency of crises that take financial rather than productive forms, and the spread of speculation and gambling into every sphere of life (2009: 245).

The fact that economic progress is being viewed through the lens of the stock exchange immediately validates this argument. Neither the threat of global climate catastrophe, nor global pandemics seem to hinder the work of the market. Some of the 'best' days recorded in recent times on Wall Street have coincided with some of the worst for the people.

The problems facing capitalism are intensifying. The profits that are being amassed are being amassed by individuals and private corporations who owe no allegiance to any national state. This simple fact has serious implications for the 'race' that is underway between the two major powers. The private nature of capitalist accumulation rarely advantages the nation-state that at best is a nominal home to that individual capitalist or corporation. This problem, alongside the others just listed, are not new for capitalism or the state. They are issues that have haunted capital from its inception and have been the triggers for growth, outward movement and expansion. The flight from the 'spectre' that these crisis points represent has traditionally meant growth in capitalist development. Expansion into new markets, the opening up of entire continents, first to produce raw materials and then to become centres of production. It had to be. There was never an escape from those same problems, contradictions and crises.

The attempt to escape the inescapable has led to imperialism, to war, to revolt and revolution. The fact always remained that each of the points of crisis, each of the contradictions facing capitalism and its state were impossible to resolve. But by the same token, there has been nowhere for capitalism to go but forward, to expand to fill the available space. That space has now been filled and filled to overflowing. It presents a new and even more chilling dilemma for capitalism. If growth is essential and it so clearly is, then how to achieve it when it seems that all avenues for growth have been exhausted?

When the stakes are survival

The fact that capitalism has nowhere to go and no room to grow is hardly a secret. States and individual capitalist concerns are equally aware of this. The necessity of movement and growth is after all what makes capitalism special. Capital, as described earlier, exists in three connected forms that have always operated as a cycle: money capital, productive capital and commodity capital. The initial money capital is used to produce goods which become commodities and finally, upon sale, become increased money capital. It has been a cycle that has been repeating since capitalism first developed.

It is also worth remembering that until quite recently production essentially took place within national borders, with the goods produced both for the domestic market and export. Workers moved to where capital existed. Today the reverse is the norm as capital moves to where the lowest-wage regime can be found. This quest for the most fruitful places to do business has meant greater competition between the major capitalist players and has led to some of the more obvious points of friction between the USA and China.

While the drive for profits has led to a scouring of the earth for new sources of labour to produce the goods to keep the wheels of capital turning, it has meant the destruction of manufacturing in the original traditional centres of production.

Since the 1970s there have been massive dislocations and

the loss of industry and jobs across the developed economies. Job losses in manufacturing in OECD countries have been devastating. The USA recorded a cut of 25 per cent of all manufacturing jobs as a result of the global push to maintain profitability (Bernard 2009). These figures further underwrite Beverley Silver's (2006: 3-23) analysis that the quest for profitability, and the consequent flow of capital, builds working-class movements in developing states. Dirk Pilat et al (2006), in describing the changing nature of manufacturing in OECD economies, note that manufacturing has become more clearly integrated at the global level.

Capitalism's relentless globalisation and the dislocation that accompanies it is intrinsically linked to its striving to maintain profitability in the face of constant threats of falling rates of profit. Empirical evidence indicates a growing degree of inequality, alongside a contraction of profit rates over time (Basu and Manolakos 2010). The crisis in which capitalism finds itself is dire. Is it possible for capitalism to break free from this seemingly all-encompassing straitjacket? Throughout its turbulent history, capitalism has been portrayed as being resilient and innovative. Has it reached the end of the road? There are few options that remain, short of war. The increasing trend towards authoritarian rule would seem to be another.

Capitalist economies are only able to exist while-so-ever they grow. It is abundantly clear that this is becoming more difficult, given the 'shrinking' global marketplace and the strained relationships between leading capitalist states. When capitalism first made its appearance as a ruling idea, it was met with opposition from those whose labour provided the profits. The relationship between capital and labour has traditionally been antagonistic. The state quickly came to realise that any on-going and open struggle between the opposing classes would end badly for capital. Open, flagrant and brutal oppression could not be countenanced as a long-term strategy. To this end, the organisations of the working class were progressively co-opted into the state and became legitimate institutions of the state. As capitalism spread beyond national borders, profitability was, at least for a time, relatively secure and the domestic working class was able to be convinced that its interests and those of the ruling class were in accord. As the expansion of capitalism is ultimately limited, new ways of extracting profits need to be considered. In this sense the wheel has turned and increasingly profits are being derived from increasing exploitation aided and abetted by the state and its institutions. This has meant for the state, introducing policies of austerity and dismantling welfare state mechanisms. Understandably these policies have not been met with acclaim from those most adversely affected. Authoritarian forms of rule are, therefore, almost inevitable, given the crisis within which capitalism now dwells.

Actions by some states and representatives of states have been described as fascist. It is one of those pejoratives that are freely and wildly thrown about. It had become almost a running joke on the left. Anyone you disapprove of could be dismissed as a 'fascist'. The time for jokes is now past. There is a sense that the tide of authoritarianism has a very real fascistic tendency about it. Peter Sinclair, writing in 1976, described a pathway from authoritarian populism to incipient fascism and from there to fascism (1976: 102-5). He is not alone in such a consideration. Samir Amin (2014) writes of a fascist 'choice' that capitalism adopts in managing capitalist society in crisis and of how the economy is 'managed' through the institution of fascism.

That series of steps, from the development of populist movements, to authoritarian regimes, to incipient fascism, to the establishment of fascist regimes is decidedly possible. At the same time, it needs to be borne in mind that fascism is a political manifestation of an economic crisis. It does not appear of itself but is a response to a very real set of political and economic considerations. Fascism enjoyed wide-spread political support in earlier times. The economic realities had seen the middle class lose privilege and be 'cast down' to join the ranks of the working class. The working class were also becoming less and less secure. Conditions demanded radical change. The ruling class, under such conditions, actively manipulated discontent. After all, the survival of capitalism was at stake.

Unless dramatic changes take place, such a progression becomes possible again. It is not that individual political figures, or even governments, have been secretly harbouring such desires, although there might well be such examples. Any move to such a political perspective is determined by economic factors. The simple and undeniable fact of the matter is that capitalism is in a state of crisis that is irresolvable.

Capitalism is like that shark that just must keep moving. To stop means to die. Crisis confronts our economic system on all sides. All the old ways of seeking to overcome crisis and to side-step contradictions have been exhausted. Capitalism and by definition the state is compelled to continue what is rapidly becoming a dance of death. Countless millions of lives are being imperilled as poverty, insecurity and anxiety confront people in the developed and developing worlds alike. It is one more piece of evidence to suggest that capitalism has nowhere to go.

A future of poverty, insecurity and anxiety

Capitalism cannot realistically expect to continue to expand by 'conquering' new markets, new sources of raw materials and creating new centres of production. In an attempt to maintain profit levels and to amass further profits, capitalism has been forced to turn its attention to the working class to extract a little more than its 'pound of flesh'. In this it has been supported by the state and the various institutions of control, both national and international. While ever smaller numbers of individuals have grown wealthier, the working people and entire states have become stretched and impoverished. Debt stalks individuals and nation states alike. Relief packages from the IMF are delivered but policies of intense austerity are enforced which exacerbates the growing feelings of fear and anxiety among the populations of those debt-laden states. There are no optimistic signs on the horizon. Inequality and insecurity are not isolated to this or that country. Developed or developing nations alike share this same precarious existence.

The disintegration of what was once a given, that things would slowly improve, is now a fact of life. The collapse is happening at an astonishing pace. Figures and statistics concerning the growth of inequality and the concentration of wealth become obsolete as soon as they appear but they are still worth contemplating. A United Nations Human Development Report from 1999 and cited by Fred Dallmayr (2002: 144) showed that just three of the world's richest families had an income equivalent to the poorest 600 million. As alarming as that figure is, things deteriorated steadily in the ensuing decades. Oxfam's 2018 report pointed to the odious fact that just 26 individuals have wealth equivalent to that of the poorest 3.8 billion people.

The UN figures from 1999 were also used by Jan Pieterse (2002: 1025) to show the rise in inequality that has occurred since the industrial revolution. He describes a situation in 1820 which saw a gap between the richest fifth of the world's population and the poorest fifth steadily grow from a ratio of 3:1 to 74:1 in 1997. This trajectory has been steadily accelerating and explosively so, especially since the 1970s. Pieterse asks, 'what kind of world economy grows and yet sees poverty and global inequality rising steeply?' (2002: 1036). History and political economy can sometimes move at an astonishing speed. The answer to his question in 2002 might have been a capitalist economy existing in conditions of crisis. Just a few years later that answer is more like a capitalist economy that is beyond any possible salvation. What we are left with is 'carpet-bagging' and looting on a mass scale.

The victims of all of this are the people whose very labour created the wealth that is now being so avariciously accumulated. The degree of this 'looting' is sometimes alluded to. International institutions, analysts and activists alike acknowledge that a fundamentally new stage of crisis has emerged. A report issued by the IMF in 2015 states that:

Widening income inequality is the defining challenge of our time. In advanced economies, the gap between the rich and poor is at its highest level in decades. Inequality trends have been more mixed in emerging markets and developing countries (EMDCs), with some countries experiencing declining inequality, but pervasive inequities in access to education, health care, and finance remain (Dabla et al 2015: 4).

The OECD (2015) has similarly reported that inequality in OECD countries is at its highest since records began to be kept. The same report indicates that the rise in inequality has been reflected in a growth of part-time and casualised labour. Joint ILO/OECD (2015) research has shown that for decades, labour's share of income has lost ground to capital. OECD (Cingano 2014) reports are also clear that inequality is growing steadily with wealth differentials between rich and poor at their highest in more than 30 years.

As many as 75 per cent of all workers across the globe now fall into the informal category – either as temporary or short-term employees. The growth of capitalist globalisation is mirrored in the growth of the global working class which now sits at about 3.5 billion. One factor that the working class in the OECD and the developing world have in common is a growing sense of insecurity.

This sense of insecurity is exemplified in the relationship between capital and labour. In responding to the tendency that exists for a fall in the rate of profits, capital has sought, as it always has, and as it always must do, to maximise the levels of surplus value at its disposal. What appear to be 'changes' in the very nature of work are observable as qualitative changes in capitalism have developed. Traditional labour/capital relationships have been altered. There has been a dramatic rise in the casualisation of labour, 'flexible' working arrangements have been introduced, and workers are increasingly regarded as 'sub-contractors'. Despite these 'changes', the reality of that essentially exploitative relationship between capital and labour remains unchanged.

In the endless propaganda war between the two competing economic powers, the working class is often overlooked. At times the supporters of the United States' position might point to the level of exploitation, the low wages, the long hours, the repression that so obviously exist in China and quickly link these with the one-party state and that China is 'socialist' or 'communist'. China is hardly a paragon of virtue in its treatment of its workers. Following global trends, it has seen a dramatic increase in casualisation from 24 per cent to 42 per cent in recent years (Liang, Appleton and Song 2016). Chinese workers are entitled to pensions from age 60 for men and 50 for women. The social wage has, however, been significantly reduced since its journey to capitalism commenced. By contrast American workers can access pensions at age 62, although this is moving out to 67 for both sexes for those born after 1960. Twenty per cent of Americans aged 65 and over are working either on a full-time or part-time basis and fully 59 per cent are non-salaried workers, working on an hourly basis. These figures are reflected in all capitalist economies as the crisis in capitalism has led to greater degrees of exploitation.

These are the realities with which we all live. All nations share certain common features, not the least of which is the economic system of capitalism. There are no shining lights upon the hill. There is just that dawning understanding that things are getting progressively worse. As far as capital is concerned, there is no option but to wring as much as possible from the living labour before it. The state has no option but to play its part in maintaining the economic system upon which it sits. Capitalism has reached the point beyond which there is no more 'stretch'. Even so, the two dominant players remain locked in a struggle for supremacy, for power, for hegemony. If one does come to dominate the world, the same problems and crises will remain. The elusive new horizon with markets aplenty will not materialise. The working class will still be forced into an exploitative existence and relations between labour and capital will only become more antagonistic. And then, even if one power does assume the mantle of hegemon without resorting to global war, the planet will still be faced with climate crisis and the threat of pandemics.

Capitalism's scorched earth

In 1964 the song *Eve of Destruction* sought to alert people to a range of threats: the Vietnam War, and the possibility of nuclear destruction for a start. The threats were unfolding, even as capitalism was enjoying its ever so brief golden age. If we move the clock forward half a century, then what have we to fear? Certainly, a little more than fear itself. As capitalism runs out of options, the 'doomsday clock' has moved closer to midnight than at any time in its history. Peter Maurer (2020) cites a recent survey of 16,000 millennials across 16 countries showing that 54 per cent feel a nuclear attack is likely in the next decade, and that the percentage who feel that nuclear war is likely in their lifetime is even higher. And then there is the crisis of a warming planet that capitalism has absolutely no way of resolving.

The past couple of decades have been marked by the speed with which climate change is being felt and by a near universal acceptance of its all-consuming importance. There are no longer serious debates as to whether it is happening. Sceptics and deniers exist, but in ever shrinking numbers, even if some of these occupy powerful positions within society. The point remains that the awareness of this huge contingent of humanity is astonishing. It is an awareness that springs from observing the obvious. Weather, fires, destruction, the images that daily fill our screens, have all served to form a mass-opinion and mass-consciousness. It has also coalesced around a stated and unstated demand that something must be done.

There is, however, a monumental disconnect between the overwhelming mass of humanity wanting change and those who can effect change. Nothing of any real substance is being done to combat this most existential of the crises that face humanity and the very economic system that is creating the crisis. The UN World Meteorological Organization (WMO) Secretary-General Petteri Taalas, citing the WMO's annual report, stated that 'greenhouse gas concentrations are once again at record levels and if the current trend continues, we may see temperature increases of 3-5 degrees C by the end of the century' (Taalas 2019). The teenage activist Greta Thunberg, speaking at the 2019 COP 25 conference, drew attention to the inaction on the part of both politicians and CEOs. All of this raises serious questions. Why is nothing significant being done? How can those being held to account by Thunberg and so many others go on doing so little, and why are the people, so justly angry, unable to make these same people respond?

What makes things even more interesting is that those same politicians that Thunberg castigates invariably acknowledge that there is a problem. As a consequence of the obvious evidence and the quiet neighbour to neighbour exchange of views, the percentages of people across the world who recognise that change must happen is astonishingly high and astonishingly similar. Two-thirds of opinion poll respondents in the UK, US and Australia have called for climate action. The figures are higher in Canada and Germany. It is an issue that unites rather than divides communities. Political theorists might well take note of all this. Responses to climate change and the calls for climate action are political issues. How political forces react to the demands being made by the people become significant. Of equal significance is how the political demand that climate change is both developed and focused on by the people on the ground. All of these things, based as they are on political considerations, ought to be able to be remedied. The problem, and it is an unsurmountable problem, comes from how the world is configured by capitalism and how its contradictions and crises are being played out.

If ever there was a problem that warranted a global response it is the problem of global climate change. It hardly needs mentioning that international meeting after international meeting has done little to fix the problem. There have been resolutions aplenty but how to implement action? There are a range of factors that come into play. While all recognise the magnitude of the problem, the world is still dominated by capitalist relations. This might remind us of one of Marx's primary contradictions of capitalism, the social nature of production and the private nature of ownership. This is generally considered from the point of view of a producer and his or her workforce. If we extrapolate out for a moment, we can see the population of the planet on one side of the contradiction and private capital on the other. To further compound the problem is the existence of the nation-state system of governance that exists to promote and facilitate the smooth operations of capitalist economics. At the last count there were 193 individual member states of the United Nations. Each of these make various appeals to 'national interest' and almost exclusively they are capitalist or at varying degrees of capitalist development. Those 'interests' remain national, even when the problems are global.

Each of these economies, large or small, developed or

developing, share that same overarching desire to promote capitalist relations to their own benefit. It is how the game has been played since capitalism first burst upon the scene and the evolution of the global nation-state system emerged. If that were not bad enough, there are the all but uncontrollable operations of an increasingly stateless global capitalism that owes allegiance only to profitability.

None of this changes the fact that billions of people across the planet are demanding action and that many representatives of the people in government accept the need for change. Without change there is no future and yet the very essence of capitalism would seem in this case to mitigate against change. This exposes another and even sharper contradiction facing capitalism and the world. Capitalism has always responded to crisis in one form or another, either to move around problems, to move away from problems, to develop new mechanisms to best maintain the system, but always with an eye to survival and reproduction of the system itself. If capitalism cannot adapt, change or offer meaningful solutions to such a crisis then it simply shows the truth of the idea that economic systems have a finite life and that this one has reached the end of the line. Suggestions of ethical capitalism, of green capitalism, of a more sharing version of capitalist economics have all surfaced, but the fact remains that capitalism can only survive by growing, expanding and returning increasing profits in a highly competitive marketplace. It seems highly unlikely that the leopard will be changing its spots anytime soon.

The devastation that is being wrought because capitalism can no longer avoid its own crisis has come to haunt the people of the planet and is haunting capitalism itself. There is a link between climate change and the rise and spread of pandemics. This in turn can effectively close down entire economies and devastate global trade as the Covid-19 epidemic has shown. Should such a spiral continue then Marx's letter to Ludwig

Kugelmann, where he commented that, 'every child knows a nation which ceased to work, I will not say for a year, but even for a few weeks, would perish' (Marx 1868), has an ominous ring of finality about it.

Destruction – global pandemics

Capitalism in its relatively short history gave much that was positive to the world. It revolutionised production, allowed for remarkable achievements in health and education, lifted countless millions out of poverty, opened up entire continents and changed forever the way people lived and thought. None of this was done through any sense of altruism. Each forward step was primarily a forward step for capital. The working people benefited coincidentally but not without enormous suffering being attached. Capitalism's progress has been described as creative destruction. Each new crisis necessitated a new response but now the earth is exhausted, the people are in despair, inequality has never been higher, pollution and a warming planet threaten new and ever more devastating pandemics. In the face of these crises, capitalism offers nothing but pain and misery. When Covid-19 erupted in 2020, the response from leading economies was to briefly lock things down, hope for the best, seek a vaccine and as quickly as possible drive people back to work, regardless of the loss of life that would accompany such a move.

Marx's words that economic death will follow if a nation stops working seemed to ring loudly in the collective ears of capital. Stock markets made profits even as mass graves were being dug and temporary morgues were being erected. Production simply had to be maintained. The results were an indictment of how economies and governments view human life. Mark Williams (2020) cites figures from the UK Office of National Statistics to show that mortality rates in poorer areas of the UK were double those of more affluent communities. The death rate in the early months of the pandemic was 55.1 per 100,000 as opposed to 25.3 per 100,000 according to the class divide. Blue collar workers in the UK according to these statistics account for 34 per cent of all jobs in the country but make up 43 per cent of all Covid-19 deaths. White collar workers total 43 per cent of UK workers and 28 per cent of Covid-19 deaths. These figures can be replicated across states. The demands from business and governments to find ways to 'open up' the economy as quickly as possible has led to the loss of many thousands of innocent lives. The pandemic is a look into the future for us all. While it has been handled well by some states and poorly by others, it is a direct by-product of capitalism in the twenty-first century and symptomatic of its incapacity to function.

Robin Marantz Henig, in *National Geographic* (2020), writes of how scientists had been warning for decades that something very like Covid-19 would eventuate. She cites her own book, *A Dancing Matrix*, which was published in 1990 to prove her point. That book and other reports, expressing the thoughts and research of so many experts in the field, was blithely ignored. Nothing was done. Governments avoided spending money in the vain hope that the threats just would not come to pass. Even as governments ignored the warnings, the threats were becoming reality. There is a clearly identified link between capitalism, climate change, global disease and pandemic and it is no secret. The World Health Organisation (WHO) has produced numerous reports and publications all pointing to the potential dangers associated with climate change and its relationship with human health. These reports formed the basis of much that was presented to the COP 24 meeting in Poland in 2018. What is disturbing is that organisations such as the WHO, and the hundreds of well-credentialled participants at such meetings, have been effectively ignored in a delusional hope that things will simply get better. It is reminiscent of a political cartoon from the early 1980s. A top-hatted, cigar smoking caricature of capitalism sees a billboard and orders his chauffeur to reverse in order to reread the sign. It read, 'the world will end in 30-40 years.' 'What a relief. I thought it said, 3-4 years,' comments our cartoon character. Satire has become reality.

Capitalism did once offer something positive. It was a step forward. Its forward movement has now not merely slowed but has become stagnant and worse. It offers the people a life of insecurity, worsening living standards, poor health outcomes, anxiety and death. The people and their labour over centuries have provided every tangible thing that can be given a value. The planet has provided the materials from which that labour has produced the value. Today both the people and the planet are exhausted, just as capitalism has exhausted its usefulness. And yet capitalist regimes and individual capitalist enterprises, zombie-like, go through the motions of continuity. A monstrous charade is enacted, and capitalist nations still vie with each other for supremacy.

Future and the prize

Capitalism, like each economic formation before it, has a time limit. Despite the best endeavours of its apologists, the simple fact remains that capitalism exists in a line of progression. It starts at a certain point on the continuum, moves forward, gathers momentum, grows in stature and power but the line it is running along is not an infinite one, any more than the line upon which feudalism ran was infinite. The sun rises and the sun sets. We happen to be living in an historical moment that is the sunset moment. How long this moment is remains to be seen. It is clear that capitalism and its state will do all in their power to forestall the inevitable day. Those who grow rich will not be convinced to slip quietly into retirement and nor will those who struggle to maintain the edifices that support capitalism quietly pick up their hats and coats and lock the door behind them. None of these individuals and institutions have a terribly bright future but while-so-ever they remain at the helm, the future for the rest of humanity is even bleaker.

This presents very few options. The *status quo* might be able to be maintained for years or even decades and with it more pain, misery and destruction. The problems will not go away. Some hope that capitalism might be reformed. A more rational capitalism, greener, sharing, ethical, might emerge, but this flies in the very face of how capitalism has developed. It is the antithesis of the logic that drives capitalism. War might be waged between those who seek to cling to power and prominence against those who seek to acquire power and prominence. Assuming that one power manages to subjugate the other and secure what remains of the world's markets, resources and labour, it will be a pyrrhic victory and the problems that drove them to war will still remain. Fascism might come to control economies and states, but fascism must, as an extreme form of nationalism, turn on other fascist states for greater control and economic power and so the war scenario is repeated. All of these are bleak, grim and depressing possibilities and none of them can resolve the crisis that exists for an economic formation that has simply run out of ideas, time and creative force.

The only rational solution is to accept that the end has arrived and acknowledge that change is knocking ever so loudly at the door. The lives and well-being of billions of people must be taken into consideration at some point. Now is the right time to consider those lives, and to consider the potential, the creative capacity that exists and which could resolve problems on a planet that sustains life. If the working people have, by their labour, created every tangible thing that has value, and the earth has provided every resource that has been used to produce all things of any value, then another way of thinking is required. Capitalism does not provide and cannot hope to provide any way out of the mess that it has created. If we are witnessing the end of an economic formation, then it is time to consider what comes next.

That 'next' is generally called socialism. It stands as the very opposite to all that we know and experience on a daily basis. It has gained a bad reputation over the past century. Some of this by the machinations of its enemies and some by the practices of many who have proclaimed themselves as 'socialists', 'communists' and 'Marxists'. Socialism, despite its less than illustrious past, has been enjoying a change of fortune. The vigorously anti-communist *Victims of Communism Memorial Foundation* (2019) conducts an annual survey of attitudes towards socialism, communism and collectivism. Its most recent survey found that 70 per cent of American millennials would vote for a socialist candidate if one were to be found on the ballot. This follows Gallup polls that show that the majority of young people are viewing the ideas of socialism in a favourable light. Such an idea, even just 10 years ago, would have been dismissed as little more than the mutterings of fantasists. How such change is to be brought about is a question for others, but one thing is certain. Change will have to be forced upon those who will not relinquish power.

And while the people, in order to survive, will turn their attention to new ways of managing lives and livelihoods, the immediate future will be marked by an insane quest by capitalist powers to secure the prize.

Chapter 10

Conclusion

A rather bleak picture has been painted. The bleak present, however, need not become a dystopian future. We live in an age that is marked by monumental changes and challenges. How the world and how the people respond to those challenges will largely shape the future. The period in which we find ourselves has been described in the book as being a period of fundamental change. The economic formation that has dominated life for the past 3 centuries has reached a point of crisis so deep that it is unrealistic to assume that there might be anything like recovery. This view has motivated much of the thinking behind this work and has been validated.

Capitalism, it has been shown, is not some immutable structure, but exists in an historical moment and for a finite time. Capitalism made its entry upon the world stage, grew, developed, effected huge changes, was progressive for a time, and began a slide into decay. It replaced an earlier economic formation and will in turn be replaced. While there is an air of inevitability in this, it is impossible to put time frames upon such momentous events and the changes certainly do not happen of themselves. Feudalism and the economic structure that supported it did not simply disappear. The economic conditions that sustained and nourished it could no longer permit such a formation to continue and so, new forces, the bourgeois, capitalist forces, seized power. Even the most cursory glance at the world around us confirms that the existing economic structures can no longer be maintained.

All of this formed the logic that is presented in this book. While the primary focus might be the observation of an end of an entire economic formation, changes within the capitalist world cannot but occupy our immediate attention. The fact is that the economic and political balance of power has been shifting now for some decades. The pace of this paradigm change has quickened and the world watches with a sense of alarm as the United States continues its slide and China appears set to become the dominant economy in the world. The alarm that is being felt is due to the potential for conflict that may very well accompany such changes. Historically empires have never relinquished power without a struggle. The United States is exhibiting all the same responses as its sun continues to set.

There are parallels between the end of empires and the end of entire economic formations. The former is, in so many ways, a microcosm of the latter. A major focus of this work has been to draw those parallels between the fall of empire and that of economic formation, especially as the two seismic shifts appear to be occurring almost in concert. A primary task and motivation of this book was to make those observations and, by doing so, to offer some observations about the state and its relationship with capital, the rivalry between the USA and China, and of the price that is likely to be paid for the questionable prize for which the two economies strive.

As a means of achieving this aim, it became necessary to outline the history and trajectory of these two titans now locked in economic and political struggle. There are, of course, limitations that will have an impact on a work such as this. While the history and development of both the USA and China were very much to the fore and form the basis of much of the analysis in the book, the work was by no means conceived as a history of either country. There are many such histories and within them much contention and conflict. The historian will doubtless find much to criticise in this work. Events and issues have been presented with rather broad-brush strokes. No, it is not a history, but it does offer a glimpse into the processes that each of the two nations underwent as they travelled along their separate paths. It allows for an examination of how each developed and how their sense of self in the world emerged. Importantly the book focused on the economic development of each state, of what is different and what is similar. It also focused on how capitalism developed in each country and how states ultimately conform to capitalist norms, even while recognising cultural, geographic and historical moments that are obviously very different. What draws the two nations into potential conflict is not any inherent differences that might be observed but a much more dangerous set of similarities that derive from a shared economic world view.

Some readers might find fault with the book's depiction of China. It is not easy to take a dispassionate stance in relation to China. Some choose to damn it and some to defend it. In doing so, sides are taken. The problem in such an approach is that it reduces issues to a simple and simplistic choice between two 'options'. The book consciously sought to avoid this. While the United States, as an economic superpower, is clearly in decline and it is a decline that is not to be lamented, its replacement by another economic superpower is hardly cause for celebration. Capitalism has, after all, left more than its share of suffering, inequality and exploitation in its wake. Replacing capitalism with capitalism hardly seems a solution.

The 'China threat' thesis is a dubious one, unless seen from the point of view purely of capitalist expansion, although few observers have shown much interest in this reality. Equally the arguments that China represents a better option because it is notionally a 'socialist' state and therefore less avaricious is hardly a satisfactory analysis. The greater the threat to American hegemony that China represents, the stronger the language that has been used to decry China's 'socialism', its 'communism', its rule by the communist party. When Hong Kong was returned to China in 1997, China's economy was on the rise but as far as the USA was concerned, this was a minor issue. Hong Kong's economy at that time represented 23 per cent of the total economic power of China. In 2020 that figure had shrunk to just 3 per cent. China is now, despite its obvious capitalist credentials, being perceived as more 'socialist' than in 1997 and even more than when the 'iron rice bowl' welfare statism of Mao's rule was in force.

Some writers, scholars and many in governments around the world look with alarm at China and its rise. For them China is a 'communist' state with a communist ethos and a communist party at its head. Those who use such epithets should know better, although more than a few careers have been built and enhanced by loudly denouncing China. The veritable tsunami of anti-China rhetoric that has consumed our media has been doing its work. The Lowy Institute, an influential think tank based in Australia, issued its annual survey in 2020. It showed that in just 2 years the percentage of Australians with a positive view of China had shrunk dramatically to just 23 per cent and that 90 per cent wanted Australia to find alternative trading partners (Kassam 2020). The anti-China propagandists have successfully staked many of their claims on China's alleged 'socialism'. It is an alarming situation as the potential for conflict is real and the mindsets of people are being assiduously moulded.

China is many things but certainly not socialist. Yes, it is led by a communist party, but it is simply a vehicle by which the Chinese government manipulates nationalist aspirations. China is as much a communist state as is the United States. Even the use of the term 'communist' is ludicrous as such a depiction presupposes that the particular state has already achieved socialism, which China did not and certainly will not. The book is critical, highly critical, of China and of its political and economic course. At the same time it is equally wrong to depict China as a threat. It is, under current conditions, a capitalist economy that began its road to capitalism at a very much later stage than most and via a very different path, through the distorted political theories of Maoism and Stalinism.

China has been and remains firmly rooted in a nationalist sense of itself and of its place in the world. So too does the United States. Each invoke nationalist symbolism to promote their own perceived interests. Each vie for prominence as the leading economy in the world and each have rather similar problems and face similar threats. Capitalism has long moved beyond the confines of national borders and exists beyond the control of governments. Globalisation impacts on how states operate. Capitalism has expanded to the very furthest corners of the planet. There is no longer any room for forward movement. To share hegemony is unthinkable for these powers or any other competing capitalist states. What drove the world to war in 1914 was a vain attempt at finding a way out of the dilemma of a globalising capitalism and coalitions of nation states all seeking individual power. The book showed that nothing has significantly changed in the past hundred years, except that the stakes are so much higher.

Yes, the present is bleak and even if it were simply a question of this or that economic superpower taking control of the various institutions on the planet, then there would be little to enthuse about. The planet, as the book described, is in crisis as never before. The economic structures provide no hope. Poverty, anxiety, alienation, inequality and insecurity plague the population. Capitalism and its misuse of the resources of the earth is leading to such mayhem through climate change as to make life even more difficult or even impossible. Pandemics threaten us all. Change has to be wrought if there is to be a future beyond the miserable dystopian vision that capitalism offers through authoritarianism, potential fascism and war.

So then, how to bring about change? Can there be any possible light on the horizon? Throughout 2019, hundreds of millions of people were in open revolt at what they saw as the 'future' under capitalism. Strikes, riots, revolts shook the world. The streets of the USA erupted in 2020. That trigger, that spark, was the death of one man at the hands of police. That spark flared across the globe, far beyond any issue of race or police brutality. And beyond that, there are billions of people demanding a planet that will sustain life and provide a future. While these movements are spontaneous in nature and often leaderless, they signal a change in thinking, a desire for something better. People are recognising their strength and the weakness of an economic system that can no longer even begin to meet their needs.

And while this unfolds before the eyes of the world, two economies, two titans of capital square off and struggle for a prize, and such a prize it is. The winner will briefly take all but it will be a pyrrhic victory and short lived.

Author biography

William Briggs has been variously a teacher, a journalist and political activist. He worked as a teacher of English and History for a number of years, and as a journalist. For 3 years he lived and worked in the Soviet Union as a foreign correspondent. Later, he resumed full-time study, completing an MA and a PhD in International Relations from Deakin University. Since then he has remained affiliated with Deakin and written extensively on issues of political theory, international politics and political economy. He is the author of three previous books, two of which have been with Zero Books. He is a regular contributor to online newsletter Pearls and Irritations and contributes to the online magazine Independent Australia. Much of this has been around the broad issue of the rise of China, its ramifications for Australia and the USA, and on the rising tensions and threats of war that stem from the United States' policies towards China, while still maintaining a critical position in relation to Chinese domestic policy. He lives in Melbourne.

Also by William Briggs

Classical Marxism in an Age of Capitalist Crisis: the Past is Prologue, Routledge, 2019
Can capitalism survive?
Capitalism has always lived in and with crisis. Wars, revolutions, economic depression, the threat of nuclear annihilation and ecological disaster have all failed to break the dominance of this economic and political system.
This book returns to classical Marxism as a means of finding the way to challenge the rule of capitalism.
A search for 'something better', this volume is an engaging read for scholars, researchers and all who share an interest in politics, political theory and socialism.

Removing the Stalin Stain, Zero Books, 2020
Can Marxism emerge from the long shadow cast by Stalinism, and challenge capitalism?
There is undoubtedly a growing interest in Marxism and socialism. Opinion polls show a majority that regard socialism as a real option. It is against this reality, and as a contribution to growing debates, that this book has been written. Marxism, as an ideological force and instituted to lead the charge against capitalism, has been poorly served in the past century. Many of its core messages have been obscured.
This defence of Marxism calls for a return of the working class to the centre of potential struggle and the healing of the damage done to Marxism, in the name of Marxism, over generations past.

A Cauldron of Anxiety, Zero Books, 2021
The veritable tsunami of anxieties that are affecting individual lives, the increasingly dysfunctional nature of society and the

potential catastrophes of global conflict and of climate change have a common cause. The inability of capitalism or the state to respond to existential crises and internal contradictions is the cause of this cauldron of anxiety. The book defends a Marxist perspective that would challenge this and provides an optimistic vision for the future.

From the author

Thank you for purchasing *China, the US and Capitalism's Last Crusade*. If you have a few moments, please feel free to add your review of the book at your favourite online site for feedback. Also, if you would like to exchange views with me, don't hesitate to contact me at briggsw00@gmail.com

Sincerely
William Briggs

Bibliography

Abraham Lincoln Online 2020 'The Gettysburg Address' *Abraham Lincoln Online*, Retrieved 4 May 2020, http://www.abrahamlincolnonline.org/lincoln/speeches/gettysburg.htm

Alison, G 2017 *Destined for War: Can America and China Escape Thucydides' Trap?* Scribe Publishers, Melbourne and London

American Enterprise Institute, 2020 'China Global Tracker' *American Enterprise Institute*, Retrieved 26 May 2020, https://www.aei.org/china-global-investment-tracker/?ncid=txtlnk usolp00000618

Amin, S 2014 'The Return of Fascism in contemporary Capitalism' *Monthly Review* vol.66, no. 4: 1-12

Anderson, B 2006 *Imagined Communities: Reflections on the Origin and Spread of Nationalism*, Verso, London and New York

Aronowitz, S 1990 *The Crisis in Historical Materialism: Class, Politics and Culture in Marxist Theory*, The Macmillan Press, London

Bader, JA 2012 'China and the World', Brookings, Retrieved 25 June 2020, https://www.brookings.edu/blog/up-front/2012/02/23/china-and-the-united-states-nixons-legacy-after-40-years/

Basu, D and Manolakos. PT 2010 'Is There a Tendency for the Rate of Profit to Fall? Econometric Evidence from the US Economy, 1948-2007' *University of Massachusetts – Amherst ScholarWorks@UMass Amherst*, Working Paper 2010-04 Retrieved 17 May 2020 http://scholarworks.umass.edu/cgi/viewcontent.cgi?article=1098&context=econ_workingpaper

Bell, D 1975 'The End of American Exceptionalism' *The Public Interest*, Issue 41 (Fall)

'Belt and Road Initiative Forum', 2017 *Overview*, Retrieved, 30 May 2020, http://www.beltandroadforum2019.com/conference-profile/overview/

Berberoglu, B 2003 *Globalization of Capital and the Nation State: Imperialism, Class Struggle, in the Age of Global Capitalism,* Rowman & Littlefield Publishers Inc., London, Boulder, New York, Oxford

Bernanke, B 2006 *Global Economic Integration: What's New and What's Not?* Speech at the Federal Reserve Bank of Kansas City's Thirtieth Annual Economic Symposium, Jackson Hole, Wyoming, Retrieved 23 March 2020, https://www.federalreserve.gov/newsevents/speech/bernanke20060825a.htm

Bernard, A 2009 'Trends in Manufacturing Employment' *Perspectives,* Statistics Canada, Retrieved 10 June 2020, www.statcan.gc.ca/pub/75-001-x/2009102/article/10788-eng.htm#a1

Bieler, A Morton, AD 2018 *Global Capital, Global War, Global Crisis,* Cambridge University Press

Board of Governors, Federal Reserve 2016 'Survey of Consumer Finances' *Board of Governors of the Federal Reserve System,* Retrieved 5 May 2020, https://www.federalreserve.gov/econres/scfindex.htm

Boucher, G 2012 *Understanding Marxism,* Acumen Publishing Ltd., Durham, UK

Brooks, DH Hill, H 2003 'Divergent Asian Views on a Multilateral Framework for FDI' *OECD* Retrieved 10 June 2020 http://www.oecd.org/dev/pgd/20354697.pdf

Bukharin, N 2003 *Imperialism and World Economy,* Bookmarks Publications, London and Sydney

Bush, GW 2005 'President Bush's Second Inaugural Address' NPR 20 January 2005, Retrieved 5 May 2020, https://www.npr.org/templates/story/story.php?storyId=4460172

Cannon, JP 1946 'The Coming American Revolution' Speech Delivered at the Twelfth National Convention of the Socialist Workers Party (Chicago, 15-18 November 1946) Marxist Archive, Retrieved 5 May 2020, https://www.marxists.org/

archive/cannon/works/1946/comamrev.htm

Cannon, JP, 1951 'From Karl Marx to the Fourth of July' *The Militant*, 16 July 1951 Retrieved 4 April 2020, https://www.marxists.org/history/etol/newspape/themilitant/1951/v15n29-jul-16-1951.pdf

Carver, T 1991 'Reading Marx: Life and Works' in T Carver (ed) *The Cambridge Companion to Marx*, Cambridge University Press, Cambridge, New York, Port Chester, Melbourne, Sydney: 1-22

Ceaser, JW 2012 'The Origins and Character of American Exceptionalism' *American Political Thought*, vol 1, no 1: 3-27

Chang, J Halliday, J 2005 *Mao: The Unknown Story*, Vintage Books, London

Chesneaux, J Kagan, RC 1983 'The Chinese Labor Movement: 1915-1949' *International Social Science Review*, vol. 58, no. 2: 67-87

China Labour Bulletin, 2020 'The State of Labour Relations in China, 2019' China Labour Bulletin, Retrieved 25 February 2020, https://clb.org.hk/content/state-labour-relations-china-2019

China Power 2016, 'Does China dominate global investment?' CSIS, Retrieved 15 June 2020, https://chinapower.csis.org/china-foreign-direct-investment/

Cingano, F 2014 'Trends in Income Inequality and its Impact on Economic Growth', *OECD Social, Employment and Migration Working Papers*, No. 163, OECD Publishing Retrieved 10 June 2020 http://dx.doi.org/10.1787/5jxrjncwxv6j-en

Claessens, S Kose, MA 2013 'Financial Crises: Explanations, Types, and Implications' *IMF Working Paper*, Retrieved 9 May 2020, https://www.imf.org/external/pubs/ft/wp/2013/wp1328.pdf

Clark, C 2014 *The Sleepwalkers: How Europe Went to War in 1914*, Penguin Books, London

Colby, E 2018 'If You Want Peace, Prepare for Nuclear War: A

Strategy for the New Great Power Rivalry' *Foreign Affairs*, vol. 97, no. 6: 25-32

Cox, RW 1993 'Gramsci, Hegemony and International Relations: An Essay in Method', in S Gill (ed), *Gramsci, Historical Materialism and International Relations*, Cambridge University Press: 49-66

Credit Suisse 2015 *Global Wealth Report 2015*, Credit Suisse Research Institute, Retrieved 23 May 2020 http://www. protothema.gr/files/1/2015/10/14/ekthsi_0.pdf

Dabla, E Kochhar, K Suphaphiphat, N Ricka, F Tsounta, E 2015 'Causes and Consequences of Income Inequality: A Global Perspective' *IMF Strategy, Policy and Review Department*, Retrieved 5 May 2020 https://www.imf.org/external/pubs/ft/ sdn/2015/sdn1513.pdf

Dahl, R 1967 *Pluralist Democracy in the United States: Conflict and Consent*, Rand McNally, Chicago

Dallmayr, FR 2002 'Globalization and Inequality: A Plea for Global Justice', International Studies Review, vol. 4, no. 2: 137-56

Deng, KD 2011 *China's Political Economy in Modern Times: Changes and Economic Consequences,* 1800-2000 Routledge Taylor and Francis, London and New York

de Tocqueville, A 2002 *Democracy in America*, The Floating Press, Auckland New Zealand

Deng, P 2004 'Outward Investment by Chinese MNCs: motivations and implications' *Business Horizons* vol. 47, no. 3: 8-16

Dietze, MC Orr, G King, J 2008 'How Chinese Companies can Succeed' The McKinsey Quarterly, Retrieved, 28 May 2020, http://fcollege.nankai.edu.cn/_upload/article/43/8a/1c 01c01245ea896e4da689527a3b/70927c82-a85a-424d-a8e8-ed082f57ba29.pdf

Dorn, JA 2008 'The Danger of Economic Nationalism: The United States should treat China as a normal rising power, not a probable adversary' *Beijing Review*, June 26, 2008 No 26

Dumenil, G Levy, D 2004 'The Economics of US Imperialism at the Turn of the 21st Century' *Review of International Political Economy*, Vol. 11 No. 4: 657-76

Dunn, B 2009, *Global Political Economy: A Marxist Critique*, Pluto Press, London UK

Eagleton, T 1991 *Ideology: An Introduction* Verso, London and New York

Easterly, W 2008 'Capitalism works because it is self-correcting' in M Kinsley & C Clarke (eds) *Creative Capitalism: a conversation with Bill Gates, Warren Buffett and other economic leaders*, Simon & Schuster, New York, London, Toronto, Sydney

Elster, J 1995 *An Introduction to Karl Marx*, Cambridge University Press, Cambridge UK

Engels, F 1966 *Socialism: Utopian and Scientific*, Progress Publishers, Moscow

Engels, F 1976 *The Dialectics of Nature*, Progress Publishers, Moscow

Engels, F 1984 *The Condition of the Working Class in England*, Progress Publishers, Moscow and Lawrence & Wishart, London

Engels, F 1886a 'Engels to Florence Kelley Wischnewetsky In Zurich, January 7' *Marxists.org* Retrieved 3 April 2020 Retrieved 4 May 2020, https://www.marxists.org/archive/marx/works/1886/letters/86_02_03.htm

Engels, F 1886b 'Engels to Florence Kelley Wischnewetsky In Zurich, 3 June' *Marxists.org* Retrieved 3 April 2020 https://www.marxists.org/archive/marx/works/1886/letters/86_06_03.htm

Engels, F 1959 *Anti-Duhring*, Foreign Language Publishing House, Moscow

Engels, F 1969 'The Principles of Communism' in *Marx & Engels Selected Works Volume 1*, Progress Publishers, Moscow: 81-97

Engels, F 1999 'Letter to Bloch, Marx-Engels Correspondence

1890' *Marxists.org* Retrieved 3 March 2020 https://www.marxists.org/archive/marx/works/1890/letters/90_09_21.htm

Engels, F 2000 'A Letter to Franz Mehring' Retrieved 5 March 2020, *Marx-Engels Correspondence 1893*, http://www.marxists.org/archive/marx/works/1893/letters/93_07_14.htm

Forbes, S Ames, E 2009 *How Capitalism Will Save US: why free people and free markets are the best answer in today's economy*, Crown Publishing, New York

Foster, JB 'Capitalism has Failed – What Next?' *Monthly Review: An Independent Socialist Magazine*, vol. 70 no. 9: 1-24

Frenkel, J 2020 'Is China overtaking the US as a financial and economic power?' *The Guardian*, May 19 2020 Retrieved, 29 May 2020, https://www.theguardian.com/business/2020/may/29/is-china-overtaking-the-us-as-a-financial-and-economic-power

Fukuyama, F 1992 *The End of History and the Last Man*, Penguin, Random House, UK

Gaido, D 2006 *The Formative Period of American Capitalism: a materialist interpretation*, Routledge Taylor and Francis Group, London, New York

Garrison, J 2004 *America as Empire: Global Leader or Rogue Power?* Berrett-Koehler Publisher Inc., San Francisco

Gellner, E 1964 *Thought and Change*, Weidenfeld and Nicholson, London

Giddens, A 1983 *A Contemporary Critique of Historical Materialism*, McMillan, London

Gilpin, RG, 1987 *The Political Economy of International Relations*, Princeton University Press, New Jersey

Gilpin, RG 2000 *The Challenge of Global Capitalism: The World Economy in the 21st Century*, Princeton University Press, Princeton

Goodwin, D 2001 'The Way We Won: America's Economic Breakthrough During World War II' *The American Prospect*, December 19, 2001, Retrieved 5 May 2020, https://prospect.

org/health/way-won-america-s-economic-breakthrough-world-war-ii/

Gordon, RJ 2016 *The Rise and Fall of American Growth: The US Standard of Living Since the Civil War*, Princeton University Press, Princeton and Oxford

Gould, J 2019 'Pentagon finally gets its 2020 budget from congress' *Defense News*, Retrieved 8 June 2020, https://www.defensenews.com/congress/2019/12/19/pentagon-finally-gets-its-2020-budget-from-congress/

Greenfeld, L 2009 *The Spirit of Capitalism: Nationalism and Economic Growth*, Harvard University Press

Gregor, AJ 2019 'Classical Marxism and Maoism' *Communist and Post-Communist Studies*, vol 52, no. 2: 81-91

Gregor, AJ Chang, MH 1978 'Maoism and Marxism in Contemporary Perspective' *The Review of Politics*, vol. 40, no. 3: 307-27

Guluzade, A 2019 'Explained, the role of China's state-owned companies' *World Economic Forum*, Retrieved 25 May 2020, https://www.weforum.org/agenda/2019/05/why-chinas-state-owned-companies-still-have-a-key-role-to-play/

Guthrie, D 2000 'Understanding China's Transition to Capitalism: the contributions of Victor Nee and Andrew Walder' *Sociological Forum*, vol. 15 no. 4: 727-49

Halliday, F 2002 'The pertinence of imperialism' in M Rupert and H Smith (eds) *Historical Materialism and Globalisation*, Routledge, London and New York: 75-89

Hamilton, IA 2020 'Jeff Bezos' wealth has exploded to $150 billion since the beginning of the pandemic' Business Insider Australia, Retrieved 24 June 2020, https://www.businessinsider.com.au/jeff-bezos-wealth-150-billion-since-pandemic-2020-6?r=US&IR=T

Hardt, M and Negri, A 2000 *Empire*, Harvard University Press, Cambridge Ma, London England

Harman, C 1991 'The State and Capitalism Today' *International*

Socialism, Summer 1991: 3-54

Harman, C 1999 *A People's History of the World*, Bookmarks, London, Chicago and Sydney

Harman, C 2010 *Zombie Capitalism: Global Crisis and the Relevance of Marx*, Haymarket Books, Chicago and Illinois

Harrison, JP 1972 *The Long March to Power: A History of the Chinese Communist Party, 1921-1972*, Praeger Publishers, New York

Hay, C 1999 'Marxism and the State' in A Gamble, D Marsh and T Tant (eds) *Marxism and Social Science*, University of Illinois Press, Urbana and Chicago

Hay, C 2020 'Does Capitalism (Still) come in Varieties' *Review of International Political Economy*, vol. 27, no. 2: 302-19

Hedges, C 2003 *What Every Person Should Know About War*, Free Press, New York, London, Toronto, Sydney

Held, D 2008 *Models of Democracy*, 3rd edn., Polity Press, Cambridge, UK and Malden Mass

Henig, RM 1994 *A Dancing Matrix: How Science Confronts Emerging Viruses*, Vintage Publishing, New York

Henig, RM 2020 'Experts Warned of a Pandemic Decades Ago: why weren't we ready?' National Geographic, April 2020, Retrieved 20 June 2020, https://www.nationalgeographic.com/science/2020/04/experts-warned-pandemic-decades-ago-why-not-ready-for-coronavirus/

Hilferding, R 1981 *Finance Capital: a study of the latest phase of capitalist development*, Routledge and Kegan Paul, London

Hobsbawm, E 2004 'Introduction: Inventing Traditions' in E Hobsbawm and T Ranger (eds) *The Invention of Tradition*, Cambridge University Press, Cambridge: 1-14

Hobson, JA 2005 *Imperialism: a Study*, Cosimo, New York

Hodgson, G 2009 *The Myth of American Exceptionalism*, Yale University Press, New Haven Connecticut

Hou, Chi-Ming 1963 'Some Reflections on the Economic History of Modern China (1840-1949)' *The Journal of Economic History*, vol. 23, no. 4: 595-605

Huntington, SP 1997 *The Clash of Civilisations and the Remaking of World Order*, Simon & Schuster, New York

ICRC 2020 'Millennials think World War Three is likely in their lifetime' News Release 16 January 2020, *International Committee of Red Cross*, Retrieved 22 January 2020, https://www.icrc.org/en/document/red-cross-millennials-think-world-war-three-likely-their-lifetime

IHS MARKIT 2020 'Impact of a Global Trade War on the Economy' *HIS Markit*, Retrieved 28 February 2020, https://ihsmarkit.com/solutions/us-china-trade-war-impacts.html

IISS 2019 'Prospectives' *Strategic Survey Journal* 2019, vol. 119, no. 1: 11-18

Institute for Policy Studies 2015 'Fighting for a US federal budget that prioritizes peace, economic stability and shared prosperity' National Priorities Project, Retrieved 8 May 2020, https://www.nationalpriorities.org/campaigns/military-spending-united-states/

IMF 2019 'World Economic Outlook Database, October 2019' IMF, Retrieved 26 March 2020, https://www.imf.org/external/pubs/ft/weo/2019/02/weodata/weorept.aspx?pr.x=29&pr.y=5&sy=2017&ey=2021&scsm=1&ssd=1&sort=country&ds=.&br=1&c=924&s=NGDPD%2CPPPGDP%2CNGDPDPC%2CPPPPC%2CPCPIPCH&grp=0&a=

International Labour Organization/Organisation for Economic Co-operation and Development 2015 'The Labour Share in G20 Economies' *ILO/OECD* Retrieved 20 March 2020 https://www.oecd.org/g20/topics/employment-and-social-policy/The-Labour-Share-in-G20-Economies.pdf

Jeet, H 2018 'Are We Witnessing the Fall of The American Empire?' *New Republic*, March 2018, Retrieved 3 April 2020, https://newrepublic.com/article/147319/witnessing-fall-american-empire

Jellissen, SM and Gottheil, F 2009 'Marx and Engels: In Praise of Globalization' *Contributions to Political Economy*, vol. 28:

35-46

Jessop, B 1990 *State Theory: Putting Capitalist States in their Place*, The Pennsylvania State University Press, University Park, Pennsylvania

Jianhua, L 2015 'The Practical Logic of the Comintern From the Perspective of World Revolution' *Social Sciences in China*, vol. 36, no. 4: 24-39

Jowett, P 2013 *China's Wars: Rousing the Dragon, 1894-1949*, Osprey Publishing, Oxford UK

Kahan, A 1967 'Nineteenth-Century European Experience with Policies of Economic Nationalism' in H Johnson (ed) *Economic Nationalism in Old and New States*, Chicago University Press: 17-30

Kaletsky, A 2010 *Capitalism 4.0: The Birth of a New Economy*, Bloomsbury Publishing Plc., London

Kane, T 2001 'China's Foundations: Guiding Principles of Chinese Foreign Policy' *Comparative Strategy* vol. 20, no. 1: 45-55

Kassam, N 2020 'Lowy Institute Poll 2020' *Lowy Institute*, Retrieved 20 June 2020, https://poll.lowyinstitute.org/report

Kautsky, K 1914, 'Ultra-imperialism' Marxist Internet Archive, Retrieved 29 January 2020, https://www.marxists.org/archive/kautsky/1914/09/ultra-imp.htm

Kegley, CJ 2008 *World Politics: Trend and Transformation (12th Edition)* Wadsworth Publishing, California

Kemp, T 2013 *The Climax of Capitalism: The US Economy in the 20th Century*, Routledge, Abington Oxon and New York

Kennedy, P 1989 *The Rise and Fall of the Great Powers: economic change and military conflict from 1500-2000*, Harper Collins Publishers, London

Keyser, CH 1984 'Three Chinese Leaders: Mao Zedong, Zhou Enlai and Deng Xioaping' *Focus on Asian Studies*, vol. IV, no. 1 Retrieved 2 April 2020 http://afe.easia.columbia.edu/special/china_1950_leaders.htm#deng

Lapavitsas, C 2009 'Financialised Capitalism: Crisis and Financial Expropriation' *Historical Materialism*, vol. 17, no. 2: 114-48

Lardy, NR 1995 'The Role of Foreign Trade and Investment in China's Economic Transformation' *The China Quarterly*, no. 144 (December): 1065-82

Lebowitz, MA 2004 'What Keeps Capitalism Going' *Monthly Review*, vol. 56, no. 2: 19-25

Legarde, C 2016 'Legarde warns Trump-style protectionism would hit world economy' *Financial Times*, Retrieved, 17 March 2020, https://next.ft.com/content/134aac12-4403-11e6-9b66-0712b3873ae1

Leitenberg, M 2006 Deaths in Wars and Conflicts in the 20th Century, Cornell University Peace Studies Program, Occasional Paper #29, Retrieved 20 March, 2020, https://www.clingendael.org/sites/default/files/pdfs/20060800_cdsp_occ_leitenberg.pdf

Lemieux, P 2018 'The Tyranny of the National Interest' The Library of Economics and Liberty, Retrieved 30 April 2020, https://www.econlib.org/Columns/y2018/Lemieuxnationalinterest.html

Lenin, VI 1977a 'Imperialism, The Highest Stage of Capitalism: a Popular Outline' in *VI Lenin Selected Works in Three Volumes, Volume 1*, Progress Publishers, Moscow

Lenin, VI 1977b 'Karl Marx: a brief biographical sketch with an exposition of Marxism' in *VI Lenin Selected Works in Three Volumes, Volume 1*, Progress Publishers, Moscow

Lenin, VI 1977c 'The Three Sources and three Component Parts of Marxism' in *VI Lenin Selected Works in Three Volumes, Volume 1*, Progress Publishers, Moscow

Liang, Z Appleton, S Song, L 2016 'Informal Employment in China: Trends, Patterns and Determinants of Entry', IZA Discussion Paper no. 10139, Retrieved 25 April 2020, http://ftp.iza.org/dp10139.pdf

Lipset, SM 1996 *American Exceptionalism*, WW Norton & Company, New York, London

Loffmann, G 2016 'The Pivot Between Containment, Engagement, and Restraint: President Obama's Conflicted Grand Strategy in Asia' *Asian Security*, vol. 12, no. 2: 92-110

Lorimer, D 1999 *Fundamentals of Historical Materialism*, Resistance Books, Sydney

Lovejoy, PE 2012 *Transformations in Slavery* (3rd edition) Cambridge University Press, Cambridge

Lowe, DM 1966 *The Function of 'China' in Marx, Lenin and Mao*, University of California Press, Berkeley California

Lukacs, G 2000 *A Defence of History and Class Consciousness: Tailism and the Dialectic*, Verso, London and New York

Lum, T et al 2008 'Comparing Global Influences: China's and US Diplomacy, Foreign Aid, Trade, and Investment in the Developing World', Retrieved, 30 April 2020, https://fas.org/sgp/crs/row/RL34620.pdf

Luxemburg, R 1982 *Reform or Revolution*, Pathfinder Press, New York

Ma, J 2008 'Economic Growth in the Lower Yangzi Region of China in 1911-1937: A Quantitative and Historical Analysis' *Journal of Economic History*, vol. 68, no. 2: 355-92

Macesich, G 1985 *Economic Nationalism and Stability*, Praeger, New York

Madsen, DL 1998 *American Exceptionalism*, Edinburgh University Press, Edinburgh

Maito, EE 2014 'The historical transience of capital: the downward trend in the rate of profit since XIX century' *Munich Personal RePEc Archive*, Retrieved 20 May 2020, https://mpra.ub.uni-muenchen.de/55894/1/

Mann, M 1973 *Consciousness and action among the Western working class*, Macmillan, London

Manning, P 1998 'The Slave Trade: The Formal Demographics of a Global System' in JE Inikori and SL Engerman (eds) *The*

Atlantic Slave Trade: Effects on Economies, Societies, and Peoples in Africa, the Americas, and Europe: 117-44 Duke University Press, Durham US

Mao Z 1957 'Speech at a Meeting of the Representative of Sixty-four Communist and Workers' Parties' *Wilson Center Digital Archive*, Retrieved 5 June 2020, https://digitalarchive. wilsoncenter.org/document/121559.pdf?v=d41d8cd98f00b20 4e9800998ecf8427e

Marx, K 1865 'Address of the International Workingmen's Association to Abraham Lincoln, President of the United States of America' *Marx and Engels Internet Archive*, Retrieved 5 April 2020, https://www.marxists.org/archive/marx/iwma/ documents/1864/lincoln-letter.htm

Marx, K 1868 'Letter to Kugelmann' *Marx and Engels Internet Archive*, Retrieved 5 April 2020, https://marxists.org/archive/ marx/letters/kug/index.htm

Marx, K 1881 'Marx to Friedrich Adolph Sorge in Hoboken' Marx-Engels Correspondence 1881, Retrieved 5 May 2020, https://www.marxists.org/archive/marx/works/1881/ letters/81_06_20.htm

Marx, K 1918 *A Contribution to the Critique of Political Economy*, (translated from the second German edition by NI Stone) Charles H Kerr & Company, Chicago

Marx, K 1974 *Grundrisse: Foundations of the Critique of Political Economy (Rough Draft)* Penguin Books, Harmondsworth, Middlesex, England

Marx, K 1986a *Capital: A Critique of Political Economy, Volume 1*, Progress Publishers, Moscow

Marx, K 1986b *Capital: A Critique of Political Economy, Volume 2*, Progress Publishers, Moscow

Marx, K 1986c *Capital: A Critique of Political Economy. Volume 3*, Progress Publishers, Moscow

Marx, K 1986d 'Preface to a Contribution to the Critique of Political Economy' *in Marx Engels Selected Works*, Progress

Publishers, Moscow: 180-4

Marx, K and Engels, F 1964 *The German Ideology*, Progress Publishers Moscow

Marx, K and Engels, F 1975 *Articles on Britain*, Progress Publishers, Moscow

Marx, K and Engels, F 1977 *Manifesto of the Communist Party*, Progress Publishers, Moscow

Maurer, P 2020 'Millennials Fear Catastrophic War: it's time for the world to act on their concerns' *World Economic Forum*, Retrieved 15 June 2020, https://www.weforum.org/agenda/2020/01/millennials-concerns-war-conflict-fear-survey/

McMahon, RJ 2003 *The Cold War: A Very Short Introduction*, Oxford University Press, Oxford

Mearsheimer, J *The Tragedy of Great Power Politics*, WW Norton & Company, New York and London

Mehta, A 2020 'Trump's New Nuclear Weapon Has Been Deployed' *Defense News*, Retrieved 26 February 2020, https://www.defensenews.com/smr/nuclear-arsenal/2020/02/04/trumps-new-nuclear-weapon-has-been-deployed/

Mehring, F 1975 *On Historical Materialism*, New Park Publications, UK

MIC 2020 '2016 US Military Defense Spending' Military Industrial Complex, Retrieved 7 June 2020, https://www.militaryindustrialcomplex.com/2016-totals.asp

Michels, R 1962 *Political Parties: a Sociological Study of the Oligarchical Tendencies of Modern Democracy*, The Free Press, New York, Collier-Macmillan Ltd., London

Milanovic, B 2019 *Capitalism Alone: The Future of the System that Rules the World*, Belknap Press of Harvard University Press, Cambridge Mass, London

Miller, RW 1991 'Social and political theory: Class, state, revolution' in T Carver (ed) *The Cambridge Companion to Marx*, Cambridge University Press, Cambridge: 55-105

Mills, CW 1963 *The Power Elite*, Oxford University Press, New York

Mitter, R 2004 *A Bitter Revolution: China's Struggle with the Modern World*, Oxford University Press, Oxford and New York

Modongai, S 2016 'Development of Nationalism in China' *Cogent Social Sciences*, vol. 2 no. 1

Moore, B Jr 1978 *Injustice: The Social Bases of Obedience & Revolt*, The Macmillan Press Ltd., London

Morrison, WM 2019 'China's Economic Rise: History, Trends, Challenges, and Implications for the United States' Congressional Research Service June 2019, Retrieved 26 February 2020, https://fas.org/sgp/crs/row/RL33534.pdf

Murphy, A Tucker, H Coyne, M Touryalai, H 2020 'Global 2000: The World's Largest Public Companies' *Forbes*, Retrieved 18 June 2020 https://www.forbes.com/global2000/#15f70c9f335d

Murray, G 2012 'Australia's ruling class: a local elite, a transnational capitalist class, or bits of both' in G Murray and J Scott (eds) *Financial Elites and Transnational Business*, Elgar Publishing, Cheltenham, UK: 193-219

National Archives, 2019 'Declaration of Independence: A Transcription' National Archives Retrieved 3 April 2020, https://www.archives.gov/founding-docs/declaration-transcript

National Defense Strategy 2018 'Sharpening the American Military's Competitive Edge' *National Defense Strategy of the United States of America*, Retrieved 22 January 2020, https://dod.defense.gov/Portals/1/Documents/pubs/2018-National-Defense-Strategy-Summary.pdf

Naughton, B Tsai, K (eds) 2015 *State Capitalism, Institutional Adaptation, and the Chinese Miracle*, Cambridge University Press, NY

Noland, M 1996 *US-China Economic Relations, Working Paper Series*, Peterson Institute for International Economics,

Washington DC

O'Brien, R 2004 'Globalisation, Imperialism and the Labour Standards Debate' in R Munck (ed) *Labour and Globalisation: Results and Prospects*, Liverpool University Press, Liverpool: 52-70

OECD 2015 'In it Together: Why Less Inequality Benefits All' *OECD Publishing*, Paris Retrieved 20 July 2020 http://dx.doi.org/10.1787/9789264225120-en

Oxfam 2014 'Still the Lucky Country? The Growing Gap Between Rich and Poor is a Gaping Hole in the G20 Agenda' *Oxfam Australia*, Retrieved 15 May 2020 www.oxfam.org.au/wp-content/uploads/2014/06/2014-66-g20-report_fa_web-2.pdf

Oxfam 2016 *An Economy for the 1%: How privilege and power in the economy drive extreme inequality and how this can be stopped*, 210 Oxfam Briefing Paper, January 2016 Retrieved 7 April 2020 https://www.oxfam.org/sites/www.oxfam.org/files/file_attachments/bp210-economy-one-percent-tax-havens-180116-en_0.pdf

Oxfam 2019 *5 shocking facts about extreme global inequality and how to even it up*, Oxfam International, Retrieved 20 May 2020, https://www.oxfam.org/en/5-shocking-facts-about-extreme-global-inequality-and-how-even-it

Peet, R 2009 *Unholy Trinity: The IMF, World Bank and WTO*, ZED Books

Peet, R 2011 'Contradictions of Finance Capitalism' *Monthly Review*, vol. 63 no. 7: 18-33

People's Daily 2012 'Market Fundamentalism is Unpractical' edited and translated by *People's Daily on-line*, Retrieved 5 April 2020, http://en.people.cn/90780/7719657.html

Perkins, DH 1983 'Research on the Economy of the People's Republic of China: A Survey of the Field' *Journal of Asian Studies*, vol. 42, no. 2: 345-72

Petras, J 2020 *US Imperialism: The Changing Dynamics of Global Power*, Routledge Taylor and Francis Group, New York and

London

Pieterse, JN 2002, 'Global Inequality: bringing politics back in', *Third World Quarterly*, vol. 23, no. 6: 1023-46

Pilat, D Cimper, A Olsen, K Webb, C 2006 'The Changing Nature of Manufacturing in OECD Economies', *STI Working Paper, 2006/9*, OECD Directorate for Science, Technology and Industry, Retrieved 10 March 2020, www.oecd.org/science/innol/37607831.pdf

Platt, SR 2018 *Imperial Twilight: The Opium War and the End of China's Last Golden Age*, Atlantic Books, London

Plekhanov, G 1976 *Selected Philosophical Works, Volume 3*, Progress Publishers, Moscow

Post, C 2011 *The American Road to Capitalism, 1620-1877: studies in class-structure, economic development and political conflict*, Brill, Leiden and Boston

Popper, KR 1985 *Popper Selections* (ed D Miller) Princeton University Press, Princeton, New Jersey

Pryke, S 2012 'Economic Nationalism: Theory, History and Prospects' *Global Policy*, vol. 3 no. 3: 281-91

Pun, N 2019 'The new Chinese working class' *Dialectical Anthropology*, Retrieved 24 April 2020, https://link-springer-com.ezproxf.deakin.edu.au/content/pdf/10.1007/s10624-019-09559-0.pdf

Raiklin, ER 2013 'On the Meaning of the PRC's Development Since 1949' *Sage Open*, vol. 3 no. 2: 1-12

Ranson, R and Sutch, R 1988 'Capitalists Without Capital: the burden of slavery and the impact of emancipation' *Agricultural History*, vol. 62 no. 3: 133-160

Rees, J 1997 'Marx in the modern world', *Socialist Review*, Issue 210, July/August 1997

Rees-Mogg W 2003 'The Transatlantic Gulf' Daily Reckoning 19 February, Retrieved 5 February 2020, https://dailyreckoning.com/the-transatlantic-gulf/

Reich, R 2010 'America's biggest jobs program: the US military'

Christian Science Monitor, Retrieved 7 March 2020, https://www.csmonitor.com/Business/Robert-Reich/2010/0813/America-s-biggest-jobs-program-The-US-military

Reinsch, W 2017 'Global Trade Policy: Opportunities for US-China Trade Cooperation' in Parallel Perspectives on the Global Economic Order, Center for Strategic and International Studies: 40-5, Retrieved 30 April 2020, https://csis-prod.s3.amazonaws.com/s3fs-public/publication/170922_Remler_ParallelPerspectives_Web.pdf?JUYh7r7rMJGc0rv1bx8yGdH mi3B67TKk

Restad, HE 2015 *American Exceptionalism: an idea that made a nation and remade the word*, Routledge, Oxon, New York

Roberts, JAG 2011 *A History of China*, (third edition) Palgrave Macmillan, Hampshire, UK

Roberts, M 2020 'The Debt Dilemma' *The Next Recession*, Retrieved 20 May 2020, https://thenextrecession.wordpress.com/2020/05/10/the-debt-dilemma/

Robinson, WI 1998, 'Beyond Nation-State Paradigms: Globalization, Sociology, and the Challenge of Transnational Studies', *Sociological Forum*, Vol. 13, No.4: 561-94

Robinson, WI Harris, J 2000 'Towards A Global Ruling Class? Globalization and the Transnational Capitalist Class' *Science and Society*, vol. 64, no. 1: 11-54

Rummel, RJ 2017 *China's Bloody Century: Genocide and Mass Murder Since 1900*, Routledge, Taylor and Francis Group, London and New York

Sayer, D 1985 'The critique of politics and political economy: capitalism, communism and the state in Marx's writings of the mid-1840s' *The Sociological Review*, vol. 33, no. 2: 221-53

Schram, SR 1981 'To Utopia and Back: A Cycle in the History of the Chinese Communist Party' *The China Quarterly*, vol. 87 (September): 407-39

Schram, SR 2002 'Mao Tse-tung's Thought' in M Goldman and L O-F Lee (eds) *An Intellectual History of China*, Cambridge

University Press, Cambridge UK: 267-348

Science Council 2020 'Our Definition of Science' Science Council, Retrieved, 26 February 2020, https://sciencecouncil. org/about-science/our-definition-of-science/

Screpanti, E 1999 'Capitalist Forms and the Essence of Capitalism' *Review of International Political Economy*, vol. 6 no, 1: 1-26

Selden, M 1995 'Labor Unrest in China, 1831-1990' *Review (Fernand Braudel Center)* vol. 18, no. 1: 69-86

Selwyn, B 2013 'Karl Marx, Class Struggle and Labour-Centred Development' *Global Labour Journal*, vol. 4, no. 1: 48-70

Serwer, A 2019 'The Fight Over The 1619 Project Is Not About The Facts' The Atlantic, Retrieved 5 May 2020, https://www. theatlantic.com/ideas/archive/2019/12/historians-clash-1619-project/604093/

Setrakian, L 2008 'Fmr. Weapons Inspector On Nuclear Iran, Syria, And Barack Obama' *ABC News*, Retrieved 8 February 2020, https://abcnews.go.com/International/story?id=6424308&page=1

Shaffer, L 1981 'Modern Chinese Labor History, 1895-1949' *International Labor and Working Class History*, Vol.20, Fall: 31-7

Shambaugh, D 2012 'Are China's Multinational Corporations Really Multinational?' *East-Asia Quarterly Review*, vol. 4, no. 2: 7-9

Silver, B 2006 *Forces of Labor: Workers' Movements and Globalization since 1870*, Cambridge University Press

Silverstein, J 2019 'Why We Published The 1619 Project' *New York Times Magazine*, Retrieved 5 May 2020, https://www. nytimes.com/interactive/2019/12/20/magazine/1619-intro. html

Sinclair, PR 1976 'Fascism and Crisis in Capitalist Society' *New German Critique*, vol. 9 Autumn; 87-112

SIPRI 2018 'The SIPRI Top Arms-Producing and Military Services Companies, 2017' Stockholm International Peace Research Institute, Retrieved 5 April 2020, https://www.sipri.

org/sites/default/files/2018-12/fs_arms_industry_2017_0.pdf

Smith, D 2006, *Globalization: the hidden agenda*, Polity Press, Cambridge and Malden MA

Smith, H 2002 'The politics of regulated liberalism: a historical materialist approach to European integration' in M Rupert and H Smith (eds) *Historical Materialism and Globalization*, Routledge, Taylor and Francis Group, London and New York

Smith, KW 2019 How Slavery Hurt the US Economy, Bloomsburg, August 2019

Smith, MEG 2104 *Marxist Phoenix: Studies in Historical Materialism and Marxist Socialism*, Canadian Scholars' Press Inc., Toronto

Solomon, S Rupert, M 2002 'Historical materialism, ideology, and the politics of globalizing capitalism' in M Rupert & H Smith (eds) *Historical Materialism and Globalization*, Routledge, London and New York: 284-300

Spence, JD 1990 *The Search for Modern China*, W W Norton & Co., New York and London

Spinazze, G 2020 'It is Now 100 Seconds to Midnight' Bulletin of the Atomic Scientists, 2020 Retrieved 26 January 2020, https://thebulletin.org/2020/01/press-release-it-is-now-100-seconds-to-midnight/

Subramanian, A 2011 'The Inevitable Superpower: Why China's Dominance is a Sure Thing' *Foreign Affairs*, vol. 90, no. 5: 66-78

Summers, L 2016 'Voters deserve responsible nationalism, not reflex globalism' *Financial Times*, July 10 2016 Retrieved 17 March 2020 https://next.ft.com/content/15598db8-4456-11e6-9b66-0712b3873ae1

Szakonyi, D 2007 'The Rise of Economic Nationalism under Globalization and the Case of Post-Communist Russia' *Vestnik: The Journal of Russian and Asian Studies*, 16 May 2007

Taalas, P 2019 'Greenhouse gas concentrations in atmosphere reach another high', *World Meteorological Organization*, Retrieved 20 May 2020, https://public.wmo.int/en/media/

press-release/greenhouse-gas-concentrations-atmosphere-reach-yet-another-high

Therborn, G 2012 'Class in the 21st Century' *New Left Review*, vol. 78

The World Bank 2019 'The world bank in China' *The World Bank*, Retrieved 25 February 2020, https://www.worldbank.org/en/country/china/overview

Tian, N et al 'Trends in World Military Expenditure, 2019' *SIPRI Fact Sheet, April 2020*, Retrieved 29 June 2020, https://www.sipri.org/sites/default/files/2020-04/fs_2020_04_milex_0_0.pdf

Tooze, A 2015 *The Deluge: The Great War, America and the Remaking of the Global Order, 1916-1931*, Penguin Books, New York

Trescott, P 2010 'Western Economic Advisers in China, 1900-1949' in JE Biddle and RB Emmett (eds) *Research in the History of Economic Thought and Methodology*, Emerald Group Publishing, Bingley UK: 1-38

Trotsky, L 1972 *On Marxism and the Trade Unions: Trade unions in the epoch of imperialist decay*, New Park Publications, London

Trotsky, L 1973 *The Bolsheviki and World Peace*, Hyperion Press Inc., Westport, Connecticut

Trotsky, L 1996 'The War and the International' *Marxists' Internet Archive*, Retrieved 5 March 2020, http//ww.marxists.org/archive/Trotsky/1914/war

Trotsky, L 2004 *The Revolution Betrayed*, Dover Publications Inc., Mineola, New York

Tseng, W Zebregs, H 2002 'Foreign Direct Investment in China: some lessons for other countries' *IMF Policy Discussion Paper*, Retrieved 27 April 2020, https://www.imf.org/external/pubs/ft/pdp/2002/pdp03.pdf

Twitchett, D Fairbank, JK (eds) 1980 *The Cambridge History of China: Vol II, Late Ch'ing, 1800-1911, Part 2*, Cambridge University Press, Cambridge UK

Updike, J 1990 *Rabbit at Rest*, Random House, New York

Victims of Communism Memorial Foundation 2019 'US Attitudes Toward Socialism, Communism, and Collectivism' Retrieved 20 June 2020, https://www.victimsofcommunism. org/2019-annual-poll

Wallerstein, I 1986 'Marxisms as Utopias' *American Journal of Sociology*, vol. 91, no. 6: 1296-1308

Walter, CE Howie, FJT 2012 *Red Capitalism: The Fragile Financial Foundation of China's Extraordinary Rise*, John Wiley & Sons, Singapore

Warren, B 1980 *Imperialism: Pioneer of Capitalism*, NLB and Verso, London

Washington Times 2007 'Beijing likens Cheney criticisms to nosy neighbor' *The Washington Times*, March 1 2007, Retrieved 25 February 2020, https://www.washingtontimes. com/news/2007/mar/01/20070301-104826-2978r/

Weber, M 2004 *The Vocation Lectures: Science as a Vocation, Politics as a Vocation*, D Owen and TB Strong (eds) Hacket Publishing Company, Indianapolis, Cambridge

Weinberg, M 2003 *A Short History of American Capitalism*, New History Press

Weiner, R 1980 'Karl Marx's Vision of America: A Biographical and Bibliographical Sketch' *The Review of Politics*, Vol. 42 No. 4: 465-503

Weisbord, A 1937 'The Conquest of Power' *Marxists Internet Archive*, Retrieved 17 March 2020, https://www.marxists.org/ archive/weisbord/conquest17.htm

Wells, W 2003 *American Capitalism, 1945-2000* Ivan R Dee, Publishing, Chicago

White, H 2012 *The China Choice: Why America Should Share Power*, Black Inc., Melbourne Australia

White House 2017 'A New National Security Strategy for a New Era' White House national security and defense, Retrieved 30 April 2020, https://www.whitehouse.gov/articles/new-national-security-strategy-new-era/

Williams, K 2017 'What George Orwell Wrote About the Dangers of Nationalism: on facts, fallacies, and power' Literary Hub, Retrieved 14 February 2020, https://lithub.com/what-george-orwell-wrote-about-the-dangers-of-nationalism/

Williams, M 2020 'Coronavirus class divide – the jobs most at risk of contracting and dying from COVID-19' Medicalxpress, May 19 2020, Retrieved 11 June 2020, https://medicalxpress.com/news/2020-05-coronavirus-class-jobs-dying-covid-.html

Wolf, M 2004 *Why Globalization Works*, Yale University Press, New Haven Connecticut

Wood, EM 1998 'Capitalist Change and Generational Shifts' *Monthly Review: An Independent Socialist Magazine*, vol. 50, no. 5: 1-10

WTO 2016 *Report on G20 Trade Measures (mid-October 2015 to mid-May 2016)* WTO-OMC, Retrieved 22 March 2020 https://www.wto.org/english/news_e/news16_e/g20_wto_report_june16_e.pdf

Xinhua, 2015 "China unveils action plan on Belt and Road Initiative' Xinhua News Agency, Retrieved, 30 May 2020, http://english.www.gov.cn/news/top_news/2015/03/28/content_281475079055789.htm

Yale Law School, 2008 'The Monroe Doctrine 1823' The Avalon Project, Retrieved 5 May 2020, https://avalon.law.yale.edu/19th_century/monroe.asp

Ye, X 2019 'Rediscovering the Transition in China's National Interest: A Neoclassical Realist Approach' *Journal of Current Chinese Affairs*, vol. 48 no. 1: 76-108

Yeung, HW 2004 *Chinese Capitalism in a Global Era: towards a hybrid capitalism*, Routledge, London, NY

Yoshino, K 2016 'The possibility of Power Sharing between China and the US: implications for Japan's national interests', *Indo-Pacific Strategic Papers*, Centre for Defence and Strategic Studies, Canberra, Retrieved 26 February 2020, https://www.defence.gov.au/ADC/Publications/documents/

IndoPac/2016/Yoshino_sep16.pdf

Yu, GT 1991 'Revolution: Past, Present, and Future' *Asian Survey* vol. 31, no. 10: 895-904

Zakaria, F 1999 *From Wealth to Power: The Unusual Origins of America's World Role, Princeton University Press,* New Jersey

Zimbalist, A Sherman, HJ 1984 *Comparing Economic Systems: a political-economic approach,* Academic Press Inc., Orlando Florida

Zitelmann, R 2019 'State Capitalism: No, The Private Sector Was And Is The Main Driver Of China's Economic Growth' Forbes, Retrieved 25 March 2020, https://www.forbes.com/sites/rainerzitelmann/2019/09/30/state-capitalism-no-the-private-sector-was-and-is-the-main-driver-of-chinas-economic-growth/#435d28e327cb

CULTURE, SOCIETY & POLITICS

The modern world is at an impasse. Disasters scroll across our smartphone screens and we're invited to like, follow or upvote, but critical thinking is harder and harder to find. Rather than connecting us in common struggle and debate, the internet has sped up and deepened a long-standing process of alienation and atomization. Zer0 Books wants to work against this trend. With critical theory as our jumping off point, we aim to publish books that make our readers uncomfortable. We want to move beyond received opinions.

Zer0 Books is on the left and wants to reinvent the left. We are sick of the injustice, the suffering and the stupidity that defines both our political and cultural world, and we aim to find a new foundation for a new struggle.

If this book has helped you to clarify an idea, solve a problem or extend your knowledge, you may want to check out our online content as well. Look for Zer0 Books: Advancing Conversations in the iTunes directory and for our Zer0 Books YouTube channel.

Popular videos include:

Žižek and the Double Blackmain

The Intellectual Dark Web is a Bad Sign

Can there be an Anti-SJW Left?

Answering Jordan Peterson on Marxism

Follow us on Facebook
at https://www.facebook.com/ZeroBooks and Twitter at https://twitter.com/Zer0Books

Bestsellers from Zer0 Books include:

Give Them An Argument
Logic for the Left
Ben Burgis
Many serious leftists have learned to distrust talk of logic. This is a serious mistake.
Paperback: 978-1-78904-210-8 ebook: 978-1-78904-211-5

Poor but Sexy
Culture Clashes in Europe East and West
Agata Pyzik
How the East stayed East and the West stayed West.
Paperback: 978-1-78099-394-2 ebook: 978-1-78099-395-9

An Anthropology of Nothing in Particular
Martin Demant Frederiksen
A journey into the social lives of meaninglessness.
Paperback: 978-1-78535-699-5 ebook: 978-1-78535-700-8

In the Dust of This Planet
Horror of Philosophy vol. 1
Eugene Thacker
In the first of a series of three books on the Horror of Philosophy,
In the Dust of This Planet offers the genre of horror as a way of
thinking about the unthinkable.
Paperback: 978-1-84694-676-9 ebook: 978-1-78099-010-1

The End of Oulipo?
An Attempt to Exhaust a Movement
Lauren Elkin, Veronica Esposito
Paperback: 978-1-78099-655-4 ebook: 978-1-78099-656-1

Capitalist Realism
Is There No Alternative?
Mark Fisher
An analysis of the ways in which capitalism has presented itself
as the only realistic political-economic system.
Paperback: 978-1-84694-317-1 ebook: 978-1-78099-734-6

Rebel Rebel
Chris O'Leary
David Bowie: every single song. Everything you want to know,
everything you didn't know.
Paperback: 978-1-78099-244-0 ebook: 978-1-78099-713-1

Kill All Normies
Angela Nagle
Online culture wars from 4chan and Tumblr to Trump.
Paperback: 978-1- 78535-543-1 ebook: 978-1-78535-544-8

Cartographies of the Absolute
Alberto Toscano, Jeff Kinkle
An aesthetics of the economy for the twenty-first century.
Paperback: 978-1-78099-275-4 ebook: 978-1-78279-973-3

Malign Velocities
Accelerationism and Capitalism
Benjamin Noys
Long listed for the Bread and Roses Prize 2015, *Malign Velocities*
argues against the need for speed, tracking acceleration
as the symptom of the ongoing crises of capitalism.
Paperback: 978-1-78279-300-7 ebook: 978-1-78279-299-4

Meat Market
Female Flesh under Capitalism
Laurie Penny
A feminist dissection of women's bodies as the fleshy fulcrum of
capitalist cannibalism, whereby women are both consumers and
consumed.
Paperback: 978-1-84694-521-2 ebook: 978-1-84694-782-7

Babbling Corpse
Vaporwave and the Commodification of Ghosts
Grafton Tanner
Paperback: 978-1-78279-759-3 ebook: 978-1-78279-760-9

New Work New Culture
Work we want and a culture that strengthens us
Frithjoff Bergmann
A serious alternative for mankind and the planet.
Paperback: 978-1-78904-064-7 ebook: 978-1-78904-065-4

Enjoying It
Candy Crush and Capitalism
Alfie Bown
A study of enjoyment and of the enjoyment of studying. Bown asks what enjoyment says about us and what we say about enjoyment, and why.
Paperback: 978-1-78535-155-6 ebook: 978-1-78535-156-3

Color, Facture, Art and Design
Iona Singh
This materialist definition of fine-art develops guidelines for architecture, design, cultural-studies and ultimately social change.
Paperback: 978-1-78099-629-5 ebook: 978-1-78099-630-1

Neglected or Misunderstood
The Radical Feminism of Shulamith Firestone
Victoria Margree
An interrogation of issues surrounding gender, biology, sexuality, work and technology, and the ways in which our imaginations continue to be in thrall to ideologies of maternity and the nuclear family.
Paperback: 978-1-78535-539-4 ebook: 978-1-78535-540-0

How to Dismantle the NHS in 10 Easy Steps (Second Edition)
Youssef El-Gingihy
The story of how your NHS was sold off and why you will have to buy private health insurance soon. A new expanded second edition with chapters on junior doctors' strikes and government blueprints for US-style healthcare.
Paperback: 978-1-78904-178-1 ebook: 978-1-78904-179-8

Digesting Recipes
The Art of Culinary Notation
Susannah Worth
A recipe is an instruction, the imperative tone of the expert, but
this constraint can offer its own kind of potential. A recipe need
not be a domestic trap but might instead offer escape – something
to fantasise about or aspire to.

Paperback: 978-1-78279-860-6 ebook: 978-1-78279-859-0

Most titles are published in paperback and as an ebook.
Paperbacks are available in traditional bookshops. Both print and
ebook formats are available online.
Follow us on Facebook
at https://www.facebook.com/ZeroBooks
and Twitter at https://twitter.com/Zer0Books